THE NEW MUCKRAKERS

Other Books by Leonard Downie, Jr.

Justice Denied
Mortgage on America

THE NEW MUCK-RAKERS

Leonard Downie, Jr.

The New Republic Book Company, Inc.

Washington, D.C.

Published in the United States of America in 1976
by The New Republic Book Company, Inc.
1220 Nineteenth St., N.W., Washington, D.C. 20036
Copyright © 1976 by Leonard Downie, Jr.

Library of Congress Cataloging in Publication Data
Downie, Leonard.
  The new muckrakers.

  Includes index.
  1. Reporters and reporting. I. Title.
PN4781.D6   070.4'3   76-4832
ISBN 0-915220-13-X

Printed in the United States of America

For Pearl, Leonard, and Mary

For their essential roles in bringing this book to fruition, I thank Joan Tapper, an extraordinary editor who strongly managed this manuscript while successfully launching New Republic Books; *Lois Decker O'Neill, formerly the Washington editorial director of Praeger Publishers, who helped conceive the idea and form for* The New Muckrakers; *Geraldine Rebach, who once again helped interview, edit, and keep the project on track; Stephen Isaacs, who caused me to become an investigative reporter and showed me many of the techniques; Harry Rosenfeld, who taught by example what I know as an editor and especially impressed on me the great value of vigilant professional skepticism; Howard Simons, my strong leader who encouraged this project—and, finally but most importantly, all the reporters, editors, and authors quoted herein who generously shared their time and thoughts with me.*

Bob Woodward (left) and Carl Bernstein (right) in the *Post* newsroom.

Seymour Hersh

Donald L. Barlett

James B. Steele

Mike Baxter

James Savage

I.F. Stone

Jack Anderson

Mel Chamowitz

Les Whitten

Chamowitz

Jean Heller

Cullen Photo

Carey McWilliams

Contents

1. The Stardust Twins of the Washington Post

Bob Woodward was already twenty-seven years old when he first went to work for a newspaper, and he was quite anxious to finally be doing something that seemed significant. He regretted spending his first decade of adulthood in college and the U.S. Navy—even though college had been Yale and service had included prestigious posts at sea and in Washington. After his departure from the Navy, Woodward tried Harvard Law School, where he only grew more impatient waiting for his life to really begin. So he impulsively quit to become a newspaper reporter, choosing that trade for no other particular reason than "I thought it was something I could do." Returning to Washington, which had fascinated him, Woodward tried unsuccessfully to talk his way onto the staff of the *Washington Post.* He had to settle instead for the weekly *Sentinel* in nearby Montgomery County, Maryland, where he quickly tired of writing about local PTA and civic groups, while his editor strenuously insisted it was good experience for a beginning reporter and a necessary service for readers of a suburban weekly.

"We were always having arguments about the scut work, which I refused to do," Woodward remembered. "I thought it was a waste. So eventually I started assigning myself to better stories. I'd go out and get them on my own, and they turned out to be good stories so he published them." Woodward quickly found that the stories his editor liked best were those that revealed examples of local government waste and bureaucratic incompetence, each of which attracted a little more attention to the *Sentinel* and its new reporter. "I was not a good writer," Woodward recalled. "But I was a good, fast reporter and I did more stories than anyone else on the *Sentinel.*" Meanwhile, he kept pestering editors of the *Washington Post* for a job there. He finally prevailed, after a year-long telephone campaign, only to be unceremoniously assigned to the newspaper's traditional 7 p.m.-to-3-a.m. scut work beat at police headquarters. While most new reporters sent there contented themselves with keeping up with each night's

1

" . . . neither of us ever takes 'no' for an answer."

robberies, murders, and fires, Woodward again assigned himself to better stories, which he pursued during his daylight time off. As he had at the *Sentinel,* Woodward found it easy to uncover small-to-middling scandals other *Post* reporters had overlooked: illegally fatty meat sold in supermarkets, outdated and mislabeled prescriptions dispensed by drugstores, health law violations found in the most expensive downtown restaurants, doctors profiteering from Medicaid, landlords and merchants violating the 1972 federal price and rent freeze, a Cuban exile-run drug ring smuggling narcotics into Washington via Miami, and corruption flourishing in the elite unit of the police department that was supposed to investigate the honesty of the rest of the force.

In this way, during his first nine months at the *Washington Post,* all *before* the Watergate burglary, Bob Woodward accumulated more front-page by-lines than any of the other sixty reporters on the newspaper's metropolitan staff. "I just sat down and thought of what I ought to be going after—it was all obvious stuff," Woodward later explained with his characteristic Midwestern bluntness. "I was always astounded that more reporters didn't do the same thing. I guess you have to have a compulsive need to succeed. You have to be insecure and to want desperately to please your boss."

Woodward had not set out to become what was known in newspapering as an "investigative reporter." He was only vaguely aware of the Teddy Roosevelt era of "muckraking" journalism and never for a moment thought of himself as heir to the likes of Lincoln Steffens. Having been raised in the traditionally strict but close and comfortable middle-class suburban household of an Illinois judge, Woodward was nearly apolitical and definitely not fired by any rebellious reformer's zeal. Rather, just as he had always tried to please his father, even though he ultimately turned away from both the Navy and the law, Woodward worked primarily to please his editors and win for himself ever greater freedom to do what the

Washington Post rewarded most: good stories for the front page.

"After you get done working each day," Woodward advised a group of young, new *Post* reporters years later, "do some reporting on your own. It takes a little extra time, but you can line things up and tell an editor the next morning—'Look, if I don't have to do that duty coverage today, I'm going to have this story, and it says this, and I can have it done by seven o'clock,' and if it's a front-page story or close to a front-page story, there's no editor in this place who's going to make you do the duty coverage instead. No editor here that I know of has ever turned down a front-page story. For the editors, the most important page of the *Washington Post* is Page One. The paper is built and lives and dies on Page One."

Woodward also pleased his editors with his shyly deferential manner and conservative dress and habits, which were a welcome change from the brash flamboyance and abrasive egotism of many other young *Post* reporters. His almost adulatory appreciation for all editorial direction, including frequently extensive reworking of his tortuous writing, gave Woodward's editors the rare, satisfying feeling that they were playing important roles in the development of a star reporter. Barry Sussman, the *Post*'s city editor when Woodward arrived, later recalled in *The Great Coverup*, "Ordinarily I kept some distance from those who worked under me, but Woodward and I became quite close. He had distinguished himself as an excellent investigative reporter, bright, aggressive and hard-working. If he had a single shortcoming, it was that his writing was sometimes awkward. He could do everything else by virtue of hard work and an incomparable nose for news." So it was not surprising when Sussman was awakened at 8:30 a.m. on Saturday, June 17, 1972, by news of the Watergate break-in arrests, that he first thought of Woodward, who had been at the *Post* less than a year, as the best reporter he could find to put on the story.

"There are only two similarities between me and Woodward, and the rest is all different," Carl Bernstein told me long after their names, Woodward and Bernstein—"Woodstein"—had been forever linked in the public mind. "One thing," Bernstein said, "is that neither of us ever takes 'no' for an answer. And the other is that we usually made up our own assignments. Long before Watergate."

By refusing to take "no" for an answer, Bernstein was given a job at the *Washington Star* as a copyboy at sixteen. By volunteering colorfully written stories about characters and curiosities he had discovered while growing up around Washington, the precocious

Bernstein went from that position to telephone dictationist to full-fledged reporter at the *Star* by the time he reached nineteen. By coming up with richly anecdotal stories about life in New Jersey and across the river in New York City for the *Elizabeth Daily Journal,* where he later worked for a time, Bernstein won several newswriting awards and used his clippings to win a job at the *Post* back in Washington.

Contrary to the boy police reporter image created for him since the Watergate story broke, Bernstein had, by the summer of 1972, been on the *Post*'s metropolitan staff for six years and covered several beats—from police and the local courts to the District of Columbia government and the Virginia state legislature. However, his best work still derived from assignments he made up for himself: beautifully written and unusually evocative magazine-style portraits of Washington neighborhoods, perceptive explorations of the problems of guns, random violence, narcotics abuse, and slum housing in the city, and "investigative" articles on the police, local prosecutors, slum landlords, and fraudulent fly-by-night "career schools." Other young Washington reporters envied Bernstein for the variety, originality and occasional great strength of his work, as well as the unusual freedom he seemed to enjoy at the *Post.*

But unlike Woodward, Bernstein had not been rewarded with such freedom by admiring editors. Instead, he had simply established himself beyond their control. He alternately patronized and argued arrogantly with editors, no matter how senior in years and experience they were. He treated with contempt most assignments they tried to give him and haughtily disapproved of editorial changes they tried to make in his writing, which often differed sharply in style and length from the norm. Bernstein saw himself as an unappreciated newspaper pioneer of the "new journalism," in which long, dramatic, and somewhat subjective narrative recreations of events would replace terse, dry, just-the-facts reporting, which Bernstein contemptuously dismissed as "this idea of reporting as stenography."

Bernstein's lifestyle also alienated his editors, who tended to comprise a quite different middle-class, college-educated, managerial class of journalists than their *Front Page* predecessors. Bernstein was an iconoclastic throwback, cast in the reporter-as-social-misfit mold. He was a college dropout who learned from the old-timers at the *Star* how to drink and chase women while he was still a teenager. He adapted to the 1960s by growing his hair long, dressing sloppily, smoking marijuana, and sometimes allowing his tendency to identify with the new radical counterculture to show up as something

suspiciously resembling advocacy in his cop
out all night entertaining himself and wom
from friends and never returned. This
somewhat erratic and sometimes sleepy
with co-workers to whom he eventually
money. Even worse, he was sometimes
scrapes with editors, which lent worrisome credence
from a few news sources that Bernstein had misquoted them,
misrepresented their positions, or written things they said they had
told him off the record.

But two qualities helped keep Bernstein afloat at the *Post*: his
strong drive, born of his own insecurity, to produce Page One stories,
and his ability to talk anything he wanted, including information, out
of almost anyone. These were two other important similarities
between Bernstein and Woodward, although Bernstein would
scarcely admit to his own insecurity, and Woodward would
disassociate himself from Bernstein's guile. "You act differently with
different people," Bernstein told me. "I can get along with a cop or a
Cabinet officer. You adapt different roles and ploys depending on
who you're talking to. You get to know their prejudices and play to
them. You've got to bullshit some."

Bernstein also had an unnerving habit of somehow materializing in
the newsroom day or night or on a weekend when a big story was
breaking and muscling his way unassigned into the coverage of it.
Whenever someone prominent died, a spectacular crime was
committed, or a major disaster occurred, there was Bernstein,
clippings from the newsroom library in hand and the names of
appropriate news sources on his lips. He was usually successful in
maneuvering to share the writing and top billing of the main story or
carve out a related "sidebar" story of his own, even occasionally
managing to bite off a piece of breaking national stories this way,
although he was on the metropolitan staff.

So it also was not surprising that when Bob Woodward was
summoned to the *Post* newsroom to begin reporting on the
Watergate burglary, he found Bernstein already there, moving in
unassigned on the story. "That morning," they later wrote in *All the
President's Men*, "Bernstein had Xeroxed copies of notes from
reporters at the scene and informed the city editor that he would
make some more checks. The city editor shrugged his acceptance, and
Bernstein had begun a series of phone calls to everybody at the
Watergate he could reach—desk clerks, bellmen, maids in the
housekeeping department, waiters in the restaurant."

Thus began the curious partnership between these two quite different and yet similarly persistent, insecure, ambitious, resourceful, and manipulative reporters that was ultimately to produce such profound changes in the course of the nation and journalism. As they finally realized themselves with numbing shock on the August night in 1974 when President Richard M. Nixon announced his resignation from office, Woodward and Bernstein eventually transcended the traditional observer role of the reporter to help shape history. They themselves became newsmakers, best-selling authors and celebrities whose professional and personal lives are eagerly followed in titillating detail by readers of gossip and media columns in newspapers and magazines. They are recognized and stopped on the street, beseeched for autographs, and overwhelmed with mail and invitations for public speaking, radio, and television appearances. Now, with their portrayal in the motion-picture version of *All the President's Men* by two of Hollywood's most popular actors, Robert Redford (Woodward) and Dustin Hoffman (Bernstein), they are becoming romanticized characters of legend.

"It's inherent in the story of Carl and Bob that they have become a kind of contemporary myth," explained Alan J. Pakula, the director of *All the President's Men*. On the screen, Pakula said, their story "could take the place of the Westerns" in film folklore, because its theme is "that American belief that a person or small group can with perseverence and hard work and obsessiveness take on a far more powerful, impersonal body and win—if they have truth on their side."

The investigative reporter is "the new American folk hero," *New York* magazine proclaimed while the Watergate drama was still unfolding in real life. "Armed only with his conscience and his wits," the chronicle of pop culture expounded with its usual hyperbole, the investigative reporter "makes whole governments tremble, not to mention politicians. He is the glamour boy of journalism in a country suddenly without glamour anywhere. To a nation unsure of its leaders and itself, he seems to offer certitude. He has never been bought, sold out—at least not yet."

Shortly after President Nixon's forced resignation, Alistair Cooke, the British-born television journalist and popular historian, declared that we had entered "the great age of muckrakers" in which "anything a public official does wrong winds up on the front pages." In a more measured tone, but with even greater historic significance, U.S. Supreme Court Justice Potter Stewart stated in a November 1974 address at the Yale Law School that "the established press in the past ten years, and particularly in the past two years, has performed precisely the function it was intended to perform by those who wrote the First Amendment of our Constitution."

There can be little doubt that a great upsurge of investigative reporting during the past decade has considerably influenced the course of the nation. In addition to the impact of Woodward and Bernstein's reporting of Watergate, the public disgrace and eventual resignation of President Nixon was hastened by at least two other young reporters, John Blackburn of the Santa Ana, California, *Register*, who first reported how Nixon acquired his palatial estate in nearby San Clemente with unusual financial assistance from business friends and then lavishly remodeled it at taxpayers' expense, and John White of the Providence, Rhode Island, *Journal-Bulletin*, who revealed that Nixon had paid very little personal income tax during the years he was President. Seymour Hersh, probably the best-known investigative reporter other than Woodward and Bernstein, helped turn around public opinion on the war in Indochina with his revelations of the My Lai massacre in Vietnam and the secret bombing of Cambodia and later touched off a national debate on the role of the Central Intelligence Agency with his exposure of the CIA's domestic spying activities. William Lambert, a member of the investigative reporting team assembled by *Life* magazine in the late 1960s, drove President Lyndon Johnson's crony, Abe Fortas, off the U.S. Supreme Court with his *Life* story about Fortas's $20,000 retainer from the private foundation of an indicted financier. Numerous other investigative reporters for newspapers and news magazines have exposed the involvement of countless local, state, and federal officials in almost every kind of corruption from local zoning bribery to conspiracy to obstruct justice in the Watergate cover-up.

Journalists have not had such a telling impact on the country's affairs since the brief golden age of the original "muckrakers" just after the turn of the century. From roughly 1902 to 1912 Lincoln Steffens, Upton Sinclair, David Graham Phillips, Ida Tarbell, Ray Stannard Baker, and others focused the attention of the nation on corruption in government and private business, including the powerful and largely unregulated oil, railroad, banking, insurance, and food-processing industries. At a time when no newspaper reached beyond its local audience, these journalists published their revelations of monopoly practices, bribery, conflicts of interest, election rigging, stock manipulation, racketeering, abuse of labor, and health dangers in books and newly popular national magazines like *McClure's, Everybody's, Collier's,* and William Randolph

Hearst's *Cosmopolitan*, which for the first time reached millions of readers across the country and influenced public opinion. They helped create the political climate for Teddy Roosevelt's trust-busting, congressional passage of the landmark Pure Food and Drug Act, and ratification of the Seventeenth Amendment, which provided for popular election of the U.S. Senate.

Along the way, however, President Roosevelt became disenchanted with the increasingly wide investigations of these bold journalists. He was particularly upset by a series of articles in *Cosmopolitan*, "The Treason of the Senate," in which David Graham Phillips accused a number of powerful senators, including needed Roosevelt allies, of being the venal tools of big corporations in which they were deeply involved financially. In setting out to discredit Phillips and the others, Roosevelt inadvertently christened them and their work in a fiery 1906 speech, in which he compared "these reckless journalists" to the Man with the Muckrake in John Bunyan's *Pilgrim's Progress*.

Bunyan had warned against narrow concentration on worldly concerns, to the exclusion of the spiritual, when he described "the man who could look no way but downward, with a muckrake in his hands; who was offered a celestial crown for his muckrake, but who would neither look up nor regard the crown he was offered, but continued to rake to himself the filth of the floor." But Roosevelt, choosing to interpret Bunyan in his own way, told his audience that the Man with the Muckrake

typifies the man who in this life consistently refuses to see aught that is lofty, and fixes his eyes with solemn intentness only on that which is vile and debasing. Now, it is very necessary that we should not flinch from seeing what is vile and debasing. There is filth on the floor, and it must be scraped up with the muckrake; and there are times and places where this service is most needed of all the services that can be performed. But the man who never does anything else, who never thinks or speaks or writes save of his feats with the muckrake, speedily becomes, not a help to society, not an incitement to good, but one of the potent forces of evil.

At first Roosevelt's attack only spurred the muckrakers on defiantly, as they burrowed deeper into government and big business and continued on to labor unions, prisons, and other subjects. But Roosevelt may also have planted doubts about the work of the muckrakers in the minds of their readers, who seemed eventually to tire of so much bad news. The national magazines turned to other fare by the time World War I began, and penetrating investigative reporting virtually disappeared from most of the popular press for decades during both world wars, the Great Depression and through the McCarthy era.

Most reporting during that time was restricted to "objective" coverage of events, with news of wrongdoing confined largely to after-the-fact coverage of celebrated crimes and trials. Only a few journalistic rebels kept muckraking alive from the 1920s through the 1950s—Paul Y. Anderson and Clark Mollenhoff among newspaper reporters, Fred J. Cook among free-lance writers, and Heywood Broun and Drew Pearson among syndicated columnists. In the early 1960s what appeared to be investigative stories about the hidden illegal activities of organized criminals and corrupt labor leaders began appearing in newspapers with some frequency. Much of this information though had actually been "leaked" to certain receptive reporters by government investigators who had been frustrated in attempts to deal with such people in court. Nevertheless, these stories attracted the attention of other ambitious reporters, who allied themselves with local investigators in uncovering police misconduct and ticket-fixing corruption in local governments.

Meanwhile, a new adversary relationship between reporters and the national government was being fostered by the realization by the press that it had been badly used in some circumstances—notably Senator Joseph McCarthy's red-hunting, the Eisenhower administration's lying about the U-2 spy plane incident, and President Kennedy's chiding of the *New York Times* for agreeing to suppress a story on preparations for the ill-fated Bay of Pigs invasion of Cuba. It required a new kind of calculated leak of government information, however—Daniel Ellsberg's delivery of the Pentagon Papers to the *New York Times* and the *Washington Post*— to activate the skepticism of most reporters about the candor and conduct of the federal government, which had escaped muckraking scrutiny since the Teapot Dome Scandal of the 1920s. And it was still not until after Woodward and Bernstein's initially belittled investigative reporting of Watergate had been proven out by events that the American press was really ready to enter a new era of unbounded muckraking.

Then, for the first time in more than half a century, as though at some signal an invisible barrier had suddenly been lifted, the new muckrakers rushed out to find new targets for investigation: government at all levels, political campaign practices, the military and the intelligence establishment, the police and the FBI, the courts and the prisons, the stock market and some big businesses, doctors and hospitals. Editors became more willing to print most of these stories as they found investigative reporting helped enlarge newspaper reputations and win more prizes. In 1974 four of the six Pulitzer Prizes for newspaper writing were awarded for investigative reporting, prompting *Time* magazine to declare it "a Year of the Muckrakers," and investigative reporters joined columnists and political writers in receiving higher newspaper salaries, greater public recognition, offers from book publishers, and invitations for public speaking and television appearances. Muckraking spread to news magazines and other popular periodicals, and even spawned new magazines, like the *Washington Monthly* and *New Times*, that specialized in investigative stories.

The impact and fame of the new muckrakers filled university journalism schools to overflowing with young people aspiring to become the next Woodward or Bernstein. "Students see what's been done on Watergate and want a piece of the action," explained a Stanford University journalism professor after a record 50,000 students enrolled in journalism schools in 1974. The *Washington Post* and other large newspapers were inundated with hundreds of applications for every news staff opening. For the first time many of these came from law school graduates and holders of other advanced degrees seeking to enter journalism because they believed investigative reporting to be an effective, ego-satisfying way to change society.

Nothing could be more misleading, however, than the image of the investigative reporter as Robert Redford and Dustin Hoffman in *All the President's Men*, Woodward and Bernstein holding forth on a special hour-long segment of the *Today* show devoted entirely to them, Bernstein starring as a panelist at a national convention, or Woodward playing in a celebrity doubles tennis match as the partner of a Ford administration Cabinet member. In reality—especially during the years before Watergate when I worked as an investigative reporter for the *Washington Post*—investigative reporting has more often been lonely, frustrating, tedious, and emotionally draining work. Starting out doubtfully with a flimsy hunch or an improbable-sounding tip, the investigative reporter must find out what someone else does not want him to know. He must make countless telephone calls to persons who will refuse to answer his questions, hang up on him, or never return his calls. He must knock on doors that will never be opened for him, even when he knows the person he is after is inside, with the shades pulled down and doors bolted tight.

The investigative reporter must spend hours on end in dreary

"Being lied to becomes so much a part of the investigative reporter's life that once in a while he asks himself, 'Why is this guy telling me the truth?'"

courthouse file rooms and other record repositories, searching through thousands of barely intelligible legal and technical documents to find small clues that often raise more questions than they answer. He must learn how to read and understand complicated lawsuits, real estate deeds and mortgages, thick books of government regulations on highly technical subjects, and involved financial records of private businesses—all with little help from experts in these fields who likely as not will resent his snooping or will try to mislead him. He must doggedly make his way through bureaucratic mazes to request other government records that may ultimately be denied him through a legal loophole or a stubborn cover-up, even after he has finally determined exactly what he is looking for, where it is kept, and who has custody of it.

With somewhat greater difficulty, the investigative reporter must be able to recognize and disregard more lies than are told to a police detective in an entire career on the homicide squad. Many of these lies come from very respectable people—government officials, top business executives, judges, and lawyers—people who would never be suspected of such duplicity. "Being lied to becomes so much a part of the investigative reporter's life," remembered Robert M. Smith, an investigative reporter for the *New York Times* in pre-Watergate Washington, "that once or twice a year he asks himself, 'Why is this guy telling me the truth?' "

From a precious few facts the investigative reporter must be able to project the shadowy outlines of the truth and then flesh out that specter with little or no help from those who know the whole story. He must decide when he has enough information to go into print, despite continuing, genuine-sounding denials from important people the story may hurt. He knows that everyone who has refused to talk to him while he was working on the story will now be waiting for just one small mistake they can pounce on with dramatic public indignation. Great apprehension washes over the reporter as the story is finally finished and he waits to see how it will stand up the next morning in the glaring light of day.

The investigative reporter must face the fact that his stories *will* hurt people. While he was working on his story, these people were the enemy—the "targets" of his investigation. They had betrayed the public trust or wronged some individual. They had lied to him or refused to tell him their side of the story. But following publication, after weeks or months of tense investigative reporting, these same people may suddenly reappear before the reporter's eyes as ordinary, frail beings like himself—people with loving families and friends and human hopes and aspirations. When, during the mid-1960s, I wrote a series of articles about systematic injustices, administrative chaos, and incompetent judges in the District of Columbia's federally supervised local court system, judges I had known well stopped talking to me and passed the word that I had maliciously betrayed and humiliated them. After the Justice Department and Congress subsequently imposed several major reforms on the D.C. court system, I was told that the former chief judge, who was replaced in a shakeup, was left a "broken man" and that his grown sons vowed to take physical revenge if they ever ran across me.

The investigative reporter must be ready for the targets of his stories to strike back in any way possible to try to ruin his reputation, estrange his editors, or gag his sources. Lawyers who practiced in the D.C. courts, for example, instigated a local bar association investigation of me and my sources of information, rather than looking into what I had revealed about conditions in the courts. Lawyers and judges who were suspected of having cooperated with me were ostracized by the rest of the legal community. Several judges on the court met with my editors to try to convince them that my stories were malicious distortions that should be retracted in print on the *Post*'s front page. Another series of articles I wrote revealing corruption among officers of several local savings and loan associations cost the *Post* hundreds of thousands of dollars in revenue lost when the city's entire savings and loan industry retaliated by withdrawing all its advertising from the paper. Other investigative projects drew the usual obscene letters and phone calls and veiled threats to me and harassment of those persons who were believed to have been my sources.

At the *Washington Post*, everyone involved in the reporting, writing, and editing of the Watergate stories suspected that all our telephones were tapped, that at least Woodward and Bernstein and probably executive editor Benjamin Bradlee and publisher Katharine Graham were being followed constantly, and their private lives thoroughly investigated for any hint of something that could be construed as scandal. Indeed, friends of Richard Nixon, at what appeared from the White House tapes to be the specific direction of the President, did challenge the licenses of the *Post*'s television stations in Florida. White House aides publicly branded Bradlee as a Kennedy family "coat holder" who they said was working ruthlessly to destroy Nixon. Bob Woodward was accused of abusing in an unpatriotic way contacts he may have made with White House aides while he was a Navy liaison officer there. There were whisperings in Washington that Carl Bernstein might be trying to avenge his parents, who had been active in the labor movement and were accused during Nixon's Red-baiting years of being Communist sympathizers. Someone Bernstein had never met before tried to sell him marijuana on a busy downtown Washington street in what appeared suspiciously like a set-up.

It also has since become known that other investigative reporters disliked by the Nixon administration were the subjects of telephone taps, FBI investigations, and Internal Revenue Service tax audits. Elsewhere in the country investigative reporters working on local stories have been ordered to appear before judges and grand juries to explain what they have been up to and who their sources are. Some have been jailed for refusing. In an outrageous act of retaliation, two members of the 1975 Pulitzer Prize-winning *Indianapolis Star* investigative reporting team that exposed police corruption and inefficiency in the prosecutor's office in the Indiana capital were themselves charged with bribery in an obviously trumped-up case concocted by the police and local prosecutor.

In most instances, however, retaliation against investigative reporters takes more subtle, although sometimes even more effective, forms. Sources simply dry up overnight. Friends the reporter has made over years on a beat suddenly turn away from him. He gets a cold, unproductive reception from officials he contacts for the first time but who already know his name and reputation. It becomes more difficult for the investigative reporter to find information and

"It's almost a perverse pleasure. I like going out and finding something that is going wrong . . . and then putting it into the newspaper."

put stories together. His editors become displeased with his decreased production, and the reporter begins to doubt himself, sliding into a professionally paralyzing depression. It has happened to me and to investigative reporters who have worked with and for me.

The alternative to these dark periods for the normally manic-depressive investigative reporter are the adrenalin-pumping highs, produced by what Robert Smith called "the thrill of the chase," and the subsequent feeling of triumph over great adversity when an investigative story of some impact is finally finished and published The need to experience such satisfaction again and again can turn the best and most determined investigative reporters into scandal-hungry fanatics who live for the next front-page victory that only the raking of more muck can produce. "It's almost a perverse pleasure," Bob Woodward admitted. "I like going out and finding something that is going wrong or something that isn't the way other people are saying it is, and then putting it into the newspaper."

For most investigative reporters, just seeing their latest exposé in print on their newspaper's front page is soon not enough. They want outrage in reaction to the injustice they have exposed and some evidence that something will done about it. Someone must be indicted, forced to resign from office, or defeated at the next election, and Congress or the state assembly or the city council must pass remedial legislation. Nothing can depress an investigative reporter more than to have his stories met with silence. He would sooner spend time in jail for not revealing his sources than be ignored. Seymour Hersh regularly solicited officials' reactions to his own exposés for follow-up stories for the front page of the *New York Times* and freely expressed his outrage when it seemed that little would be done. Other reporters have slipped information to prosecutors to help induce indictments. Still others, like Miriam Ottenberg of the *Washington Star*, who during the 1950s and 1960s pioneered investigative reporting of consumer fraud, have actually helped write and lobby for corrective legislation in Congress. Becoming an active, and sometimes brash, advocate can damage a reporter's reputation for fairness and warp his perception of his purpose. It can lead him arrogantly to justify his own overstepping the bounds of propriety to uncover wrongdoing by others.

Carl Bernstein was brash, arrogant, and uncontrollable long before the Watergate story brought him fame and influence. He never really matured during a footloose adolescence cut short by his early entry into the adult working world. "I was a terrible student," Bernstein remembered. "The only thing I could do in school was write. I'd pass the essay exams and flunk the true and false. So I worked a lot." He had quit a job in a local variety store, "selling black people terrible goods on credit and hating it," when his father, who knew a *Washington Star* executive, suggested a copyboy's job there. The editor turned Bernstein down when he realized he was just sixteen, but Carl kept calling back until he was finally hired "to get me off his back."

"I immediately fell in love with the *Star* newsroom," Bernstein said. "It was the biggest room I had ever seen in my life," and it seemed to exude excitement. Bernstein looked for every opportunity to do more than just run errands for his $44-a-week salary, and he soon was covering night civic meetings at an extra $7.50 for each story he got into the next afternoon's *Star*. He was still only sixteen when he broke into the paper with the first of those stories—without a by-line, as was the custom there for nonreporters—and soon went from copyboy to city desk clerk to the *Star*'s bank of news dictationists. The dictationists, who typed up breaking stories telephoned in by reporters on the street or out of town, were encouraged to rewrite press releases into short stories and turn out obituaries from information called in by funeral homes and relatives of the deceased.

"The dictation bank was how you got to the reporter training program," Bernstein said, "so it was highly competitive. I was a lot younger than most of the others on the dictation bank, who had already gone to college and were in their twenties." Bernstein was not yet eighteen, and looked even younger with his freckled, cherubic face. "The city editor treated me like a son. He was stern and good to me at the same time," recalled Bernstein, whose own father was away from home on business much of the time. "He sent me out on crime stories to hospitals to make sure nobody died between editions without our knowing it, and I used the opportunity to get good stories."

Bernstein rapidly rose to head dictationist on the day shift and was regularly sent out at night to cover crimes, fires, and suburban government meetings, where he wound up competing against veteran reporters for the morning *Washington Post*. He often ran across Tom Wolfe, the "new journalist" who was then a brilliant but frustrated young reporter at the *Post*. "I'd meet Wolfe at fires, which he hated," Bernstein said. "It drove Wolfe crazy to be covering fires along with a kid dictationist from the *Star*."

Bernstein, always a restless, nocturnal person, liked hanging around with the older, ambulance-chasing night reporters, photographers, and television cameramen, and he bounced around night spots with them in the city's tenderloin districts. He was fascinated with Washington, a city that newcomers often found forbidding or dull, and walked all over town in both black and white neighborhoods, gregariously striking up conversations with anyone he met. He became interested in the city's history and the old buildings and neighborhoods that remained from its past. Always a voracious reader, Bernstein examined everything he could find on the capital's history and became so expert that in later years he could write authoritative reviews of books about the city, including the collected records of the Columbia Historical Society of Washington, D.C.

One of the city's Runyanesque characters Bernstein grew to know was Annie Crim, a poor peddler who ran two small newsstands downtown, gossiped with the commuters who bought papers from her, and fed the ubiquitous pigeons. When she died and her body turned up unclaimed in the D. C. morgue, Bernstein recognized her name. "I used to pass by her every day," he said, "and I wrote a flowery obit, and they put it on the front page. It was my first by-line. It also was a big breakthrough at the *Star* because dictationists didn't get by-lines before then."

Bernstein started college as a commuting student at the University of Maryland in nearby College Park, but he devoted more time to his work at the *Star* than to his studies, volunteering stories about life on and around the campus. Wherever he went, Bernstein saw story ideas. "It's a cliché," he told me, "but every day as you walk around, you see fascinating things that haven't been written about."

By the time he was nineteen Bernstein was put on the reporting staff of the newspaper full-time as a summer replacement. At that time the *Star*'s editors featured a brightly written human-interest story across the top of the front page of the local news section every day. With his ability to spot feature stories all over town and bring them to life with colorful writing, Bernstein dominated this spot week after week into the fall.

The *Star*'s newsroom, which still had much of the ambiance and camaraderie of *Front Page* newspapering, became Bernstein's real home. "It was fun, the most fun I've ever had in this business," Bernstein remembered. "I really grew up in that newsroom. Two martinis were standard at lunch," and after work for each day's editions ended at about 4 p.m., everyone moved to a nearby bar to "wait out the rush hour," drinking for another four or five hours. Bernstein's acceptance and premature success in this glamorous-seeming grown-up world was not unlike the experience of a child actor slipping unknowingly into adulthood. "All my friends," he recalled, "were reporters and editors at the *Star*, people ten or more years older than me."

The *Star*'s editor at the time, William Hill, decided that Bernstein should finish college before becoming a permanent member of the newspaper's reporting staff and ordered him back onto the dictation bank. But Bernstein had had enough of school and knew he was already good enough to be a reporter, so when an assistant city editor left the *Star* that autumn to become editor of the Elizabeth, New Jersey, *Daily Journal*, Bernstein went along. "He had a magnificent plan to rebuild the Elizabeth paper with me as his top reporter," Bernstein said. "Elizabeth is the worst city there ever was, but it was great for me, because I could do anything I wanted there. I started doing really long pieces on life in and around Elizabeth, and I even wrote a column."

Bernstein is now embarrassed by the sophomoric excesses of much of his free-wheeling writing there, although he won three first prizes in the 1965 New Jersey newspaper association's awards competition. One of those prize-winning stories was a long, rambling account—which took up the entire *Daily Journal* front page on November 10, 1965—of his experiences in New York City during the massive northeastern U.S. power failure the night before. "I happened to be in Manhattan that night visiting a friend when the lights went out," Bernstein said. "I started taking notes right away and ran all over the city, hitchhiking and riding motorcycles and whatever to see what was going on. Then I wrote all night and the next morning to get the story into the afternoon edition. It was an overdone, obvious imitation of Tom Wolfe, filled with exclamation points and everything."

I was at a friend's apartment at 110th Street and Riverside Drive and the lights fell asleep and I woke up.

We looked out the window and—Dig We Must—this crazy, unbelievable scene with half the lights in Manhattan out.

Half the lights hell! We made our way up to the roof by candlelight and somebody had stolen the Empire State Building. And the Chrysler Building and Harlem, and Jackie Kennedy's apartment house, and Queens, and Lincoln Center and Temple Emanuel . . .

The story began that way; yet as Bernstein went on to describe the giddy, New Year's Eve liberation of the great city in the dark, the ebullient mood of his writing, when a little more controlled, seemed particularly suited to the event.

Later in the story, describing one of his hitchhiking experiences that night, Bernstein wrote:

Then came Tom Sabatino, a truck driver, of 233 Hillside Ave., who owns a big Checker station wagon which seats nine. Mr. Sabatino, as his grateful nonpaying patrons made clear, is clearly one of the world's greatest sports.

He loaded 15 of us into the oversized automobile and started heading uptown. Everytime we would stop to let somebody out, others would crowd around the big Checker wagon. "You going to Flushing?" "How about the Bronx?" "Mister, I'm only going to 42nd Street, but I've been walking since Wall Street." Even at our final stop at 47th Street, the car was still loaded.

And what a ride! By now the police had put up huge searchlights at some important intersections and people were walking in the middle of the street and hitchhiking. Grown men in Brooks Brothers suits walking backwards on Eighth Avenue with their thumbs out like they were sailors on the Turnpike.

The hotels. Who could ever forget the hotels on the night of the Great Blackout? I walked into the lobby of the Americana, that grand monument to the nation's conventioneers, and it was a human parking lot.

One thousand people, the hotel's PR man said, were sprawled out in the lobby. It looked like two thousand and it was the damnedest thing I have ever seen in my life. The hotel had provided them all blankets and they were sleeping, talking, joking, drinking, crying, kissing in every imaginable nook and cranny of the Americana's multi-level lobby.

How many people were in the Americana's lobby? How many of the hitchhiking executives were wearing Brooks Brothers suits? Were there really fifteen people packed into Tom Sabatino's Checker? With Bernstein, you could never really be certain about the little details. Yet he clearly captured the essence of the New York blackout experience with dramatic if overwritten verity. This story is illustrative of the kind of writing, later to become considerably more mature in style, that Bernstein has always liked best—colorful language and human vignettes used to recreate an event or portray a locality.

The blackout story also provides an early example of Bernstein's compulsive eagerness and great excitement at being at the center of a great event, rather than merely a note-taking spectator on the sidelines. Both reporter and participant, he wrote about the blackout in Manhattan as a Bernstein Odyssey. It foreshadowed the time when, after returning to Washington as a reporter for the *Post,* Bernstein would invariably get mixed up with the participants in protest demonstrations, be himself manhandled by the police, and spend nights in demonstrators' encampments, sharing their experiences and later offering what amounted to a diary of his adventures as story information for the *Post*. Eventually, of course, he would manuever himself into the middle of Washington's biggest drama of the 1970s.

Bernstein landed at the *Washington Post* in 1966, after tiring of Elizabeth, New Jersey, and its little newspaper and then failing to get a job in New York. Bernstein's work for the *Post* in the succeeding years on a variety of local beats, including the municipal court and a suburban county, was spotty. He was summarily moved off the city hall beat when the city editor, making a surprise visit, found Bernstein curled up asleep on the press room couch at midday. It was hard for editors to keep track of Bernstein because he often came in late, disappeared on long lunches, and failed to call in to the city desk. Bernstein was among the first *Post* reporters to let his prematurely gray-flecked hair grow long, and in time his dress became sloppier and his living habits became even more chaotic. He was married for a brief time to another *Post* reporter, but he could never settle down. The long drinking sessions of his *Star* days became all-night prowls of the city, mostly in search of excitement and companionship rather than drink. He seemed to suffer a strange restlessness and loneliness, even when in the company of other people.

Bernstein became a bicycle aficionado, buying one expensive imported racing bike after another, and going almost everywhere in town on them. He was a knowledgeable rock music critic who occasionally contributed reviews to the *Post*'s "Style" section and maintained a huge tape and record collection of rock music dating back to the 1950s. He also collected classical music, to which he had been listening since he was a child, investing large sums of money in sound systems of steadily increasing size, volume, and complexity.

The cost of such possessions, plus restaurant meals, for which he had gourmet tastes, and nightly entertainment, kept Bernstein perpetually in debt. He defaulted on installment sales contracts, dodged collection agencies, and borrowed regularly from generous co-workers—from $5 to $20 for lunch or dinner to much larger sums to help cover other debts—repaying the loans slowly if ever. Although first his wife and, later, Bob Woodward, tried to help Bernstein manage money better, he was never really solvent until he later became a best-selling author and went to a professional financial adviser.

As out of step and undependable as Bernstein could be, he nevertheless graced the pages of the *Washington Post* with self-assigned stories of life in and around Washington that were unequaled by other reporters. He began with a profile of the mixed-lifestyle, multiracial downtown neighborhood in which he himself lived and then moved on to articles about Saturday street life on the Wisconsin Avenue shopping strip of restored colonial Georgetown, the chic residential life amid Victorian architecture in Cleveland Park, and the clash of working-class whites and blacks in the distant southeastern section of Washington. These stories were filled with the local history and sounds he discovered every day. They were told mostly in vignettes linked by a sense of Bernstein's own presence in each neighborhood—much as he had done in less sophisticated fashion during the blackout in New York.

Bernstein also came across ideas for what amounted to in-vestigative reporting, although he did not know it as such at the time. While covering the local courts, he noticed that prosecutors failed to follow up housing violations charged to the landlords of big, old, inner-city apartment buildings and instead allowed the landlords endless delays to make vital repairs or restore heat or water that had been cut off. One day Bernstein noticed a number of unprosecuted violations charged to the owner of Clifton Terrace, a once-elegant group of apartment buildings. Bernstein remembered Clifton Terrace "from when I was a kid as being very fancy buildings. It occupied the finest site in the city, right on Cardozo Hill with a magnificent view all the way across the river."

Bernstein asked to see the entire file on Clifton Terrace. "I didn't even know for certain if such a file existed," he said, "but there was one, and they showed me where it was. I looked, and there was a whole damn drawer full of violations at Clifton Terrace—more than a thousand of them." Bernstein and another *Post* reporter, Robert Kaiser, visited the apartments and were told by tenants that a new landlord was allowing them to go to ruin. The reason, the reporters soon discovered, was that the landlord had bought the buildings, whose tenants had changed from white to black, primarily as a tax shelter—a depreciation deduction to offset other income on his personal income tax. The city had become "a partner" in the scheme, Bernstein said, by not forcing the landlord to keep the apartments up. "The inspectors would go out and cite the damn place, but the landlord would keep getting extensions and no fines were levied."

In the city's land records Bernstein and Kaiser found how the landlord kept selling Clifton Terrace back and forth between dummy corporations and other "straw parties" to inflate its value artificially and increase the size of his deductions. They even found his federal income tax return for one year, which showed that after depreciation and other deductions he paid only $259.20 in tax on a gross income of $834,080.70. "Because of a legal dispute at one point, he voluntarily filed his tax return with the court," Bernstein said, "and by checking all the public records on him we came across this tax case and just by coincidence happened to check the file at the time his tax return was there."

Bernstein subsequently indulged in occasional investigative reporting on other subjects that interested him, including police neglect of rising heroin traffic in Washington, the proliferation of guns in the city and the victimization of young adults by private "career" schools that charged high prices but provided little useful training in paramedical, secretarial, computer operation, modeling, or merchandising skills.

One of the readers of Carl Bernstein's career school series in the summer of 1971 was Bob Woodward, who was looking for new ideas for stories that would further enhance his small but growing local reputation as an investigative reporter at the *Montgomery County Sentinel* and prove that the editors at the *Washington Post* had been wrong to turn him away.

Woodward was the eldest of six children of Chief Judge Alfred E. Woodward of the DuPage County Circuit Court in the western suburbs of Chicago. Judge Woodward, a soft-spoken but firm man, tried to maintain some influence over Bob's destiny, sending him off to Yale, from which Bob graduated in 1965. His unremarkable college career included Naval Reserve Officer Training Corps instruction he took in exchange for scholarship support.

"I had signed up for Navy ROTC at the end of my senior year in high school," Woodward explained, "both for the scholarship and because my father had been in the Navy. I had always seen his Navy uniform in the closet. Military service seemed the inevitable and honorable thing to do. I had a crisis at Yale when it became clear what the Vietnam war was really all about, but I never considered going to Canada or anything like that."

Woodward entered the Navy for the requisite four years with an ROTC commission and found that he "hated the service, especially the regimentation." But he also found ways to make the Navy bureaucracy work for him. He served his first two years as an officer aboard the presidential flagship for communications, which was a carrier fitted out to become a floating White House in case of emergency. "Then I received orders to go to Vietnam as a tactical watch officer at a jungle command center," Woodward said. "I knew it would be a death trap. To get out of that, I asked to be transferred instead to a destroyer, which apparently pleased the Navy. I was assigned to a new guided missile ship."

Along the way Woodward married and brought his wife to California, where his ship was based. When the Navy then extended his enlistment for a fifth year because of the war and transferred Woodward to Washington, his wife, who had enrolled in college on the West Coast, decided to stay behind. His new assignment, as a communications liaison officer between the Pentagon and the White House, was "awful and boring," Woodward said. "I was miserable." Then, when he finally left the Navy and went back to California, it seemed, he said later, as though he and his wife had never known each other, and they divorced.

Because his father wanted him to be a lawyer, Woodward came back east and enrolled in Harvard Law School. But Woodward quickly grew restless. "I felt as though I was behind other people my age," he remembered. "A good friend of mine was already out of law school and working as a clerk to a Supreme Court justice. I wanted to be out of school. I was looking for a shortcut. Newspaper work was something I thought I could do right away."

So one day in August 1970 Woodward suddenly showed up at the *Washington Post* to see Harry Rosenfeld, who was then the assistant managing editor in charge of the metropolitan news staff, on which all new young reporters started at the *Post*. Rosenfeld was a sharp-witted, aggressive, nervous-stomached newspaper veteran who had worked his way up from clerk to foreign editor at the old *New York Herald-Tribune* without ever being a reporter. He came to the *Post* as the *Tribune* was collapsing to work on the foreign desk and was eventually moved to the top job on the metropolitan staff to shake it out of lethargy. Although he was quite warm and compassionate in private, Rosenfeld's assumed personality on the newsroom floor was blustery, bitingly sarcastic, relentlessly demanding, and stubbornly dictatorial. In his no-nonsense approach, there was no understanding of the strange proposal made to him by Bob Woodward. Why did this over-age Yale graduate, Navy veteran, Harvard Law School dropout with no experience in journalism want to come to work immediately, even without pay?

"I wanted to start working for nothing to show that I could do the job," Woodward said. "That was unheard of at the *Post*. I remember that Rosenfeld was mystified by it. But I talked him into a two-week tryout without pay under the tutelage of another editor whom he foisted me onto in exasperation. I did some stories on my own that I thought were pretty good, but the editor wouldn't read them. My writing wasn't so good, but the information was. I wrote one story about gas stations that were accepting only exact change because of robberies. I couldn't get the story in the *Post* and later a story on the same subject appeared in the *New York Times*. Anyway, Harry Rosenfeld called me in and told me, "You're no good to us. Get yourself a job somewhere else and call back.' They helped me get a job at the *Montgomery County Sentinel*. I had failed the *Post* tryout, and I was upset by that. I had loved working in the *Post* newsroom. It was another failure coming right with my divorce."

As a $115-a-week starting reporter at the *Sentinel*, Woodward was determined to get stories that editors at the *Post* would notice and wish they had. That was why he didn't want his time taken up with press releases, civic association meetings, and the other scut work that *Sentinel* editor Roger Farquhar tried to force onto him. "He kept telling me, 'You have to learn the lesson and pay the price,'" Woodward recalled. "He said a weekly newspaper lived on scut work, that it was its life's blood. I said, 'I realize that, but I still don't want to do it.' Finally, I stopped arguing with him and went after my own stuff. I'd write up some release he wanted done and then come to him with a story he couldn't turn down."

Many of Woodward's stories were about small scandals he found while making the rounds of county government offices or asking simple questions that occurred to him, such as what happened to county cars at night. The answer, he discovered, was that many of them went home with the employees and were used by them and their families at night and on weekends. Woodward calculated the cost of the mileage put on the cars by this personal use and came up with a loss to the county's taxpayers that put the story on the front page of the *Sentinel*, which enjoyed a large circulation in Montgomery County, especially among government officials and workers.

Soon, Farquhar was passing along tips for other possible exposés to Woodward. A Montgomery County state senator who was running for Maryland attorney general told Farquhar that a lawyer close to the incumbent attorney general, Francis Burch, had been getting money from the assets of several bankrupt Montgomery County savings and loan associations that had been put in state receivership. Woodward found that none of the depositors in the institutions had yet gotten any of their money back, but that hundreds of thousands of dollars in legal fees had been paid out of the savings and loans' assets to a variety of lawyers, including Burch's law partner, with the state's approval. The story created a sensation in Montgomery County, where the bankruptcy of the savings and loans, following considerable self-dealing by their officers, had been a major scandal. The *Washington Post*, which had played a large role in revealing the original scandal, but had not been interested in the state senator's tip, was forced to pick up Woodward's story, rewrite it with a little more information, and put it on its front page. "Burch was mad," Woodward said, and came all the way from Baltimore to Montgomery County to complain in person to Farquhar. Woodward remembered watching with a mixture of apprehension and a strange satisfaction as the attorney general of Maryland argued loudly with his editor about his story.

Some time later Burch went after Woodward himself, who had reported the assertion of a rural Maryland prosecutor that conspiracy charges against H. Rap Brown had been fabricated by the government. When the story was picked up by the *Post* and the *New York Times*, Burch represented the state in a hearing on the matter, subpoenaed Woodward, and questioned him aggressively on the reliability of his reporting. Woodward and his story survived the test. It was becoming increasingly difficult to ignore this reporter for a county weekly.

Woodward created his greatest sensation at the *Sentinel* with a story he would now like to forget. He and another reporter decided to rate high school principals by interviewing students, teachers, and parents and making observations in the schools. In March 1971 they published their findings, rating eight of the twenty-two county high school principals as outstanding, eight others good, four poor, and two as unsuited for the job. One of those two principals sued the reporters and the *Sentinel* for libel and won a $356,000 damage verdict from a county jury at a 1973 trial held after Woodward had joined the *Post*. The verdict was later overturned on appeal. "It was a bad verdict," Woodward said. "But the story itself also was a bad idea. I never got as much reaction on anything I wrote about Watergate as I got on that story in the *Sentinel*, and two-thirds of the reaction was vehemently negative."

All during this time, Woodward periodically telephoned Harry Rosenfeld to apprise him of his progress and ask for a job at the *Post*. He didn't always get through, but he sent along clippings from the *Sentinel* and was strongly recommended to Rosenfeld by the *Post*'s senior reporter in Montgomery County. Finally, after nearly the year that Rosenfeld had casually mentioned as the possible length of Woodward's apprenticeship at the weekly paper, Woodward called Rosenfeld at home, where the editor was on vacation. Rosenfeld was furious at being interrupted by this nagging job-seeker, but his wife Annie observed, "Isn't that the kind of reporter you've always said you wanted?" Rosenfeld had to reluctantly agree, and Bob Woodward went to work on the *Post*'s metropolitan staff exactly 366 days after he had been sent to the *Sentinel*.

"I had perceived that there was no recruitment policy at the *Post* at that time, and that Harry didn't want to be bothered by job applicants," Woodward said, "so persistence paid off. Harry's role at the *Post* was important for me. He was a kind of stern father image. He was always asking, especially during Watergate, 'What have you got for me today?' I was always trying to please him."

The night police beat on which Woodward started out at the *Post* usually proved to be a difficult initiation rite for a new reporter. Many policemen did not like the *Post* because of what they perceived as its liberal, criminal-coddling editorial policy. They delighted in the power they had over the fresh-faced, Ivy Leaguers from the paper who depended on them for information. Some young reporters wilted under the animosity displayed toward them, while others developed their own unyielding contempt for cops. Both of these kinds of reporters did poorly on the beat.

Woodward was as Ivy League and starched-shirted as any of them, but he made himself an unusually bright success on the night police beat by reverting to the behavior that had helped him cope with the pressures of rank and regimentation in the Navy. With wide-eyed earnestness, almost obsequious deference, and quiet persistence, he ingratiated himself with the middle-level officers who ran the night shift. He tried to befriend individual policemen by taking them out for drinks or dinner or sharing a snack with them at headquarters and listening intently as they talked about themselves and the unappreciated drudgery of their work, something few reporters bothered to do. In return, Woodward got fast, accurate information about what was happening. In time he was also let in on the gossip about politics and scandal inside the police force that helped him produce some of his first investigative stories for the *Post* on police corruption.

On his own time during the day Woodward came into the *Post* newsroom to think up ideas for other stories that would get him on the front page. He remembered Bernstein's career school series and subsequent stories about a new city ordinance—proposed and passed as a result of Bernstein's articles—that required such schools to have city licenses. Woodward decided to check the city department that had the responsibility for issuing the licenses and found that three months after the new law had taken effect nearly all the private career schools in Washington were operating without licenses.

Overlooked city government offices seemed a good source of stories, too. "I sat down with a D.C. government directory," Woodward said, "and went through it department by department to see what they were doing." When a telephone call produced an interesting lead, he went out to see the bureaucrats and go through their records himself, often on his own time. In the department that manages the city's property, he found that much of the D.C. government's vacant downtown land was being used for commercial parking lots for little or no rent to the city. Both the bureaucrats and the parking firm's executives said they were not making money on the lots, so they were not paying the city much. "I went out and counted the cars on the lots for three days in a row," Woodward said, "and found that the company was making plenty of money at the city's expense."

Woodward frequently found bureaucrats "who had never seen a reporter before, except when they were being questioned about some problem." They were anxious to tell him what they had been accomplishing for the taxpayers with little or no public credit. The city's health inspectors said few people realized how many well-known, expensive Washington restaurants fail inspections. Woodward took down and published the names of the restaurants and their health deficiencies in a story that attracted considerable attention and prompted *Post* editors to make it a regular practice. Woodward's new friends in the city's health inspection office also tipped him to grocery stores selling illegally fatty meat and pharmacies selling defective, outdated, and mislabeled prescription drugs—providing Woodward with more front-page stories.

"Whenever I visited a city agency," Woodward said, "I'd start by asking what were the good things they were doing. Then I'd get around to asking them if they had any problems. In the Bureau of Condemnation, for instance, they told me they had trouble getting the buildings they condemned torn down because of legal red tape. Meantime, they said, people were still living in some of the buildings. I checked and found hundreds of condemned buildings standing all over the city, with people living in at least 10 percent of them. It made a great story."

Woodward also was not shy about biting the hand that sometimes fed him. While his sources in the police department helped lead him to front-page stories about the activities of local narcotics dealers, Woodward found that the officers working out of one particular police substation regularly parked their private cars illegally in the surrounding ghetto neighborhood. Woodward reported that "Officer John A. Malinowski (drove) his blue Camaro up and parked it by a fire hydrant." Woodward wrote that "the reporter asked Malinowski if he thought his car was parked illegally. 'Yes, if I get a ticket. But they have to catch me. I have Maryland tags and $140 in outstanding warrants (for the tickets),' he said. 'You aren't going to put that in the paper, are you?'" Woodward did, and added in his story: "Malinowski was in uniform and on his way to work for the 4 p.m. shift. His license number is GL-7912."

One day Ben Bradlee called Woodward into his large glass-enclosed office along the outside wall of the *Post* newsroom. "It was the first time I was alone with Bradlee in his office," Woodward recalled later. "Bradlee told me there was a Pulitzer in Medicaid payments fraud. He had heard something about Medicaid costs from his pharmacist in Georgetown and didn't know anything else about it." It was a typical Bradlee tip—a rumor passed along from a crony with great drama but little supporting evidence to work on. Many of those tips failed to check out.

But Woodward set out systematically to find the records the federal and local governments kept on Medicaid. Along the way he found a confidential federal audit of the local Blue Cross-Blue Shield health insurance program, which is partially supported by federal Medicare and Medicaid reimbursements. Woodward talked a federal official into giving him a copy of the audit, which showed that local Blue Cross-Blue Shield administrators had "wasted millions of dollars on unneeded staff, computers, big cars and country club memberships," according to Woodward's front-page story. Woodward also found unpublished audits of the District of Columbia's Medicaid program that showed that $500,000 was wasted "in excessive and double payments to hospitals, doctors and druggists" during the program's first year in Washington. He obtained another report showing that four Washington doctors received more than $100,000 each in Medicaid reimbursements that year, including two doctors who collected more than $220,000 each. His stories led to a government reevaluation of local Medicaid costs and a D.C. Medical Society investigation of the four doctors.

When President Nixon ordered federal wage and price controls, Woodward visited members of the Price Commission's rent advisory board and obtained copies of the commission's rent increase guidelines. He discovered that in the Washington area the guidelines would allow rent increases roughly double those that had been made by landlords the year before, when there were no price controls. This and other stories Woodward wrote with information he got from visiting staff members of the price-control bureaucracy caused considerable controversy. They also angered the *Washington Post*'s national and business editors, whose staffs were beaten to these stories.

In fact, forays into other reporters' territories produced many of Woodward's front-page stories during his first nine months on the *Post's* metropolitan staff. Aided by the ideas of city editor Sussman, with whom he had become quite close, Woodward checked into everything from local departments like the police to federal bureaucracies like the Environmental Protection Agency. A growing number of reporters came to resent Woodward for these incursions, for his special relationship with Sussman, and the unusually frequent front-page play of his stories.

At the same time, however, other metropolitan editors came to appreciate Woodward's ability to obtain information almost anywhere. He quickly became as good a bet as Carl Bernstein to wind up involved in the coverage of the big story of the moment, the only difference being that Woodward usually was invited in.

Among other *Post* reporters who unjealously admired Woodward's unusual initiative was Morton Mintz, a veteran investigative reporter who had previously labored for years in vineyards overlooked by other Washington reporters. He specialized in chronicling the shortcomings of the various federal regulatory agencies. Mintz was impressed with Woodward's ability to penetrate bureaucracy, and he passed along to the younger reporter several tips he did not have time to follow up himself. One of these tips led Woodward to a vice chairman of the U.S. Civil Service Commission who, in violation of government regulations, helped a former business associate sell hundreds of thousands of dollars of health insurance to federal employees. Woodward got the story, and it ran on the *Post*'s front page on June 17, 1972—a day now better remembered for Woodward's start on the reporting of the mysterious burglary and bugging of the Democratic National Committee's headquarters in the Watergate office building.

"I suspect if I had known on that June 17 where this story was going," Ben Bradlee told Bob Woodward and Carl Bernstein many months later, "you guys would have been lucky to have a hunk of it. If I had known then what I know today, I probably would have fought tooth and nail against involving either one of you. Sure, I would have been wrong. But there is no way I could have made any other decision."

Bradlee would have helped steer the story to any of the several star national staff reporters—Haynes Johnson, Lou Cannon, Jules Witcover, William Greider, or David Broder—whom Bradlee, after taking control of the newsroom in the late 1960s, had brought to the *Post* with what he called "breathtaking hires." Bradlee, a rakishly handsome, irreverently stylish descendant of two old Boston families, was himself a promising young reporter for the *Post* before quitting in the 1950s to go off to Paris. There he picked up the fluent French he now mixes for dramatic effect with English obscenities and a recently acquired smattering of Yiddish to gain the upper hand in almost any conversational encounter. He worked as an enterprising foreign correspondent for *Newsweek*, landing in a Paris jail after interviewing anti-French rebels in the mountains of Algeria, and later became *Newsweek*'s Washington bureau chief. Bradlee talked *Post* publisher Philip Graham into buying the then stodgy news magazine and set to work himself to remake its Washington bureau by hiring dynamic younger reporters. These efforts were noticed by Katharine Graham, who turned to Bradlee for help in running the *Post* after her husband's untimely suicide in 1963.

Bradlee pushed ahead so fast at the *Post* and made so many drastic changes that he acquired a reputation for ruthless Machiavellian decision-making. In fact, however, with the help of Howard Simons, a sensitive, intellectual, former science writer whom Bradlee eventually made managing editor, Bradlee created a kind of federal system of fairly independent middle-level editors who, in vigorous competition with each other, had great latitude in supervising their respective staffs and areas of coverage. Bradlee also worked to erase the *Post*'s reputation for putting a liberal "spin" on much of its news coverage. As opportunities presented themselves, he put Harry Rosenfeld, a determined foe of journalistic idealogues, in charge of the metropolitan staff, and made Richard Harwood, a conservative-leaning cynic, the national editor.

In 1971 the *Post* became one of the newspapers to receive the Pentagon Papers, an event that made two important impressions on Bradlee: the *Post* had been beaten to a story of major historic significance by the *New York Times*, which obtained and began writing about the Pentagon Papers first, and the federal government made a determined effort to stop newspapers from publishing stories about them, an effort that first the *Times* and then the *Post* just as determinedly resisted. Katharine Graham's "simple declarative decision, 'I say we print,' launched far more than the legal actions that ended in vindication two weeks later by the Supreme Court," Bradlee later said. "In a real sense it marked the beginning of the journey which placed the *Post* once and for all on the cutting edge of history and journalism." Bradlee had decided, after years of ambivalence (owing to his personal friendship with the Kennedys) that a strong adversary attitude toward government power was vital for a free press and the public it served.

Thus, if Bradlee had seen Watergate from the beginning as a story of even more importance than the Pentagon Papers, he would have chosen for it his best senior reporters. Such a decision would have left out Woodward and Bernstein, as Bradlee told them many months later. "I thought you were a guy who was not always running at top speed," Bradlee said to Bernstein. "I thought you had extraordinary talents that you didn't always use. And Woodward? Who the Christ was Woodward? I've always said that Woodward reminded me of when I was a beginner in this business. But I thought you were hopelessly inexperienced to tackle something like this. Who the hell am I to give the biggest story in journalism to a guy who's been in the daily newspaper business nine months?"

As it happened, Bradlee was not in the *Post* newsroom to consider such things when Woodward, Bernstein, and other metropolitan staff reporters began chasing down the Watergate story on a Saturday. Managing editor Simons was there and did notice a bizarre local story about men in business suits and wearing surgical gloves who had been arrested inside the Democratic National Committee's headquarters. He put the story on the front page and mentioned it in a telephone preview of Sunday morning's newspaper for Katharine Graham, who was at her farm in the rural hunt country of Virginia. More of their conversation, however, was devoted to another bizarre story—the tragic-comic account of an automobile crashing into the bedroom of a suburban home where a naked man and woman had evidently been making love.

More than anyone else in the newsroom that day, city editor Barry Sussman, a chunky, curly-haired, thirty-eight-year-old newspaper journeyman from Brooklyn by way of Tennessee, recognized the Watergate burglary immediately as an event of potentially great significance. Sussman, who had a sometimes wildly imaginative analytic mind, was not much interested in the predictable, if sometimes sensational events that consume so much of the average newspaper's editorial resources and newsprint. He was fascinated by the unexpected—human actions and societal trends—and left supervision of much of the day-to-day coverage of the District of Columbia news to subordinates, so that he could concentrate on the longer range, in-depth projects of a few especially resourceful journalists.

In all, Sussman put ten reporters on the Watergate burglary arrests that first day, producing three stories—the front-page account of the crime and two "sidebars," one on security guard Frank Wills, who discovered the taped door locks that revealed the burglary, and another on the backgrounds of the burglars, as illuminated by police and court records, newspaper clippings, and hasty telephone checks. Carl Bernstein pushed his way into helping report and write the sidebar story on the burglars. Woodward worked on the main story, supplying key information he got at the arraignment of the arrested men by overhearing courtroom whisperings and cornering attorneys in the hall.

During the next two weeks Woodward's name appeared over several follow-up stories on the Watergate break-in, as he forged the important link between the burglars and the White House. While checking on the scrawled "W.H" and "W. House" found by another *Post* police reporter, Eugene Bachinski, in the Howard Hunt notebook confiscated by police, Woodward found out from White House switchboard operators and secretaries that Hunt was employed there and somehow associated with presidential aide Charles Colson. Characteristically, Woodward had telephoned those on lower working levels of the White House, rather than going through its press office or higher officials.

However, "despite the *Post*'s quick start on the story," Sussman later wrote, "our coverage was becoming somewhat chaotic. The *New York Times* and the *Washington Star* were working as hard as we were, and we had to eat up time and energy simply confirming reports they carried first." The *Post*'s national staff paid little attention to the political implications of the Watergate burglary arrests, Sussman recalled, while his staff was "still investigating Watergate as a mystery story." When Sussman went on vacation early in July, Woodward's reporting was directed by Harry Rosenfeld, who told Woodward he was particularly skeptical of John Mitchell's stated reason for resigning from the Committee to Re-elect the President—that Martha Mitchell had tired of political pressures on her husband. Meanwhile, Carl Bernstein, who had been ordered back to his assigned Virginia beat by both Sussman and Rosenfeld, kept pestering to stay on the Watergate story and talked Rosenfeld into allowing him to chase down some leads Woodward was not working on. Sussman noticed while at the beach on July 3 that "a new byline appeared in the *Washington Post*: by Carl Bernstein and Bob Woodward." It was on a story about Hunt being interviewed by federal investigators and the White House assigning presidential counsel John W. Dean, III, to work "as an informal staff coordinator of White House reaction to the bugging incident."

When Sussman returned from his vacation, with Rosenfeld now away, managing editor Simons summoned him to his office to say he was worried that the *Post*'s efforts to pursue the Watergate story were drifting. Simons pointed to a story in that morning's *New York Times* and asked why the *Post* didn't have it. "Goddammit, we've got to do more on Watergate," Simons said. "I want an investigative team full-time on it and I don't care who you put on it."

At the same time Simons told Sussman he was displeased about Carl Bernstein's flagrant misuse of *Post* expense money. Among other extravagances, Simons pointed out, Bernstein was renting automobiles for assignments and leaving them parked and forgotten in downtown garages as both the parking and rental bills ran up. So Sussman did not expect Simons to be overjoyed when he told him later that day just who had been put on the special Watergate investigative team. "Now, sit down and don't go through the roof," Sussman told Simons. "Please relax. I've assigned Carl Bernstein to the team and I've sent him to Florida."

Bernstein surprised everyone, of course, both by not spending like a sailor in Miami and by making possible the next important breakthrough on the Watergate story. He talked a state prosecutor into showing him the telltale $25,000 check from a Nixon campaign contributor that had been found deposited in the Miami bank account of Watergate burglar Bernard Barker. It was from this account that Barker had withdrawn the $100 bills found by police on the Watergate burglars. Bernstein did not know that the name he found on the $25,000 cashier's check—Kenneth Dahlberg—was that of a Nixon campaign contributor. But with the information Bernstein telephoned to him, Woodward used *Post* clippings, directory assistance, and the telephone to track down the Minneapolis businessman, who acknowledged making the campaign contribution. As it happened, a *New York Times* reporter had seen the Dahlberg check shortly before Bernstein got to Miami, but he was unable to discover who Dahlberg was.

It was Woodward's and Bernstein's ability to work flat out, with little rest, and in uncanny coordination under Sussman's imaginative, constantly theorizing direction that put them well in front of everyone else. "When you got that $25,000 check and once Woodward developed his 'Deep Throat' source," Ben Bradlee later told them, "there was no way of keeping you off the story. You were working harder than the national staff is accustomed to working. Because you had no families, you were ready to do that 2 a.m. bit, which the forty- and fifty-year-olds on the national side aren't."

Woodward's and Bernstein's work habits during the long months of reporting Watergate have become legendary. They virtually lived in the *Post* newsroom, turning up there almost every day of the week. When one tried to get away on a weekend or a short vacation, a call from the other about a new development brought him right back. Once, Woodward flew to Mexico City to unwind, but after two days of nervously searching through every English-language newspaper he could find for news of Watergate he returned impatiently to Washington. Ever fastidious about his health and grooming, Woodward kept a toothbrush and toothpaste in his desk so that he could faithfully brush his teeth each evening he was staying on past dinner at the *Post*. Bernstein, who prowled the newsroom even later—often until two or three in the morning, making more telephone calls, rewriting their story for the next day's paper, or checking on what that night's *New York Times* or *Los Angeles Times* might have on Watergate—finally bought clothes he stuffed into his desk drawers for late-night or early-morning changes. Woodward told Sussman one day he had run out of soap at home and never had a chance during the day to buy it. "It's really getting to be a problem," Woodward told Sussman, "I'm taking my showers with shampoo because that's all I have to wash with." Sussman gave a copyboy money to buy soap that he sent home with Woodward that night.

While Woodward methodically filed away his information, story carbons, and clippings, Bernstein allowed them and a raft of newspapers, magazines, books, and personal mail and belongings to pile high on his desk. Months later, when he finally had an opportunity to clean it off, he found dollar bills and a pair of shoes, among other curiosities. With almost no work space on his desk, Bernstein hunched over in his rolling chair to talk on the telephone and took notes on his typewriter or by hand on any available scrap of paper. Yet he could always find any note or hastily scribbled telephone number he looked for in the mountain of debris. He chain-smoked his way through the hours of telephoning and writing, usually borrowing other people's cigarettes and matches. "He never has matches," wrote a friend of Bernstein's, free-lancer Julia Cameron, in *Washingtonian* magazine, "and a walk past his desk when he is on a call and signalling for a light is a glimpse at a talent that puts Bombay beggars to shame."

The reporters relied on two principal investigative techniques to solve the Watergate riddle. One was to trace the "money chain," which eventually led from Barker and G. Gordon Liddy to campaign contributors like Dahlberg and reelection committee officials like Hugh Sloan and Jeb Stuart Magruder to fund-raisers like Herbert Kalmbach to controllers of the Nixon campaign's secret slush fund for "dirty tricks" like John Mitchell and H. R. Haldeman. The other technique was to find low- and middle-level people in the White House and the Nixon reelection committee who could be persuaded to provide them with small pieces of the puzzle. With Sussman's help, Woodward and Bernstein fitted these together to create first theories and then, with confirmation from a few steady sources in the FBI, Justice Department, and White House itself, stories that could be safely put into the newspaper. "The thing is to work from the bottom up," Bernstein said, "finding secretaries, clerks, and middle-level aides. They're people without the vested interests of their bosses, and very often you will get a much better version of the truth from them than you would get from their superiors or the target you're after."

It is now well known how Woodward and Bernstein spent their evenings and weekends knocking on the doors of such people, "like magazine salesmen," Bernstein has said. "For every sale," he pointed out, "you had fifty rejects." It was an exhausting, ego-testing experience, especially for Woodward, who had to work to become as glib with wary strangers as Bernstein seemed naturally to be. "Your inclination is to see somebody in their office," Woodward said, "but you usually do twice as well if you can get to see them in their homes. Even in the White House, people have names and addresses, and they go home at night. Nobody else is around, and the conversation is open-ended, especially at night. No phone calls. No appointments. If you ever take one of those interviews and graph it to plot the useful information against the amount of time you spend in someone's home, you'll find the useful information comes at the end of a long interview." In several cases it required several visits—almost like a courtship—for Woodward and Bernstein to completely gain a key person's confidence and finally persuade him to answer questions.

"People can come to perceive you as a friend if you come to see them at their homes," Bernstein said. "It really involves a different kind of relationship. If you think there is a chance of their agreeing to let you in by prearrangement, you call first. Otherwise, you just go and knock on the door. We went back to several places several times, were thrown out again and again, and then maybe on the fourth time, they will say, 'Okay, we'll talk to you.'"

"Go when it's cold and wear a thin coat," Woodward interjected. "Right, and shiver a lot," Bernstein added. "It gets a little tricky," he said, "and you shouldn't make any hard rules about it, but you can get people to perceive you as the opposite of what you know their prejudices are going to be." Nixon's people, even those upset by Watergate, remained fiercely loyal to the President, right on down to secretaries at the reelection committee, for a long time, and many of them shared his hostility to the press in general and the *Washington Post* in particular. "If you can sort of say," Bernstein explained, "that I'm not one of the herd, or express a thought that hits them as being sympathetic, perhaps, to a certain position they believe in, it can be terribly helpful. I'm not talking about acting or anything like that, really, but you let people know you're a human being."

In fact, Bernstein's approach often meant expressing sympathy for the plight of Nixon loyalists and implying that he and Woodward were not out to get the President but rather were after those functionaries who had embarrassed the President. Or the two reporters would say they already knew something that could embarrass many people and, to protect those who were innocent from the wrong kind of publicity, they were seeking clarification of the information. They insisted to their editors that they never violated the *Post*'s policy against wrongly identifying themselves or

"You want to find out how many different versions of a particular set of facts there are, . . . and find out exactly where the truth lies."

misleading people about their purpose. But there was obviously enough leeway in such situations to permit considerable wheedling.

In addition, Woodward and Bernstein seldom took notes during these encounters. "We couldn't use notebooks because they would just scare people," Bernstein said. "We would rush out to the car afterwards to write it all down." After returning to the *Post*, they usually typed up those notes and everything else they remembered on the *Post*'s six-copy paper. Copies of the notes—sometimes attributed to the source by name and sometimes only to "Woodward's friend" or "a White House source" or only an initial—were then shared with Sussman, Rosenfeld, and other editors, including myself. This enlarged the circle of those enlisted in the brainstorming about just where the new information fit into the puzzle.

Even Woodward and Bernstein's most helpful sources would only tell or confirm small pieces of information in each interview, and what they would say usually depended on how much Woodward and Bernstein could show they already knew. That made it seem less like breaking a secret for the next source to add information, and it encouraged the second person to know that he or she might then not be discovered as the real source. It also created tricky psychological situations for Woodward and Bernstein, who tried on occasion to guess what might be going on and bluff a source into confirming their theory. Because the confirmation often came in a kind of code or evasion, and because, of course, any one source could be mistaken or lying about what he or she discussed, more than one source had to independently confirm any important piece of information before it could be published in the newspaper.

"The idea is that you want to triangulate information," Bernstein said later, using a word he became fond of during the reporting of Watergate. "You want to find out how many different versions of a particular set of facts there are, and you want to reconcile them and find out exactly where the truth lies."

Accomplishing that led Woodward and Bernstein to finish each day's work by "making one last call" over and over again on the story going into the next day's paper to make certain they had not misunderstood or misinterpreted anyone. They also tried once again to reach anyone named in the story who was not going to come out looking very good. Many of those calls produced only a "no comment" or no answer at all. Most calls to the White House for comment produced the notoriously circuitous denials that help make Ronald Zeigler a household name. But a precious few others prompted the person involved to supply Woodward and Bernstein, for whatever self-serving reasons, with valuable new information that occasionally improved the story. "People we wrote about who were under suspicion and later even went off to jail became good sources," Bernstein said.

"You have to bite that emotional bullet at the end of the day and call them," Woodward explained, "and say, 'Look, this is going into the paper tomorrow.' Some of the people are magnanimous enough to say, 'Good, it was nice of you to call.'"

Although Woodward and Bernstein's reporting stood the test of subsequent events well, it was difficult to be certain they were absolutely right during those long months when they and the *Post* were virtually alone on the Watergate story. Editors worried about the two reporters "reading eyebrows," as Howard Simons characterized it, in their coded conversations with sources. That concern increased after Bernstein misinterpreted a government source's long silence on the telephone as a prearranged confirmation of something that turned out not to be true—that Hugh Sloan, treasurer of the Nixon reelection finance committee, had named H. R. Haldeman in his grand jury testimony as one of the White House officials with control over disbursements of the secret "dirty tricks" slush fund. It turned out to be Woodward and Bernstein's one glaring error of fact, and the White House came down hard on it the next day. When Bernstein then telephoned Sloan to find out what was really true, I was listening in on the strange, meaningful, and yet uncertain communication taking place between Bernstein and one of his most important sources. As Bernstein went over and over the problem, Sloan would only state directly that he had never mentioned

Haldeman's name before the grand jury. In answer to all of Bernstein's never-ending, imaginatively rephrased questions about whether he nevertheless knew that Haldeman helped control disbursement of the money, Sloan would only say things like, "I'm not trying to influence your pursuit of the story." The denial was strictly low-key, purposely low-key. What was he *really* saying? Bernstein thought he knew. He thought as indeed turned out to be the case, that Sloan was pointing to Haldeman, but that he had never told the grand jury, and that was the only way in which the *Post*'s story had been wrong.

Woodward and Bernstein's writing methods also did not always add to their credibility in the newsroom. As they repeatedly rewrote each other's drafts of almost every story—Bernstein to smooth out Woodward's prose and better underscore the story's meaning, and Woodward to try to excise what he believed to be Bernstein's overreaching of the facts in hand—they sometimes fell to bickering about what a particular story should really say. It appeared, as Harry Rosenfeld often complained, that Woodward and Bernstein themselves did not fully understand what information they had.

When Barry Sussman became involved in the reporters' arguments over what to say and how to write it, "generally, but not always, I would decide on the path of restraint. Rosenfeld, Simons and Bradlee were generally involved in similar decisions, and they were basically even more restrained than I would have been." As it happened, Sussman later wrote, "what often seemed like rash, early judgments by Bernstein proved almost invariably to be correct, and as time passed, they found their way into the newspaper with abundant supporting material."

Bernstein continually argued with his editors, however. He wanted to get what he believed to be the whole truth out immediately. He wanted to contradict every accusatory statement put out by the White House. He wanted to underscore in his stories what he felt most readers, including his thick-headed editors, did not realize was really going on. Just when Bernstein seemed about to completely alienate his editors, Woodward would intervene and pull him off to an unoccupied corner of the vast newsroom for what appeared to be just the kind of firm but low-key parental lecture that Woodward must have received now and then from his father.

"There was some worry about what you were doing," Simons later acknowledged to Bernstein. "Accuracy. Trust. I think you were your own worst enemy. You two were the odd couple. Absolutely the odd couple."

As Bernstein especially, and Woodward to a lesser extent, became more and more emotionally involved in their struggle with the White House, the responsibility of the *Post* editors for carefully and dispassionately supervising the two investigative reporters became increasingly critical and difficult. Only Woodward and Bernstein knew just what information they had and how they obtained it, so it was necessary to go through the daily cross-examination sessions they describe in a few instances in *All the President's Men*. Every fact, every sentence, and every paragraph of every story was closely questioned—first in discussions with Sussman, Rosenfeld, and later myself about whether a story could be written, then in meetings with Simons and Bradlee in one of their offices to approve or overrule a decision to go ahead with a story, and then finally in the line-by-line editing of each story, which everyone seemed to get involved in. "Everybody wanted a piece of the action," Simons remembered. "Tempers would rise. Standing in the doorway (and stopping a story or excising something from it) got to be a very tedious job."

Editors must deal with an investigative reporter's stories in an adversary way, since an investigative reporter does not record an event in objective fashion. He subjectively presents what amounts to his theory of the evidence against someone he believes has done something wrong. He can be no more impartial about his inquiry than a good police detective or prosecutor, no matter how hard he tries. It is up to the editor to maintain the distance that the reporter has lost and bring to the story the skepticism that the reporter can no longer muster. This became difficult for Barry Sussman, who grew frustrated with an editor's limited role in getting and publishing a story like Watergate, and he eventually took time off from the *Post* in 1973 and 1974 to do his own research and write *The Great Coverup*, which remains the most insightful analysis of the entire Watergate drama.

Meanwhile, others at the *Post* were subjected to an apparent Nixon administration campaign to discredit the Watergate stories. Both Ben Bradlee and Katharine Graham were contacted by old political friends, who said they were strongly skeptical that John Mitchell or H. R. Haldeman could have been involved in such an affair. Others cautioned them to consider the effect of the stories during delicate negotiations to end the Indochina war. Henry Kissinger personally told Mrs. Graham that Haldeman had been wronged. Ken Clawson, a former *Post* reporter and national news editor who worked as a Nixon White House publicist, took Howard Simons aside in a downtown restaurant to ask how he could permit "two young punks" like Woodward and Bernstein to work on a story of such magnitude. Other officials told Bradlee that Bernstein and Woodward were "badgering" and "persecuting" people who worked for the Nixon reelection committee by repeatedly calling them at their homes. They also accused Bernstein of trying to seduce secretaries he and Woodward had contacted for interviews.

Editors and reporters on the *Post*'s national staff, who were under similar pressures from their high government contacts, also expressed doubts about Woodward and Bernstein and their anonymous sources. "You always had the doubt on the national side," Simons later recalled, "that somehow we, Ben and Howard, had been taken, that we were on a giant joy ride. Anonymous sources. Nobody stepping forward. A good newspaper would never do that."

Only Simons and Bradlee know for certain whether then national editor Richard Harwood, a close buddy of Bradlee's, actually tried to take the story away from Woodward and Bernstein by arguing that it was too big for the two metropolitan reporters and their editors. "There really wasn't any choice," Bradlee said later. "The boys had started with it and had done all the work. It was their story, and there never was a time when we seriously considered taking it away from them."

At times, when Woodward and Bernstein seemed stymied or too tired from their nonstop work, Bradlee and Simons urged Harry Rosenfeld to add other metropolitan reporters to the Watergate team. But each of the newcomers produced only analysis stories, rather than new leads, in part because Woodward and Bernstein closely guarded their sensitively placed sources.

With Richard Nixon's overwhelming reelection victory in November 1972 came administration reprisals against the *Post* and an agonizingly frustrating period for Woodward and Bernstein and their editors. Reporters from other newspapers were favored with exclusive stories at the White House, presidential aide Charles Colson made a nasty personal attack on Ben Bradlee in a speech to a group of newspaper editors, and friends of Nixon in Florida filed formal challenges against the *Post* ownership of television and radio stations there. Meanwhile, weeks went by with Woodward and Bernstein unable to put together enough new information for another major Watergate story. From the outside it looked as though the *Post* had indeed been trying only to sabotage Nixon's reelection and, once he had won, had given up active pursuit of the story. Actually, the two reporters were simply running into too many closed doors. The Watergate cover-up, Americans would later learn, was now being directed personally by the President and his top aides, and they were keeping the lid on tight.

It was during this difficult time that Woodward and Bernstein, with Bradlee's worried approval, tried to contact members of the special Watergate grand jury then hearing evidence in U.S. district court in Washington. When only the Watergate burglars themselves were indicted and there seemed to be no movement by the prosecutors or grand jury to trace criminal involvement beyond them, reporters and editors at the *Post* began to fear that the case was somehow being fixed. If that were the case, one of the grand jurors might want to complain about it. Although grand jurors were sworn to secrecy about their investigations under penalty of criminal prosecution, there appeared to be no legal bar against reporters approaching them. Woodward and Bernstein described vividly in *All the President's Men* how Woodward memorized the twenty-three grand jurors' names, addresses, and occupations from cards filed in the federal court clerk's office, later wrote them down out of the sight of a watchful clerk who had warned him against taking notes, and then went from house to house with Bernstein in a vain attempt to persuade one of the grand jurors to talk.

The whole exercise turned out to be a big mistake. None of the grand jurors volunteered any information, and one of them reported the approach to the prosecutors and Judge Sirica, who had to be persuaded not to cite and jail the reporters for contempt of court. Although Woodward, Bernstein, and Bradlee have all contritely admitted their error in this particular case, Bradlee has refused to rule out the possibility that a *Post* reporter might at some other time be quite justified in talking to a grand juror, if that were the only way for the press to reveal a monstrous miscarriage of justice—and particularly if the grand juror were to come forward voluntarily out of a sense of higher duty.

For Woodward and Bernstein during this period there were also a growing number of distractions. In late November 1972 they learned that they and Barry Sussman had won the $6000 Drew Pearson Foundation award for investigative reporting, which was presented at a December luncheon addressed by Averell Harriman. During the next several months there were many more awards—including the Worth Bingham and Heywood Broun awards for investigative reporting and the Pulitzer Gold Medal for public service—and the luncheons, dinners, and ceremonies they brought. Correspondents from *Time* and *Newsweek* wanted to interview Woodward and Bernstein for magazine profiles. The two young reporters, their long hair flowing over the collars of rented tuxedos as they sat at banquet head tables, were lured increasingly into the spotlight.

There was also the book. Bernstein had once been approached by literary agent David Obst for a book growing out of Bernstein's *Post* series on career school frauds, so in October 1972 he called Obst with a new idea. He and Woodward were contemplating a book about Watergate that would go well beyond their cautiously written stories in the *Post*. Obst, a novice book agent who had worked for leftist political causes and was fascinated by Watergate and its political implications, spent three nights working up a proposal to present to four top New York publishers. Only one, Richard Snyder, vice president of Simon and Schuster and a friend of Obst, took the idea seriously enough to come to Washington and discuss it with Woodward and Bernstein. As it happened, they had lunch the same day the Haldeman story with the mistaken information broke. Lunch with Snyder was therefore short and the conversation rather unsatisfactory for everyone. Snyder returned to New York, where he was later called by Obst who told him that McKay, an upstart second-line publisher, was offering $60,000 for the Watergate book. Obst said he was seeking a publisher that could make it a best-seller and would come down a little for Simon and Schuster. After another telephone call Snyder and Obst agreed on a deal with a $55,000 advance for Woodward and Bernstein.

It seemed large at the time, but that figure turned out to be a gross underestimate of the book's financial potential. It was a whopping best-seller for Simon and Schuster, which has paid Woodward and Bernstein much more than $55,000 in actual royalties, and the Book-of-the-Month Club, which paid $105,000 to obtain it as a featured monthly selection for club members. Foreign publication rights were sold for more than $100,000, *Playboy* magazine paid $30,000 to excerpt highlights of the book in two prepublication installments, paperback rights were sold for $1 million, and Robert Redford paid $450,000 for a movie option, with more to come.

What helped greatly to increase the value of Woodward and Bernstein's book, of course, were the big breaks that began occurring in the Watergate case in 1973. Seymour Hersh of the *New York Times* and *Time* and *Newsweek* magazines joined the reporting competition in January with stories about the Watergate burglars still receiving money from the Nixon reelection committee on the eve of their trial. These stories took some pressure off the *Post* as a newspaper—it was no longer alone in the struggle against the Nixon White House and could be less convincingly accused of pursuing a vendetta—and put new pressure on Woodward and Bernstein, who responded by coming up with their next big story. Bernstein forced his way into a taxi carrying the Cuban Watergate burglary defendants and their lawyer from U.S. district court, where their trial had begun, to the airport, and then got a seat next to one of the men on a flight to New York. The men were being pressured, the source said, to plead guilty, in return for financial support for their families and eventual executive clemency from the White House. The *Post* printed the story, and the men changed their pleas to guilty that same day.

Then things seemed to happen in a rush, even though they were strung out over many months. The U.S. Senate created its Select Watergate Committee, chaired by Sen. Sam Ervin. Convicted Watergate burglar James McCord sent his letter to Judge Sirica charging that perjury had been committed at the Watergate burglary trial. Stories by Woodward and Bernstein, Hersh, and others explained the nature and dimensions of a White House-run Watergate cover-up and its relationship to the activities of the White House "plumbers" who had been assigned by President Nixon to find and stop government leaks to reporters. The burglary of Daniel Ellsberg's psychiatrist's office was revealed at Ellsberg's Pentagon Papers trial in Los Angeles. More information about all of this, as well as the first public knowledge of the White House taping system, came out of the Ervin committee's dramatic hearings during the summer of 1973. The eventual Watergate cover-up trials, campaign finance violation prosecutions, and the presidential impeachment investigation all became virtually inevitable.

Woodward and Bernstein, meanwhile, were becoming an institution. Practically everyone was willing to talk to them now, including high-ranking figures in the White House and the Nixon reelection committee who met secretly with the pair or used lawyers as intermediaries. Some of these sources—particularly one-time White House counsel John W. Dean, III, communicating through his lawyers—tried to use Woodward and Bernstein, Hersh, and reporters for the news magazines as instruments in their bargaining for favorable treatment from Watergate prosecutors and the Ervin committee by leaking tantalizing bits of information. The prosecutors themselves became more helpful to the reporters in an effort to convince doubters that they were pursuing the Watergate cover-up vigorously and to expose and counter efforts by the Nixon White House to hamper their work. Officials inside the White House itself became dependable sources for Woodward and Bernstein as they tried first to put the best light on information that was coming out anyway and, toward the end of the Nixon Presidency, to assure the public that nothing rash would happen in the White House. Woodward told me that whenever he called for General Alexander Haig, who became Nixon's White House chief of staff following the forced resignation of H. R. Haldeman, Haig would promptly call him back personally. Transcripts of the White House tapes later showed that Nixon himself followed closely what Woodward and Bernstein were writing and tried to send threatening messages to them through his staff, particularly a young White House aide named David Gergen, who was a friend of Woodward's.

"What did Woodward say?" Nixon asked Ronald Ziegler on the evening of April 27, 1973, according to the White House transcripts.

"Woodward said they had two stories," Zeigler answered. "One was the fact that it (the Watergate investigation) was reaching a new plateau, and he was not ready to read the story because he was still working on it, and Woodward was taking the position that he was confused and needed to talk to someone to get a perception." It was just three days before the resignations of Haldeman, John Ehrlichman, and Attorney General Richard G. Kleindienst and the firing of John Dean; Woodward and Bernstein knew that something was about to happen. "What they are trying to do," Zeigler told Nixon, "is to get a fix on what's happened over here."

"Okay," Nixon decided. "Take a hard line. Gergen to Woodward. Anything on that they better watch their damned cotton picking faces."

After having labored almost alone on the Watergate story for many long months, Woodward and Bernstein were now caught up in a frantic competition among numerous Washington reporters trying to keep abreast of investigations under way on Capitol Hill, in the U.S. district court, and in the Special Watergate Prosecutor's office. To stay ahead of the pack, Woodward and Bernstein developed their own sources inside each investigating body. For example, Woodward helped get an old acquaintance, Scott Armstrong, hired as an investigator on the staff of Senator Ervin's Senate Watergate Committee, and Armstrong did not forget his friend and benefactor. Even inside the Special Watergate Prosecutor's office, the most nearly leakproof of all the groups investigating Watergate, Woodward and Bernstein found lawyers they could befriend over dinner and convince to help them with confirmation of information the reporters first learned elsewhere. In addition, whenever there was a battle between investigators and the White House—like the special prosecutor's struggle to obtain subpoenaed White House tapes— Woodward and Bernstein infiltrated the lines on both sides, offering the combatants a chance to air their side of the story.

At the *Washington Post*, national editor Richard Harwood had successfully claimed formal jurisdiction over both the Special Prosecutor's office and the House Judiciary Committee's impeachment investigation, because the Justice Department and Congress were traditional national staff beats. But Woodward and Bernstein, who were still allowed to roam anywhere they wished, came up with the *Post*'s only inside stories on these investigations. They were the first reporters, for instance, to discover that the Watergate grand jury had taken a secret eighteen-to-nothing "straw vote" (five grand jurors did not participate) in favor of naming President Nixon in the Watergate cover-up indictment if they had the constitutional authority to do so before impeachment. Bradlee and Simons blocked publication of that particular story for days, until hints of it began showing up in other newspapers, as well as Jack Anderson's syndicated column. The two editors remembered too well the fiasco over trying to contact individual grand jurors months earlier.

Bradlee and Simons had also grown wary of Bernstein's attempts to get stories past them that included what became known around the newsroom as "the-President-is-guilty paragraph." Bernstein had believed John Dean's accusations against Nixon from the beginning, and after the spring of 1973, Bernstein's pursuit of the Watergate story focused on the involvement of Richard Nixon. His versions of jointly written Woodward-Bernstein stories invariably contained an interpretative paragraph or two pointing directly at the President. Those inserts were always removed by an editor, prompting Bernstein to storm around trying to argue them back into the story. The scenario was repeated so often that it became a kind of ritual everyone expected to go through regularly.

By that time I was editing most of the metropolitan staff's Watergate stories under the supervision of Rosenfeld, Simons, and Bradlee, and I remember well hours of often angry negotiations. Deadlines would come and go—a half-finished story would have to be rushed into the first edition—as Bernstein and Woodward argued between themselves and then with the rest of us about analysis Bernstein in particular badly wanted in the story. The process inevitably became a test of stamina. Bernstein would stay late in the newsroom, repeatedly rewriting his key paragraph to win approval from me or the night editor after I had gone home. Then Bernstein would go back through the early edition versions of that night's story, castigating the amalgamation of his and Woodward's prose and revising it line by line, sometimes until 1 or 2 a.m. It was a *Post* editor who first said that at the premiere of the movie version of *All the President's Men* Bernstein would be inside the projection booth up to the last minute, making final revisions in each reel with scissors and splicing tape.

Finally, in August 1974 came what by then appeared to be the inevitable if still somewhat unsettling climax to the Watergate drama: President Nixon's resignation. Woodward and Bernstein had continued to report from their well-placed sources revealing glimpses of the extraordinary atmosphere inside the White House in the dying days of the Nixon administration. But when Nixon finally went before television cameras in the White House studio to announce the decision that Bernstein in particular had been predicting for more than a year, the two reporters became numb. After watching the speech with other *Post* reporters and editors gathered in funereal silence, Woodward and Bernstein each drifted wordlessly to his desk and sat down glassy-eyed. After a while, they each got up to wander aimlessly around the newsroom and watch distractedly as other reporters busily put together stories on the momentous event. But Woodward and Bernstein themselves were simply unable to work. Woodward said something about letting a decent interval of time pass before he could bother his inside sources. He and Bernstein typed out a few short background memos for other reporters to use, and then they disappeared. The reality of what they had been doing for more than two years finally hit them: They had helped force the first resignation of a President in American history.

Woodward and Bernstein did not return to work at the *Post* until a year later. In the interval they took a leave of absence without pay to advise on the production of *All the President's Men* and to write their new book on the last days of the Nixon administration, with a $300,000 advance from Simon and Schuster. They had already been away from the newspaper for fairly long periods during the latter stages of the Watergate story to write and promote *All the President's Men*, and for nearly two years they had been making one or two-day trips to lecture for up to $3000 an appearance each. But while working on their second book they tried to withdraw somewhat from the limelight and normalize their lives. Woodward married the Washington correspondent for the *Fort Worth Star-Telegram*, Francine Barnard, and settled down in a comfortable house he bought in a fashionable neighborhood northwest of Georgetown.

Bernstein bought a cooperative apartment downtown and concentrated on supervising its expensive redecoration.

They were unable to avoid the kind of determined media attention that concentrates on popular celebrities, however. Newspaper and magazine gossip columns featured details of their book deals, the making of the movie and the reporters' own up-and-down relationship. "A rumored rift between them is reported with the same gushing and guessing accorded Jackie and Ari, Sonny and Cher, Liz and Dick," declared the *Washingtonian*, which had indulged in much of the gushing and guessing itself.

This Hollywood aura washed over the rest of the *Post*'s newsroom inhabitants when Robert Redford and company came to prepare for the movie of *All the President's Men*. Redford had wanted to make such a film ever since he first read about Woodward and Bernstein's emergence from obscurity and their marked dissimilarities in personality. "It all clicked," he recalled later. " 'That's a movie,' I said." Redford arranged a meeting with Woodward in Washington, where he was told that they were writing a book about it all first. Redford bought the movie rights as soon as they became available and continued visiting Woodward while the reporting of Watergate was still in progress. The actor became what others at *Post* called a "newspaper groupie," enjoying vicariously the thrill of the Watergate chase. In interviews after the movie was finished, Redford even claimed that he had provided valuable suggestions for Woodward's and Bernstein's reporting.

The collaboration almost worked both ways. After screenwriter William Goldman produced a first draft for the movie that one *Post* editor described as "really nothing more than 'Butch Cassidy and the Sundance Kid Bring Down the Government,' " Bernstein decided to rewrite the script in collaboration with Nora Ephron, the *Esquire* writer with whom he was living. Director Alan Pakula finally stepped in and spent weeks in the *Post* newsroom himself, taking notes and shadowing editors and reporters as they worked. He interviewed Woodward and Bernstein so thoroughly that Woodward said, "If Pakula ever stops directing movies, he'll make a great shrink." Pakula then supervised a final Goldman draft of the script.

Redford and Dustin Hoffman next took turns prowling the *Post*, watching reporters for days, and hobnobbing with editors and publisher Katharine Graham "to get a feel for the business," as Hoffman put it. They were joined briefly by Jack Warden (who portrays Harry Rosenfeld in the movie), Martin Balsam (Howard Simons), and Jason Robards (Benjamin Bradlee), plus a bevy of production assistants who measured and photographed every inch of the huge newsroom and carted away tons of its desk-top trash for an eerily exact replica built at a cost of $450,000 on two sound stages at Burbank Studios in California. At the height of this excitement, editors offering news stories for the *Post*'s front page at the daily story conference tried to outdo each other with drama and wit as the visiting actors watched. Hoffman even listened in on one investigative reporter's telephone calls and whispered suggestions for questions he thought the reporter should ask. Although the actors generally did their research at the *Post* seriously—and Hoffman in particular captivated editors, reporters, and copykids with his earnestness, modesty, and humor—the continuing distraction made the *Post* newsroom's recovery from a predictable post-Watergate slump even more difficult.

"Beneath all this fuss," the newspaper itself philosophized in a long examination of the Watergate movie hoopla that Ben Bradlee ordered written for the "Style" section,

lie questions that gnaw at editors and reporters alike. Roles are suddenly being reversed here; actors are going to be reporters and reporters are onstage, playing themselves for the observing actors.

Professional newspaper people prefer to see themselves as detached, dispassionate observers—rumpled scribblers lurking carefully in the background. Now they find themselves bedfellows with "The Stars," emissaries from Hollywood, where self-publicity is a necessary art and the synthetic ray of the spotlight a principal source of energy.

All these considerations surface at a time when, as a side effect of Watergate, the media and the public are talking about journalists as being "stars" themselves . . . There are those who say Robert Redford isn't as big a name any more as Robert Woodward.

"The celebrity stuff is total bullshit," Bob Woodward the reporter said, as he struggled to free himself from the outer skin of the celebrity. "As soon as someone becomes a celebrity, they become less useful to the newspaper, and that includes Ben Bradlee and David Broder, too. It gives you too much independence from the institution and breaks down the hierarchy. That institutional support is important for me. I operate best in an institutional framework."

When Woodward returned to the *Post* in the autumn of 1975, while Bernstein remained on leave, he simply turned up at his desk again one day, telephoning old sources around Washington until he hit on new investigative stories for the *Post*'s front page: Howard Hunt's abortive plan to drug or poison muckraking columnist Jack Anderson, the National Security Agency's sophisticated electronic eavesdropping on long-distance telephone calls and cables of American antiwar leaders, and the blocking by Internal Revenue Service officials of recommended tax audits and investigations of Senator Joseph Montoya, whose Senate subcommittee controlled the IRS budget. All three stories led to immediate federal investigations. "Woodward really impressed me and gave the whole newsroom a lift," one *Post* editor said, "when he just came in here without any fanfare and sat right back down to work."

But for Woodward, it was the only course to take. "I'll go back to doing anything that's wanted of me," Woodward had said several months earlier, while still on a leave of absence. "I'd go right out on a murder. And then I'd go back to my old mode of operation. I'd start coming to you and say, 'I've got this other good story, and I've already talked to these people and have just these other phone calls to make before I can write it, and it will be worth page one.' That's the most salable quality a reporter has—the ability to get a good story."

2: "Scoop Artist"

"My cover is that I like scoops," Seymour Hersh said, smirking slyly. "That's what I told *Newsweek* once, and they ran with that, calling me the reporter who loves scoops." The *Newsweek* article—which was even entitled "Scoop Artist"—appeared in late June 1972, not long after he was hired by the *New York Times* for its Washington bureau and given an unusual assignment for one of its correspondents in the capital: investigative reporting.[1]

Hersh, who while a free-lancer had uncovered the My Lai massacre in Vietnam, soon rivaled Woodward and Bernstein with his explosive exposés of government wrongdoing for the *Times*: the Nixon administration's secret bombing of Cambodia; Henry Kissinger's participation in the bugging of his own staff aides; several significant Watergate revelations; the involvement of the Central Intelligence Agency in the overthrow of Chilean President Salvador Allende, and, perhaps Hersh's most important single story for the *Times*, the CIA's extensive, illegal, domestic spying activities. With these and other stories Hersh helped turn public opinion against the war in Vietnam, end the press corps' overlong honeymoon with Henry Kissinger, keep the Watergate story alive, and bring about a complete reexamination of the role of the CIA. Hersh did all this with a defiant, tenacious, often badgering, and sometimes belligerent style of reporting seldom exhibited by any newspaper's Washington correspondent, much less one for the prestigious and proper *New York Times*.

Since the 1840s, when the *New York Herald* and the Associated Press began building the first Washington bureaus of top-flight reporters, the capital's correspondents have comprised an elder elite of American journalists. Each has been specially selected by his news organization to report authoritatively on the words and actions of the nation's leaders in the tradition of Horace Greeley, Richard Harding Davis, David Lawrence, and James Reston. Because he helps decide what is news in Washington, surviving elections along with "the upper bureaucracy of the permanent government establishment," as

Stewart Alsop observed, he eventually gains what Alsop called "a certain status and authority, and on occasion, a certain pomposity as well."

Arthur Krock, who held what he described as the "elegant title" of "The Washington Correspondent" of the *New York Times* for two decades during and following World War II, wrote in his *Memoirs* that the position "confers high professional and social prestige and these provide opportunities for getting important news." Krock also acknowledged, however, that he suppressed important news whenever he or his good friends in Congress, the Cabinet, or the White House thought it would be best. Such symbiotic relationships have been the rule rather than the exception.

Washington correspondents also have tended to cling together in the capital city's highly stratified society. They work alongside each other in the House and Senate press galleries, the West Wing press room of the White House, and the many Washington news bureaus located in the National Press Building just off Pennsylvania Avenue. They eat and drink in private House and Senate dining rooms, the National Press Club bar and restaurant, the Washington establishment's Metropolitan and Federal City clubs, and certain favored restaurants and bars downtown. They see each other at the frequent cocktail and dinner parties that constitute night life in Washington. And they even live near each other and government people of similar status in preferred neighborhoods like Cleveland Park, an enclave of large Victorian frame houses on a wooded hillside in northwest Washington.

All this togetherness, Stewart Alsop noted in *The Center*, his study of power in the capital, has given Washington correspondents the tendency to "travel in a pack" with the same "anxious, preoccupied, self-important air of beagles" on a hunt. "The beagle is a highly competitive dog," Alsop explained, "but he is always ready to follow uncritically any other beagle who claims to have smelled a rabbit." News becomes what the pack of correspondents chases after, and enterprising reporting becomes merely a matter of beating the rest of the pack to this news. There is little incentive to examine critically the institutions and mores of government, because that might mean breaking friendships with trusted government contacts, missing the consensus front-page stories everyone else is after, or failing to be followed down a new path of inquiry. There have always been a few mavericks sniffing around outside the pack, who have been regarded by their colleagues as eccentrics to be barely tolerated, but generally the Washington correspondent has not been a muckraker.

When "Sy" Hersh, as he is known to news source and quarry alike, came to Washington from Chicago in 1965, an exceedingly ambitious and energetic young reporter, he had ample opportunity to slip into the traditional Washington correspondent's role. He began work in the Associated Press office and soon was assigned to cover the Pentagon, a beat encumbered by traditionally strict protocol and abundant restrictions on independent news-gathering. Eventually, he, too, moved to a modest house in Cleveland Park. But these outward trappings had little impact on Hersh's way of pursuing news. Instead, he remained conspicuously loud, brash, and aggressive, defying Pentagon protocol, giving short shrift to the formal briefings there, and wandering around alone to find low-level bureaucrats he could cajole or bully into helping him report stories the top brass wanted suppressed. When Hersh uncovered U.S. research, development, and storage of chemical- and biological-warfare weapons in a series the Associated Press found too controversial, he quit and sold the pieces as magazine articles and a book, which helped lead to a presidential order stopping production and storage of biological-warfare agents. And when he came to the *Times* Hersh brought with him a reputation as a renegade radical journalist. He had, after all, worked outside the established news media system getting such stories as the My Lai massacre and then gone out of his way to condemn the conduct of the U.S. military in Vietnam and elsewhere. Hersh had made antiwar lectures for years on campuses all over the country. He had joined in the October 1967 "March on the Pentagon" protest demonstration in Washington. He had worked for a time as press secretary in Senator Eugene McCarthy's antiwar campaign for the 1968 Democratic presidential nomination. And he had traveled as a visiting journalist to Hanoi after being invited twice by the government of North Vietnam.

Even after he had been in the *Times* Washington bureau for several years, Hersh's defiantly individualistic, strongly driven, frequently abrasive manner made him seem singularly out of place in its reserved, men's club atmosphere. He still talked loudly and excitedly on the telephone and argued with other reporters in the bureau who he thought should be more skeptical in their work. He continued to rush out of the office to meet unknown sources and usually refused to indulge in the traditional Washington correspondent's business lunch with government officials or other reporters. His most productive work was often still done late at night at home, when he phoned sources who could not talk freely in their offices or over lunch.

"One of the bad things about the newspaper business is that the stories have to be so dry and stick to proven facts."

If anything, Hersh had become more of a crusader since he had told the *Newsweek* reporter in 1972 that "I love writing stories that make everybody jump up and down." By autumn 1974 he was ready to tell me, "I can say now that I'm motivated by more than scoops." He believed the nation had entered a liberating "era of skepticism" following My Lai, the Pentagon Papers, and Watergate. "Reporters obviously have personal beliefs," Hersh said. "The question is would you lie? Does the reporter maintain his integrity? I'm not a flaming radical, but I am against war. I also think, for example, that multinational corporations are dangerous, and many of them will have to be nationalized in time."

Hersh had just written several front-page stories for the *Times* about the Central Intelligence Agency's spending millions of dollars to secretly create domestic dissension in Chile before the military overthrow and killing of its Marxist President, Salvador Allende Gossens. Hersh told me that he was also convinced, but could not then prove, that the International Telephone and Telegraph Corporation, which sought U.S. intervention in Allende's Chile to protect its investments, was involved much more deeply in the CIA's covert operations there than fragmentary press accounts of ITT-CIA contacts had yet demonstrated.

"One of the bad things about the newspaper business," he said, "is that the stories have to be so dry and stick to proven facts. That's why I want to write a book about the Chile thing, so I can present some of the conclusions I've come to that I cannot absolutely support.

"But I'm responsible; I don't print every story," Hersh added quickly. He stopped just long enough in his rapid-fire, stream-of-consciousness delivery to jerk his head up and project intent sincerity from behind his heavy, dark-rimmed glasses. "I just spent a whole month—I must have interviewed fifty people, including some who you wouldn't believe talked to me—checking out rumors that the U.S. Navy actually helped the Chilean Navy overthrow Allende. But it's not there; at least I can't find anything but rumors. I still think it was just the money we used down there that did it, and that's still fantastic. We have so much power to screw up other countries."

As he freely expressed his anger at a government that could do something like that, it became evident that it was Hersh himself who would be the first to "jump up and down" at much of what he found out in his reporting. This sense of outrage, abetted by his craving for ego-feeding attention, has in the past driven him to extraordinary lengths to push his stories before the American public. He recalled his frustration when little notice was paid to an article of his published in the *New Yorker* in 1971. Hersh had written about a Pentagon memorandum in which a U.S. Army division commander, Major General Lloyd B. Ramsey, ordered only official reprimands for American soldiers who had violated the Army's own "rules of engagement" in strafing a "friendly" Vietnamese village by helicopter for no reason and killing ten civilians.

"I still have that piece of paper," Hersh said. "An army clerk of some kind came up and gave it to me after a speech I made on the war in South Dakota. I couldn't believe it. I thought it might be a fake. But I went to work on it and discovered through intensive interviewing that it wasn't a fake. The general had been foolish enough to put it all in writing. It was a clearer example than My Lai of how this kind of thing was tolerated at the highest levels. But it didn't get picked up. NBC did call me and did something on it on their evening TV news. But they pointed out that only ten civilians were killed in this one compared to a hundred or more at My Lai."

"Hersh is a man on the run, like Sammy Glick, running all the time," one of Hersh's government sources told me. "On the phone, he is almost breathless, and I mean at two in the morning!"

This source, who worked in a sensitive federal position, did not set out to leak information. But Hersh's integrity and his unusual grasp, gained through voracious reading and unceasing questioning, of the technical knowledge of the source's field of responsibility convinced him. "He impressed me with what he knew, and with the good judgment he showed in evaluating the information he gathered. He could read disguised language well," the source said of Hersh and the codelike conversations that are a muckraker's stock in trade. "He found the secondary and tertiary meanings, and he had the background knowledge to put it into context. He had a good sense of what the story was."

Sources who are not so willing to talk are much less complimentary about Hersh's technique. Some are terrorized by his constant calling at all hours and screaming tantrums when they would not tell him what he wanted. Although he indignantly denies it, some sources have accused him of crudely insulting and threatening them over the telephone and castigating them in his conversations with their colleagues. At other times, when it suits his purpose, Hersh can be engagingly witty and charming, flattering his source into revealing important information.

Hersh insists, though, that investigative reporting "is just basic reporting—just hard work. All along I've been willing to make the extra effort." Hersh makes dozens to hundreds of telephone calls in checking out any promising tip. "You call and call," he said, "and sooner or later you find somebody who knows something and is indiscreet enough to tell you. Then you call somebody else and say so-and-so is saying this. And he says no, it's that."

Such persistent effort can produce amazing results. He described for example, how with just two phone calls and a long taxi ride—three steps no other Washington correspondent took in this particular case—he got from Air Force General John D. Lavelle himself the first story of Lavelle's secret bombing of North Vietnam. "I'm the guy who went and found the son of a bitch," Hersh said, "just by scrambling around."

Lavelle had been forced to retire for what the Pentagon announced as "personal and health reasons" in April 1972. But beyond a nine-paragraph United Press International report, picked up on the front page of the *Washington Post*, the change of command received little attention from Washington reporters, who apparently accepted the Pentagon's explanation. An even more curious May 15 statement from General John D. Ryan, Air Force chief of staff, saying that Lavelle had been relieved "because of irregularities in the conduct of his command responsibilities," went almost entirely unnoticed by the press. On Capitol Hill, however, the staff of a House investigating subcommittee decided to summon Lavelle, Ryan, and Secretary of Defense Melvin Laird to a hearing scheduled June 12.

Hersh, just returned to Washington from covering the Paris peace talks, received a call from "a guy with Air Force connections who said there might be something hot there. So (after many telephone calls) I found the name of Lavelle's executive officer and called him. He told me that Lavelle lived in an apartment in Gaithersburg (a Maryland suburb of Washington). So I made that one phone call to his apartment, something no other reporter did. He said he was on his way out to play golf with his sons. So I asked if I could go along; I told him I hit a good ball. He said okay, if I wanted to come. So I just got into a cab and went out there. None of this 'I'll see you tomorrow at 9 a.m.' stuff. I went out there that same day."

"You don't forget how to hit a golf ball, and I had always been able to hit it well," Hersh, who had played for money in his twenties, told me with characteristically earnest immodesty. "I was hitting them beautifully—180 yards with a five iron and a nice draw—and giving them lessons on how to fade and draw the ball. I don't know if that made the difference with Lavelle or not. I also joked about how, for a guy retired on disability, Lavelle hit a golf ball pretty well himself. It's always good to joke with these guys, and I like to fuck around anyway. So when we were finished I asked him if we can talk, and he sends his kids away while we go to the clubhouse for a beer. And after about an hour he just starts to tell me all about it."

Lavelle told Hersh he had been demoted to three-star status and forcibly retired because he had ordered numerous unauthorized bombing attacks on North Vietnam in January, February, and March 1972 and then falsely reported them to the American command in Vietnam and to the Pentagon as "protective reaction" strikes in defense of enemy attacks on U.S. aircraft.

"I was stunned," Hersh said. "The guy confessed that he had violated one of the most sacred principles, acting without orders. I said, 'Tell me one thing, why the hell weren't you court-martialed?' And he said, 'When was the last time you heard of a four-star general being court-martialed?' It was a little chilling."

Hersh remembered that "all this was on a Thursday, and I checked it out on Friday." The hearings of the House investigating subcommittee were scheduled for the following Monday, and Hersh wanted his story to appear first in the Sunday edition of the *Times*. Under the ground rules set by Lavelle in their interview, Hersh could use everything the general told him, but none of the information could be attributed to Lavelle. As a result, Hersh's long story was attributed to "a high-ranking military source with close knowledge of the incident," who was, of course, Lavelle himself.

Hersh then went to New York "to check the galley proofs" of the Sunday story, a precaution the *Times* at first insisted on for major stories by their new investigative reporter in Washington. Hersh also took the unusual step of reading much of the story to Lavelle on the telephone from New York to make certain he had not heard the general wrong. This was Hersh's most risky and controversial exposé in his first weeks at the *Times*, and he wanted every last detail to stand up. "Right near the top of the story I had listed some of the targets he ordered hit," Hersh said, "including air fields, radar sites, missile sites, anti-aircraft batteries, and MIG bases. Lavelle told me to cross out MIG bases and add oil storage sites. When you get down to that kind of detail, you know you really have the story."

Despite Hersh's admitted antiwar, antimilitary bias, he had come to like and feel sympathetic toward Lavelle. He also had the feeling, based on his own knowledge of the military command structure, that Lavelle may not have been acting entirely on his own. Instead, Hersh believed that Lavelle must have received some kind of secret encouragement with the understanding that he would take the full blame if it ever became necessary. Thus, Hersh's story in the *Times* included passages attributed to a "source" who was Lavelle himself, like the following:

A high-ranking military source with close knowledge of the incident said that General Lavelle was known to have received no written orders authorizing the strikes but "thought it was implied in the instructions that were given him."
The source added that the strikes ordered by General Lavelle were aimed "only at targets that could hurt the enemy." In General Lavelle's eyes, the source added, he had the authority as a battle field commander "to make a determination of how far you can stretch the rules before going up through the chain of command" . . .
In addition, General Lavelle, who is 55 years old, is known to believe that his superiors at headquarters in Saigon were aware of his bombing attacks but nonetheless accepted his reports of protective reaction strikes at face value.

After discussing the Lavelle interview, Hersh proudly showed me a letter he had kept in his desk at the *Times* bureau for more than two years since receiving it from the general's oldest son. Young Lavelle, a college student, complimented Hersh on the completeness and accuracy of that first story, which was later confirmed in detail by testimony at congressional hearings. He also thanked Hersh for his fairness in presenting his father's side of the story, something no one else had done. After letting me read the letter, Hersh put it back in his desk drawer and asked, "How can you beat that?"

Seymour Myron Hersh was born in Chicago in 1937 in a family of four children, whose parents ran a dry-cleaning store. Raised on the city's South Side, Hersh was an avid reader and a Chicago White Sox baseball fan, enjoying "a very happy childhood with no idea what I wanted to be." He was a "B" student in history at the University of Chicago, where he spent much of his time playing bridge. To see what journalism was like, he applied for work at Chicago's City News Bureau, which supplied crime and neighborhood news to Chicago's daily newspapers and broadcast stations. He was put on a long waiting list and went to work instead as a clerk selling liquor at a drugstore. "Then I decided to try law school. I applied and was accepted in a week. Can you imagine doing that today? But I hated law school and did poorly. I got decent grades at the start, but then they got worse every quarter. I finally left. I had discovered golf and was playing a lot of good, under-eighties golf in those days."

After fifteen months, Hersh was finally called back by the City News Bureau and got a job there as a copyboy. Occasionally, he was given the opportunity to chase a story. "One of the few times they sent me out," he remembered, "I found six people dead in a black neighborhood. Someone had killed five people and then killed himself. Five murders and a suicide. I got really excited and began calling bulletins back into the office. And I mean I was really running to the phone and calling up and shouting, 'Bulletin!' Now the City News Bureau was an old dry place—its reputation is really overblown—and a guy on the desk there finally broke into one of my calls. 'Ah, my good Mr. Hersh,' he said. 'Could it be that these unfortunate victims are of the American Negro persuasion?' So I said yes, and he said, 'Well, then, cheapen it up.' The story ran only a paragraph or two in the papers. I was really burned up. I guess I was a boat-rocker even then."

After six months at the City News Bureau, Hersh, who was in the Army Reserve, spent another half year on active duty as a public information officer at Fort Riley, Kansas. He gained good experience there, reporting and writing largely on his own, but when he returned to Chicago, the City News Bureau refused to take him back. Eventually, he agreed to the proposition of a friend and golfing partner named Robert Billings to start a weekly newspaper in the southwestern suburbs of Chicago. "He had the money, and I had the energy," Hersh said. "I sold ads five days a week, picked up the papers with a truck, and dropped them off to the delivery kids. Then I'd go back to the office and wait for mothers to call in and say their little Johnny is sick today, and then I had to go out and deliver the papers myself, too." Actually, Hersh did get a day off, Thursday, when he played golf from morning to dark.

The fledgling newspaper was quite successful, building quickly to a paid circulation of 8000, despite what Hersh thought were unfortunate editorials written by Billings. "I was always fighting with him about the editorials," Hersh said. "I wanted editorials about driving safely and things like that. But he wanted to be 'socially uplifting.' He wanted to urge them to do things like go see *La Dolce Vita*, and this was in a fine upstanding Catholic area, nearly all Roman Catholic. Here I am struggling for dimes and nickels selling ads and trying to tell him that he can't try to be so socially uplifting." After about a year, "just when we started getting the big national ads regularly," Hersh decided that being a suburban editor was not really his life's work. "There I was, twenty-five years old and almost a newspaper publisher, everybody's dream, but I realized that was not what I wanted. Billings was furious and wouldn't buy me out, so I quit."

Hersh went to California, where his mother had moved, and he played golf every day. "I got tired of that, came back to Chicago and got hired at United Press International by a friend who was an editor there. He sent me to Pierre, South Dakota, to run their bureau there. I was all alone. It was a small state capital, and I covered the whole legislature. I learned a lot, like how to cover a lot of committees simultaneously. I even punched the teletype to send my own stories out on the wire." Other reporters would have hated being "sent to Siberia" in a remote wire service bureau, but Hersh thought of it as an unusual opportunity. "I did a four-part series on the history of the South Dakota legislature, and I thought about doing a series on the Oglala Sioux Indians who were mistreated there. Even then I was thinking about the bigger picture. I looked around and did good features that went out over the wire, and some of them got into the *Chicago Tribune*. That was a big deal for those of us who had never been east of Chicago. So after the legislature ended in the spring of 1963, I asked UPI to send me to their Washington bureau. They said Omaha instead, so I quit—nicely and a little reluctantly—but I quit.

"Despite the stories I had gotten into the *Trib*, I still couldn't get a job on a Chicago paper," Hersh said. "But luckily I went to the Associated Press office in Chicago looking for a job about five minutes after some guy stood up after fifteen years there and said, 'Yaaahh,' and started tearing his hair out and quit. So they hired me a couple of days later. I worked for the AP in Chicago for two years, getting more good experience. I began writing the whole nightly radio wire for Illinois stations. I had to rewrite 1000 words an hour, trying to make it lively. I didn't have to punch the copy myself at AP; I just handed it to an operator."

Hersh thrived on the lonely night work. He found ways to get more attention on the night shift than he could have working in an office filled with older reporters during the day. "I looked for good features to do at night," he recalls, "and I took the stories that had been written during the day and put good new leads on them for the p.m. papers (which make their wire-service story selections early in the morning). I got them on the A-wire a lot and got good play in the afternoon papers. I was always getting into the AP weekly log, which is an in-house cheerleading sheet that all the AP reporters and editors get all across the country. I'd get mentioned for scoring big on features, getting play in 82 percent of the papers and like that. I was obviously hot shit."

In time, Hersh was sent out on important breaking news during the day, including the first big, sometimes violent, civil rights marches through Chicago's all-white suburbs. The day editors, Hersh said, tried to tone down his accounts of verbal and physical attacks by whites on black civil rights organizers. So he stayed late enough to rewrite each story the way he thought best and send it out on the overnight wire. "By the time the editors on the dayside came in and sent out substitute paragraphs," Hersh said, "it was too late. The story was already in the afternoon papers."

After work, Hersh usually stayed up into the next morning, drinking and talking with night-owl friends or reading at home. His habits changed only a little after he married his wife, Liz, in 1964, though, according to friends, the sensitive, slim, dark-haired former social worker whom Hersh first met in 1958 at the University of Chicago, had a calming, influential effect on her unpredictable husband. When she decided to go to medical school after ten years of marriage, Hersh agreed to assume responsibility for the care of their two young children, a son and a daughter, and their home while he was not at work.

By 1965 Hersh "got restless again and tried job hunting." He sent letters and résumés to several newspapers, including what was then his first choice, the *Washington Post*, but got no encouraging replies. Just in time, the AP agreed to send him to Washington. There, he knew, he would be able to get more of his stories in papers all across the country. And sure enough, he "got a 400-word story on a national

"I'd play off the Navy against the Army, or tell the Air Force, 'You hit only three bombs on target the other day. . .'"

Shriner's parade out on the wire from Washington on the day after I left Chicago."

Again he was first assigned to night duty, and again he found it an opportunity to get his by-line in more newspapers. Taking stories already written by the bureau's veteran dayside reporters for the next day's morning newspapers, Hersh made the telephone calls necessary to put later developments and new information into his rewritten version. It did not take long for AP's Washington editors to recognize Hersh as an unusually ambitious, energetic, and resourceful young reporter. In 1966 they assigned him to cover the Pentagon.

Many a determined young reporter before Hersh had been worn down by the Pentagon's tight news-management procedures and eventually become little more than an uncritical parrot of the military's official pronouncements. In a vast labyrinthine building where many areas were kept permanently off limits to anyone without high government security clearances, reporters were segregated in a hallway of their own, called "Correspondent's Corridor," on the walls of which hung color photographs of the correspondents regularly assigned there. On one side of the corridor was a large press room; across the hall was the Pentagon information office, where printed announcements were regularly posted and official reports, compilations of data, and military maps were made available. The Pentagon's information officers expected the reporters to do most of their work in Correspondent's Corridor. Once each day a public information officer would come to the press room, perch himself on a table top, and deliver the daily briefing. A number of Pentagon officials also were made available for briefings, press conferences, and interviews each week, though some would talk only if the reporters agreed not to name them as their sources. In this way an official could put out his version of a controversial military position without taking the responsibility of having his name or rank attached to it. On many other occasions, both Pentagon officials and the daily briefing officer simply refused to answer questions raised by reporters, especially on subjects potentially embarrassing to the Pentagon. They would cite national security or say simply, "I can't go into that."

Despite these restrictions, correspondents there were showered with enough official information of apparent importance that they were always able to produce a large number of stories—many of them front-page stories—without fighting the system. Their editors were generally satisfied, so long as each correspondent kept up with what everyone else was writing out of the Pentagon. They tended to leave the same reporters there for years in the belief that they needed considerable time to make key military contacts and acquire the complicated technical knowledge to understand new weapons systems, the Pentagon's huge budget, or tangled defense policy. Eventually, many of the correspondents came to accept the reporting restrictions in Correspondent's Corridor as normal and acceptable. In fact, most of the Department of Defense public information officers at any one time have been former Pentagon correspondents for major newspapers and armed forces' journals.

It is not surprising, then, that most major stories written by Pentagon correspondents on national issues reflected only the official military point of view. With a few notable exceptions, Pentagon reporters, especially at the time Hersh was assigned there, have seldom tried to balance that view with more critical appraisals from dissenters within military or civilian Pentagon ranks or from expert outside observers of the military on Capitol Hill, in the State Department, in universities, and elsewhere.

Hersh, though, quickly grew impatient at briefings and press conferences, where his sometimes impertinent questions were brushed aside. He soon made a habit of walking out in the middle of unproductive sessions and going instead to high-ranking officers in their lunch rooms, to question them, informally and uninvited, on subjects the briefing officers dodged. Hersh also found disgruntled Pentagon bureaucrats and "systems analysis guys with access to the cables" who regularly supplied him with key bits of inside information. Pentagon officials began to resent "that little ferret," as one officer called him, "who broke every rule for bureaucratic journalism" but landed important, often controversial stories for the

Associated Press. "I had more balls than most of those guys in that press room," Hersh said of his Pentagon colleagues. "I'd play off the Navy against the Army, or tell the Air Force, 'You hit only three bombs on target the other day' so that he'd tell me the truth.

"I realized right away that the briefings on the war in Vietnam were a waste of time, so after about twelve minutes of one of them I asked one question, said, 'Thank you,' and left. The other reporters walked out with me because they didn't know what was going on. (Arthur) Sylvester (then assistant secretary of Defense for public affairs) was amused, although publicly he said he was angry. But many of the other reporters were really mad. They called it a great breach of etiquette and very impolite, although I figured the briefings were for my convenience and not the briefing officer's."

Gradually, Hersh said, he began to realize that the Vietnam war briefings were not only incomplete but "were lies." (Sylvester himself later wrote—barely accepting responsibility for his own role in the deception—that "for six years I watched cover stories go down smooth as cream when I thought they would cause a frightful gargle. I don't know a newsman who has served the government as an information officer in the Pentagon who hasn't been dismayed at the evidence of shabby performance by what he used to think of with pride as his profession.")

Hersh's eyes were opened after "I attended a McNamara briefing and wrote a story about it according to the rules, without attributing the information to McNamara. The next day a young naval officer I had met said, 'Where did you get that story?' I told him he wouldn't believe it, that it was straight from a McNamara briefing. He said everything in it was wrong, and he showed me how. That incident had an impact on me.

"It was also about that time I met Izzy (I. F.) Stone. One day this funny old man showed up there, introduced himself, and asked if he could look through the AP files. Finally, the other guys in the press room asked me who the funny old man was. When I told them, they made it clear they didn't like me allowing Stone to use the files. So I began to notice what Stone was writing in his *Weekly* and saw he wrote some very good staff exposing the Pentagon's lies."

When the United States was accused of bombing civilian's homes in Hanoi and Harrison Salisbury of the *New York Times* was allowed into North Vietnam to write about the bombing damage there, it was all strongly denied by the Pentagon in unskeptical stories written by most of the regulars. According to Hersh, a small group of the regulars even "met privately with a top Pentagon official, who asked for help in writing a statement of denial that turned out to be untrue." But Hersh went to his sources in the Pentagon and found documentation that Hanoi had indeed been regularly bombed, and McNamara had quietly ruled it off limits for a time because of Salisbury's stories. Hersh's AP story made the front page of the *New York Times* that day.

"I learned how to work the *Times*," Hersh said. "I would hold off and break stories at night, right on their 6:15 deadline, with an 'urgent' sent out over the wire. I always told the AP what I'd be writing very late in the day, and I'd tell them that I had a good story but needed one more guy to confirm it. That's when they'd send the advisory out on the wire. That one last guy I had to talk to usually would be the systems analysis guy I saw after he finished work. He could always confirm stories and always gave me a little something extra in details, although he never told me anything big first.

"Neil Sheehan (the *Times* Pentagon reporter who later obtained the Pentagon Papers) helped me at the *Times*," Hersh said. "When one of my urgents came in over at the *Times*, they'd ask Sheehan to check it out," Hersh said. "So, unknown to them, he'd call me. We had a ritual. He'd ask me, 'Was that story on the wire pretty much the way you wrote it?' And I said yes. So Neil would tell his editors, 'Okay, I confirmed it,' and they'd go with my story."

Why did Sheehan do that for him? Hersh said Sheehan "was impressed with my energy and ability to get the real truth out of the Pentagon system. He tried, too, and he was a good reporter, but too often he got constipated. We became friends after one day when I took Sheehan to a guy in his cups at the Pentagon who helped me out sometimes. He told us something key that made a front-page story for Sheehan in the *Times* and for me in the *New York Post* with the AP.

"Most of the other Pentagon reporters supported the war and believed the official lies," Hersh said. "I learned to hate the war at the Pentagon. It was just one lie after another. I learned to be such a cynic. It got so I'd hear the darkest stories from my sources and figured they were probably true, so I went to see someone and made the worst case possible on hypothesis. And the guy would say, 'Well, it was not quite that way. Not two villages hit by our own bombs, but only one.' And you'd come back a little on your original hypothesis and have a story.

"I was only wrong that way once," Hersh admitted, "on a supposed McNamara memo that turned out not to be true. And I still did the hardware stories and other stuff the beat demanded, too. But the Pentagon was uptight about me, and Sylvester began calling Wes

Gallagher" (general manager of the Associated Press). Hersh is not certain what the effect of the calls were, but about that time he was transferred from the Pentagon to a new investigative reporting team the AP set up in Washington. At first unhappy about being moved out of the Pentagon, he quickly adjusted and wrote a series of articles that revealed American development of chemical and biological warfare weapons.

"I was the first to confirm that we did chemical and biological warfare like crazy at a time when it was a big secret in the United States," Hersh said. "I wrote a forty-five-page, seven-part series and turned it in to the editor of the team. He was a paper shuffler who kept pushing aside problems. Finally on the third day after I turned it in he took a look at one part and told me it was too long. That's when I decided I had to get out—nothing dramatic, no confrontation, but the AP never ran the series."

Hersh sold several of the articles to *The New Republic*, which gave them prominent display. In them Hersh described the government's research and development of chemical and biological warfare agents in detail and named the private corporations and universities doing the work under government contracts. He told where the agents were made and stored and explained how hazardous they were for workers, some of whom had been made ill or killed following undisclosed accidents. Hersh argued that the entire program was a violation of earlier promises by the government, going back to Franklin Roosevelt, that the United States would never undertake biological or chemical warfare. The articles attracted wide attention, and when Hersh was offered a contract to write a book on the subject, he took it and quit the Associated Press in June 1967.

"I guess it was a gutsy thing to do," Hersh mused seven years later. "I had just moved into a new house in Cleveland Park, and my wife was pregnant. The rent was $225 a month, and I left a $200-a-week salary for a book that got me only a $4000 advance, $1000 of it in cash." Hersh managed to earn $8000 altogether in his first year of free-lancing, including his salary for the weeks in the early spring of 1968 when he worked as press secretary in the beginning of Eugene McCarthy's antiwar campaign for the Presidency.

Mary McGrory, the *Washington Star* columnist who was herself an outspoken opponent of the war, "lived across the street from me," Hersh said, "and got me the McCarthy press secretary job. That was the children's crusade, so-called. But I didn't last, although I did a good job." Hersh stayed with the campaign through the New Hampshire primary but quit in Wisconsin just before McCarthy's stunning victory there. "I can't be anybody's press secretary," Hersh told me, although he was not ready to admit that it just might be because he always wants to be the top banana. "I was a good press secretary," he insisted, "but I couldn't stand the backbiting. In anybody's campaign, there are too many second-raters and intrigues. People said I was too blunt, and they plotted against me. It was sheer madness. I was called an unexcelled master of profanity."

Hersh returned to Washington and continued free-lancing, selling more articles about chemical and biological warfare and other national defense issues to *Ramparts*, the *Progressive,* and the *New York Review of Books.* He picked up $200 to $300 plus expenses for each of several lectures he gave at college antiwar symposia, and he started work on a book about the Pentagon to be called *The Ultimate Corporation.*

Hersh was at home working on that book in late October 1969, when he got a call from a local lawyer friend who had good sources of his own in the Washington military community. "I've got a fantastic story," the lawyer said. "The Army is court-martialing some lieutenant in secrecy at Fort Gordon, Georgia. He's supposed to have killed seventy-five Vietnamese civilians."

"I instinctively knew I was not the first reporter to hear about the charge against the lieutenant, whoever he was," Hersh later recalled. "But I also knew that I was probably one of the few who would believe it. So I simply stopped all other work and began chasing down the story."

By calling sources in and out of the military all over Washington it took him days to find out the court martial was to take place not at Fort Gordon but rather at Fort Benning. Unable to learn anything more he took an unusual chance and called the Fort Benning public information office, where a surprisingly courteous and helpful officer told him he might mean a case involving a lieutenant named Calley, who had been charged with murder in the death of some Vietnamese civilians about eighteen months earlier, on March 16, 1968. The officer told Hersh that an Associated Press story about the filing of the charges had appeared on page 38 of the September 8, 1969, *New York Times.*

Hersh found the 190-word item, which had been transmitted by the Associated Press on September 6 and published by the *Times* two days later as a filler story. It began:

> FT.BENNING, GA.(AP)—An Army officer has been charged with murder in the deaths of an unspecified

number of civilians in Vietnam in 1968, post authorities
have revealed.
    Col. Douglas Tucker, information officer, said the
charge was brought Friday against 1st Lt. William L.
Calley Jr., 26, of Miami, Fla., a two-year veteran who was
to have been discharged from the service Saturday . . .

Nothing more about the case had been published in the nearly
seven weeks between the AP story and the tip that prompted Hersh's
inquiries. In later acknowledging to a reporter from *Time* magazine
that the AP was "derelict" in not following up its own story, Wes
Gallagher pointed out that the news service did not receive a "single
call from an individual reporter or from broadcasters" requesting
additional information or stories.

Hersh went to see a friend on Capitol Hill, who, ironically, worked
on the staff of Mendel Rivers, the conservative Democrat from South
Carolina who chaired the House Armed Services Committee, "and I
began the standard newspaperman's bluffing operation: pretending
to know more than I did." Seeking to correct the wild story Hersh
gave him, the source said that Calley was charged with killing perhaps
ninety Vietnamese civilians. The congressional aide added that
Calley apparently had shot many of them himself. "Don't write about
this one," the source advised. "It would just do nobody any good. The
kid was just crazy."

Other Pentagon and Capitol Hill sources who supplied small bits
of information also pleaded with Hersh not to write anything,
because of the likely adverse effect of such a story on public support
for the war in Vietnam. The killings were an aberration, they argued,
the act of one disturbed man. "This Calley is just a madman, Sy, just a
madman," said an Army colonel in the Pentagon, who told Hersh
that the victims included many women and children. "He just went
around killing all those people. Little babies! There's no story in that.
He's just pathetic and should be locked up in an institution."

Stymied, Hersh asked for help from the lawyer who gave him the
first tip and was told the last name of Calley's defense lawyer:
"Latimer." Hersh followed the tip to the one lawyer named Latimer
listed in the Washington, D.C., Yellow Pages. He was not
representing anyone named Calley in a military court martial, he
said, but it might be George Latimer, a former judge on the U.S.
Court of Military Appeals in Washington who had moved to Salt
Lake City. Hersh called that Latimer and made "an instinctive
decision—I wouldn't talk over the telephone to any potential source
about the case. Not because of any fear of wiretapping or such, but
simply to ensure that I gave myself every chance to get as much

information as possible." He told Latimer he just happened to be going to Salt Lake City and made an appointment to see him at nine the next morning.

Hersh had no money, however, so he called James Boyd at the Fund for Investigative Journalism, a Washington, D.C., foundation set up by philanthropist and muckraker Philip Stern to help free-lance investigative reporters bear the expense of research and travel. Hersh told Boyd what he was working on and about the trip he had to take to Salt Lake City. Assured that the fund would reimburse him Hersh left Washington that night.

He began his conversation with Latimer by complimenting him on a military appeal he had just won. Then, with the lawyer at ease, Hersh once again overstated the information he had on the Calley case, making the crime sound even worse than Hersh believed it to be at the time. As Hersh expected, the exaggeration prompted Latimer to correct him with some of the facts he knew. The lawyer even showed Hersh the official court martial papers charging that Calley was responsible for the deaths of 109 Vietnamese civilians near the village of Song My in the farmland province of Quang Ngai on the northeast coast of South Vietnam.

Convinced that he had an unusually important story, Hersh returned to Washington and used his new information to find out from his Pentagon and Capitol Hill sources that many soldiers involved with Lieutenant Calley in the military operation were back home in cities scattered across the United States. Hersh would have to find and interview some of them, and he would first have to find Calley. So much travel would require still more money, and after failing to sell the story idea to *Life* and *Look* magazines, Hersh went back to the Fund for Investigative Journalism. The directors, a group of Washington writers and editors who keep their decisions confidential until each project is completed, formally approved a grant of $2000 for Hersh's further research into the Calley case.

Beginning a flurry of cross-country air travel that would take him more than 30,000 miles during the next several months, Hersh took an early morning flight Tuesday, November 11, from Washington to Columbus, Georgia, where he rented a car and drove onto the sprawling Fort Benning U.S. Army base to find Lieutenant William Calley. Hersh stayed away from the base's headquarters and public relations office; he knew they would try to hide Calley from him. Instead, wearing a suit and carrying a briefcase so that he looked like a lawyer or some other official visitor, Hersh spent the first three hours searching unsuccessfully the main prisoners' stockade and the many military police posts dotted throughout the base. Calley was not locked up anywhere, and his name was gone from Fort Benning's current resident telephone directories.

"To reassure myself that Calley did, indeed, exist," Hersh later recalled, "I made a reckless move." He went into the Judge Advocate General's office, where the Army attorneys who would prosecute Calley worked, and asked a seasoned desk sergeant where Calley could be found. When the sergeant demanded that Hersh identify himself and was told that he was a reporter, he began to telephone for a colonel. Hersh hurried out of the building. He went next to the office of Calley's military lawyer at Fort Benning, Major Kenneth A. Raby, but that encounter also ended with Raby dialing the phone for a higher-ranking officer. Hersh now was certain that Calley was somewhere on the base and that he was upsetting the brass by trying to find him.

"I had a depressing sandwich at an Army cafeteria and thought briefly of giving up," Hersh remembered, "but then I had a better thought." He convinced a base operator to look up Calley's name in an old telephone directory. There it was. Apparently Calley had been stuck away in a training unit for new recruits in a distant part of the big installation. Hersh found it after another hour's searching in his car. The unit's commander, Captain Charles Lewellen, grew agitated when Hersh identified himself as a reporter and asked for Calley. "Look, give me a break," the officer told Hersh. "I'm just a captain trying to mind my own business. If you've got any questions about Calley, take them someplace else."

Hersh slipped into the unit's barracks, where only one soldier could be found sleeping on the third floor. Deciding to take another chance, he walked over, kicked the bed, and shouted, "Wake up, Calley!"

The young soldier turned out to be a National Guardsman from Iowa. He was not with the other trainees because his files had been lost for three months. But he had a friend named Jerry, who had been busted from sergeant to private the day before and sorted mail at the message center for the battalion. Perhaps he knew where Calley was. Hersh drove to the mail-room barracks, left his car parked out front with the motor running, and went inside, carrying his briefcase. "I want to see Jerry outside in my car in two minutes flat," Hersh announced to the officer on duty with as much authority as he could muster. The busted soldier quickly appeared outside and got into Hersh's car, looking apprehensive about what new trouble he might be in. Hersh told him he was looking for Calley. The only way to find him, the ex-sergeant said, would be to steal his personnel file.

"Well?" Hersh asked.

"I'll try, Mister," the soldier answered. He returned in five minutes with the battalion commander's information sheet on Calley. It included a local address.

Hersh drove outside the base to a small house at that address, where a group of officers told him that Calley was being hounded by the Army for some reason and had been ordered to move back onto the base in certain senior bachelor officers' quarters. It was 7 p.m. when Hersh found the five two-story dormitory-like buildings, each containing about fifty rooms. "I did the inevitable," Hersh recalled. "I walked through the maze, knocking on each door and saying brightly with each knock, 'Hey, Bill, are you in?' I did this for the next hour or two, finding only a few officers and no sign of Calley. Again, I was at the end of my wits, but I wasn't about to quit. If need be, I thought, I'd stay at Benning and knock on these doors for weeks."

In desperation, he went into the parking lot in front of the buildings and began stopping cars to ask the officers inside them, as nonchalantly as possible, "Hey, I'm looking for Bill Calley, have you seen him?" Nobody admitted even knowing the lieutenant. Discouraged and worn out from his long day on the move, Hersh finally decided to find a motel where he could eat and sleep before coming back to the base the next morning to knock on doors again. As he walked toward his car he saw two men working under the hood of another auto in a far corner of the parking lot. As tired as he was, Hersh could not resist making one more try: "Hey, you guys seen Calley?"

"Yeah, he's up in 221," answered one of the men, a middle-aged Army veteran.

"Um, which building?" Hersh mumbled, giving himself away as a stranger. The officer stiffened and demanded to know who Hersh was and what he was up to. Once again Hersh went through his whole story, ending with the explanation that he merely wanted "to give Calley a chance to tell his side." The officer took Hersh up to his little apartment, shared some Scotch with him, and confessed that he was beginning to have doubts about the war in Vietnam himself. He said he thought Calley was probably being made a scapegoat somehow for a sorry mess that had occurred over there. Finally, the officer agreed to take Hersh to a party where he expected Calley to be that night.

As they left the building, a short, slight young man crossed their path. The officer with Hersh called to him: "Hey, Rusty, come over here." Hersh, exhausted and nervous, started walking quickly toward the parking lot. "Wait," the older officer called to Hersh as "Rusty" walked toward them, "That's Calley."

Calley had been told by attorney Latimer that Hersh was looking for him, and although he was apprehensive at first, he gradually relaxed and soon was giving his side of the story to the one reporter he would talk to before his court martial. They went up to Calley's room and drank beer like old friends. "As he talked, I took notes, even jotting down the number of his telephone," Hersh later recalled. "He took a shower, and I remember staring at his nude body as he toweled off and thinking, 'This is the man who shot and killed 109 people.'"

Yet Calley seemed to be a pleasant and normal enough young man. They drove to the base store, bought bourbon, wine, and steak and went to Calley's girlfriend's apartment for dinner. Later, Hersh and Calley went to an officers' party before Hersh finally left him very late that night. "Hell, he was nice," Hersh remembered. "It could have been a night with any old friend."

Calley referred to the place near Song My village where the killings took place as "Pinkville," because of its coloring on military maps. It was the first name anyone had given Hersh for the exact location, which he would later learn was the hamlet of My Lai 4. Calley told Hersh he was only following orders by shooting dangerous Viet Cong villagers before they shot him and his men. He was certain his superiors would back him up. "Pretty naive," Hersh later recalled about the baby-faced young officer.

Hersh wrote his first 1500-word story on the mass killing and Calley's court martial on the plane back to Washington the next morning, November 12. It began:

Lt. William L. Calley, Jr., twenty-six, is a mild-mannered, boyish-looking Vietnam combat veteran with the nickname of "Rusty." The army says he deliberately murdered at least 109 Vietnamese civilians during a search-and-destroy mission in March, 1968, in a Vietcong stronghold known as 'Pinkville.'

After reaching Washington, Hersh called Latimer to tell him, as he had promised, that he was ready to run the story. Hersh also took the unusual step of reading the lawyer what he had written. "This normally is a frowned-upon practice in journalism and rightly so," Hersh later acknowledged, but he wanted to go out of his way to assure Latimer that he had been fair to Calley and had not quoted him on any specifics of the case that might prejudice his military trial. Now all Hersh had to do was sell the story.

Hersh had decided to entrust that task to a young Cleveland Park neighbor named David Obst, whom Hersh had met while playing touch football. Obst ran the Dispatch News Service, a year-old news-story marketing service for a collection of free-lance writers working in Vietnam. Dispatch had been incorporated in 1968 by the best known of those writers, Michael Morrow, and others who wanted to write about the war's effect on the Vietnamese people. Obst, the son of a well-to-do Los Angeles advertising executive, was a twenty-three-year-old graduate student in Asian studies at the University of California when he met Morrow in Taiwan and decided to join his fledgling venture and become its marketing manager.

When Obst returned to the United States, he began selling Dispatch stories to a few West Coast newspapers, the *National Catholic Reporter*, and some college papers for a commission of 25 percent of the selling price. After several months, Obst decided to move east, where he believed there would be a larger market for the kind of Vietnam stories Dispatch offered. He settled in Washington, working out of his home. Obst was quite like Hersh in many ways— brash, iconoclastic, peripatetic, highly competitive, and consummately ambitious. The two quickly became friends. Even before Hersh went to find Calley, he had told Obst about his developing story about a mass killing of Vietnamese civilians. The two men had agreed to market it through Dispatch some time after the planned November 15, 1969, antiwar march down Pennsylvania Avenue in Washington. Although both were outspoken critics of the war in Vietnam, Hersh did not want what he believed to be a singularly important story of wartime atrocity, which he then believed could win the Pulitzer Prize, to appear to be mere propaganda timed to appear just before the protest march. "I didn't want the Pinkville story to get confused with the activities of the antiwar movement," Hersh said.

But at one of his stops at Fort Benning on November 11, Hersh had overheard a man identify himself as a *New York Times* reporter and ask about the Calley court martial. The *Times* reporter apparently was never able to find Calley or any details about the case, but Hersh "panicked." He rushed to a telephone, called Obst in Washington, and told him to start selling the story, which he said he would somehow get to Obst in finished form the next day. Throughout that day, Hersh kept Obst advised via long-distance telephone of his progress. After he finally found and interviewed Calley that night, Hersh made one last, very late call to Obst, shouting into the receiver: "Touchdown!"

While Hersh wrote the story on the plane north from Georgia, Obst sat in Washington with a copy of *Literary Market Place*, which lists the telephone numbers of newspaper editors, and began calling all over the country. "I'm David Obst of the Dispatch News Service, calling from Washington," he told more than fifty editors in the United States and Canada. "I've got a story I think you'll be interested in."

In most cases he had to explain at length just what the Dispatch News Service was and how he and Hersh could be certain they were right about the facts of the "Pinkville" story. After the story itself arrived, with Hersh's quotes from Calley and Latimer and the Army's official charges of murder, it was a bit easier to convince the editors. In all, thirty-six newspapers—including the *Chicago Sun-Times, Milwaukee Journal, St. Louis Post-Dispatch, Philadelphia Bulletin,* and *Washington Post*—agreed to buy the story at $100 each.

Some editors expressed concern about libel, and Obst and Hersh themselves worried that something in the story, despite Hersh's painstaking reporting, might leave them open for a disastrous lawsuit. Hersh suggested they seek out a highly successful young lawyer, Michael Nussbaum, whom Hersh remembered from the University of Chicago law school. As a junior partner in a prestigious Washington law firm, Nussbaum had done well both in lobbying the federal bureaucracy for lucrative corporate clients and in defending draft resisters against prosecution by the government. Nussbaum, a footloose bachelor who liked to travel, eat well, and stay out late, happened to be at his seldom lived-in Georgetown townhouse late in the evening of November 12, 1969, talking long distance on the telephone, when the operator broke in to tell him that a "Mr. Obst" was trying to get through to him with an emergency call.

"I had never heard of Obst," Nussbaum said later, "and I was irritated at being interrupted like that. So I told the operator to tell him to call back the next day. Then the next thing I knew, really late that night, someone was knocking on my door, and Hersh himself was there and rushed right inside. I objected loudly, but Sy told me, 'Don't say anything until after you've read this,' and handed me the first My Lai story.

"I was shocked by it. Hersh asked me to represent him whenever needed on the story. He said he expected to be sued for libel and figured he needed to be represented in his future dealings with editors on the story because he was a free-lance. I asked him questions about cross-checking, who his sources were, and all that, and Sy satisfied me that he had checked out the story thoroughly and was right. So I agreed to represent him. I became generally impressed with Hersh's concern for accuracy. I figure that is one reason why sources trust him."

Reassured by Obst that a top Washington law firm had given its blessing to the "Pinkville" story, most of the three dozen newspapers buying the story published it the next day. Several put the story on their front page. The *New York Times*, which had been tipped about the Calley court martial on November 7, printed its own, much less detailed account, without quotes from Calley or the location of the massacre. Editors at the *Washington Post* assigned a Pentagon reporter to check it out and rewrite it. Hersh said the reporter called him afterward to say angrily, "You son of a bitch, where do you get off writing a lie like that?"

Only the *New York Times* decided to pursue the story in South Vietnam, where its Southeast Asia correspondent, Henry Kamm, set out to locate "Pinkville." After two days of badgering Army investigators in Quang Ngai province, Kamm and reporters for *Newsweek* and ABC persuaded military officers to take them to a relocation hamlet in Song My village, where they found and were allowed to interview several My Lai survivors. Kamm's story reporting allegations by the survivors that 567 Vietnamese civilians had been murdered by American soldiers at My Lai appeared on the front page of the *Times* Sunday, November 16. It helped lend credence to Hersh's reporting.

Among the few other stories on My Lai that appeared over that weekend, Hersh noticed a short wire-service report in which a former soldier, Ronald L. Ridenhour, was quoted as saying that he had instigated the Army's investigation of the affair. Hersh flew across the country to California that same day to find him. Ridenhour told Hersh he had heard about the massacre from several Charlie Company eyewitnesses whom he had encountered at various times while he was in the Army during 1968. After his discharge Ridenhour returned home to Phoenix and brooded about what he had been told. He talked with his creative writing teacher at Phoenix College about writing a magazine article on it, but the teacher, according to Hersh's later account, told Ridenhour "it would cheapen what he was doing if he tried to sell the story." At the teacher's suggestion, Ridenhour instead wrote a letter about what he knew, made thirty copies, and sent them to the White House, Pentagon, State Department, and leading members of Congress in April 1969. These letters apparently prompted the secret Army investigation of My Lai and ultimately led to the charges against William Calley.

When the Army refused to answer several requests from Ridenhour about the progress of its investigation, however, he began to worry that it might end in a whitewash. Deciding to become a free-lance writer, Ridenhour tried to sell the My Lai story to a national magazine. He hired an agent who contacted several magazines, including *Life* and *Look* some months before Hersh unsuccessfully queried them about the same story. Everyone turned Ridenhour down. On October 22, just as Hersh began work 3000 miles away on the telephone tip he received about Calley, Ridenhour received a note from his agent saying, "Quite frankly, Ron, I am doubtful of my ability to be of much more help. I honestly feel the matter is best handled at this stage by waiting until your next response from the Army."

At their meeting three weeks later, Ridenhour showed Hersh a copy of the letter he had sent to officials in Washington and filled in more details. He also gave Hersh the names and addresses of the soldiers, most of whom were now discharged and back in the United States, who had told him about the massacre. During the next twenty-four hours, Hersh somehow flew to Utah, Washington, and New Jersey to find and interview three of these soldiers, all of whom had been at My Lai. They told Hersh everything they saw and heard there. One of the soldiers had witnessed the entire encounter from a helicopter gunship called in to provide air cover for the Pinkville attack. The others saw the bodies stacked in open ditches, reminiscent of a Nazi concentration camp.

"One of the reasons I think Hersh did so well in getting these kids who were at My Lai to talk," Michael Nussbaum told me, "was that he went right to their homes to see them. He met them inside their homes with their parents and other relatives, and he impressed them as being sincere, I think, because he is so sincere."

Hersh stopped back in Washington just long enough to write a long story filled with grim descriptions from the young Vietnam veterans. Obst was back on the telephone November 19 successfully selling it to several dozen newspapers for the same $100 fee. But with the exception of the *New York Times* and the few papers that put Hersh's Dispatch News Service stories on their front pages, My Lai was not yet a consensus "big story."

One of the Pentagon reporters for the *Washington Post* wrote a story that seemed to belittle Hersh's disclosures by arguing that "for

Company C, in March, 1968, the Pinkville rice paddies and battered hamlets were a nightmare of booby traps and mines." An Associated Press story contended that "in Vietnam the killing of civilians was a practice established by the Viet Cong as a major part of the war long before the first U.S. ground troops were committed in March, 1965." Many newspapers "barely noted the alleged massacre or ignored it completely," according to a *Time* magazine "Press" section report two weeks later.

This could not have pleased the Pentagon more. It had been bracing for months for a backlash of bad publicity its officials were certain would be produced by eventual disclosures of the My Lai massacre. "In talking to some Pentagon officials before I wrote my first story," Hersh recalled in an article he later wrote for the American Society of Newspaper Editors' *Bulletin*, "one general officer told me: 'Pinkville had been a word among G.I.'s for a year. I'll never cease to be amazed that it hasn't been written about before.'" Hersh said many reporters later admitted to him they had heard something about "the Pinkville incident" during 1968 and 1969 but had not followed it up. Even after he had found Ridenhour and the three My Lai eyewitnesses, Hersh pointed out in his book, *My Lai 4: A Report on the Massacre and Its Aftermath,* "there was little investigative reporting on the part of the American press to determine exactly what had happened, perhaps because newspapers did not try to locate former members of Charlie Company."

Hersh kept trying, and on November 21 he found in New Goshen, Indiana, near Terre Haute, a wounded veteran of My Lai who admitted actually participating in the mass killing himself. Paul Meadlo, twenty-two, told Hersh in stark detail "how he had calmly executed, under orders, dozens of Vietnamese civilians." Meadlo, a religious young man who was tormented by what he had done, "wanted to confess publicly," according to Nussbaum. So when CBS news called Hersh to ask if any of his sources would go on television to talk about My Lai, Hersh, Obst, and Nussbaum thought about Meadlo, whose story Hersh had not yet written.

Hersh felt that Meadlo should go on television to shock the nation into paying attention to the My Lai disclosures, although he later said he felt uneasy about selling Meadlo's story to the highest bidder. "Hersh knew he had the kind of story he'd never have again," Nussbaum recalled, "and because as a free-lance he needed the money, he saw this as a rare opportunity to be compensated for extraordinary work. So we told CBS about this guy from the Midwest, a religious guy who wanted to confess." Obst, who later

"We have the front-page story of the world."

became a highly successful Washington literary agent known as a "deal freak" who hungered for the ultimately satisfying financial deal for a hot property, told a CBS vice president, "We have the front-page story of the world."

"After long negotiations with the CBS vice president in a New York hotel," Nussbaum recalled, "I wrote out in longhand a contract for CBS to pay $10,000 for an exclusive appearance by Meadlo, although we did not use his name in the negotiations to protect ourselves."

"It was a cash deal for Dispatch," Hersh recalled. "Meadlo, who had been fully informed of the possible dangers to him and to his rights in the matter, was not paid one cent. But even more important was the fact that television was needed. Somehow, just relying on newspapers to sear the conscience of America hadn't been working."

In a four-minute interview with Walter Cronkite on the CBS Evening News, Paul Meadlo, with the camera focused in tightly on the soft features of his young face and the look of shame in his eyes, told millions of Americans how he shot women and babies with his automatic rifle until he could continue no longer and finally wounded himself in his feet so he could stop without disobeying orders. Hersh's subsequent, more detailed Dispatch News Service interview with Meadlo was sold by Obst to newspapers all over the world, most of which put the story on their front page. The *Washington Post*, which bought and rewrote the Meadlo story, devoted three pages to My Lai in its next Sunday edition.

Hersh's telephone suddenly was ringing with requests from Washington correspondents for the names of Charlie Company veterans in their newspapers' towns. "The newspaper profession, in one of those collective changes of mind that can only be found in the business, decided each man's testimony was important enough to play all over the front pages," Hersh later told the American Society of Newspaper Editors. "The indiscriminate use of eyewitness statements amazed me. I had carefully attempted to get some kind of 'feel' from each of my interviews before quoting them."

Hersh typically has minimized what other reporters did in following trails he blazed. Like most of the boldest of the new muckrakers, he has trusted only his own instincts and work. Besides being a manifestation of his extraordinary egotism, this trait has been a strong motivating force for Hersh, who is convinced that if he did not do what needed to be done, it would never be done right.

The impact of the Meadlo interview also made Hersh himself a hot property. His next several stories for the Dispatch News Service about My Lai and a similar mass killing of civilians at a nearby Vietnamese village sold quite well. The My Lai book he wrote for Random House (in place of the Pentagon book), was completed by the spring of 1970 after several more months of cross-country interviews with Charlie Company veterans, and earned $40,000 for Hersh from newspaper serialization rights alone. He was in greater demand as a campus speaker criticizing the Vietnam war and his fee went up to $1500 per appearance. Reporters and television talk-show producers sought him out for reactions to new developments in the My Lai investigation, including the court-martial conviction of Calley: "My immediate reaction is guilt. If I hadn't written the story, Calley might not be where he is today . . . I think he's as much a victim as the people he shot."

Hersh was twice featured in the "Press" and "Media" sections of *Time* and *Newsweek*, first in December 1969, just after Meadlo appeared on CBS, and later in May 1970, after Hersh won the Pultizer Prize for international reporting without ever having left the United States. He turned down an offer from producer Joseph Strick to buy film rights to the My Lai story. ("I said, 'Nope, I don't want to do it. It's immoral.' I don't want to exploit these kids—well, I have exploited them already, but there was a higher goal to be realized.") And he took on "a good agent in New York who made sure I made as much as I would if I were a top-flight reporter for one of the big newspapers" with the income from his book, speaking appearances, and the magazine articles he wrote on his reporting of the My Lai story, his opinions on the American military's conduct of the war in Southeast Asia, and evidence he uncovered of other atrocities in Vietnam.

Hersh was grateful for his unexpected financial windfall, which enabled his family to move into a larger house on the edge of Cleveland Park. He also reveled in the extent and intensity of his personal fame. "I was at the University of Minnesota for a seminar at the journalism school," Hersh recounted during an interview he gave Washington free-lance writer Richard Lee, in the midst of it all. "They set up a speech—filled the second biggest hall on campus—and the students gave me a *standing ovation—fifteen minutes*—I'm a fucking *celebrity!*" Even the hectic travel from one disorganized talk show to the next failed to temper his buoyant enthusiasm. During a quick Chicago trip, he told Lee, there were "fourteen talk shows—all those hot kleig lights—awful scheduling, with Ashley Montagu, talking sex and the women's world, and then I had to fly back to New York in the middle of it, to do '60 Minutes' . . . They told me I was great—I'm stupendous on television—never get rattled." After taping a "Today" Show segment in NBC's Washington studios, Hersh concluded, "Boy, was I good. *Sensational.*"

For a time the Dispatch News Service prospered along with Hersh, and he and Obst moved it into a three-room suite of offices in the National Press Building paid for by the revenue from the My Lai stories. Hersh remembered that during this period he met another free-lance celebrity, muckraking author and lawyer Ralph Nader, who had a smaller office down the hall. "We'd get together after 11 p.m. and talk into the night," Hersh said. Obst, meanwhile, paid to fly Michael Morrow, the Dispatch founder, to Washington, so they could draw up new incorporation papers for their suddenly prosperous enterprise.

Seven months later, however, the two became adversaries in court in Washington when Morrow filed suit charging that Obst used the reincorporation of the news service to put himself in control of the money from the My Lai story. Morrow sought $100,000 for himself and other founders of Dispatch plus a court injunction preventing Obst from continuing to use the name. Michael Nussbaum, representing Obst, helped arrange a settlement in which Obst paid far less to Morrow, who left to create Dispatch New Service International, which survived for another three years and syndicated Morrow's stories on his thirty-nine days of Communist captivity in Cambodia.

Meanwhile, Hersh went his separate way, and "the My Lai stories not only brought me $1500 speaking fees, but also things like the Peers documents." During the Pentagon's long investigation of the My Lai affair and its apparent cover-up by the Army, one of Hersh's military sources regularly passed to him the still-classified findings of the investigating panel, which was headed by Army Lieutenant

General William R. Peers. "Twice a week a guy working on the report would meet me and we would Xerox another bunch of pages," Hersh said. "This went on for about a year. By that time I had made a contact at the *New Yorker* magazine, for which I wrote the piece on General Ramsey's memo. So I began writing about the Peers report for the *New Yorker*. I wound up writing a book, which really was done for the *New Yorker*." *Cover-up*, Hersh's third book, was published by Random House in 1972, several months after two excerpts ran in the *New Yorker* on January 22 and 29.

They caused a new controversy over My Lai by revealing the startling conclusions of the Peers report more than two years before its official release by the Army in the autumn of 1974. The report stated that Army investigators counted 347 Vietnamese civilian victims at My Lai, plus an estimated 155 more peasants killed as part of the same Army operation in the nearby Mykhe 4 hamlet where American soldiers indiscriminately burned and blew up the residents' huts. Hersh contended that these could not have been isolated, aberrational incidents but instead raised serious questions about how the American Army treated civilians generally in Vietnam. He also showed how field officers broke Army rules, and soldiers in ranks all the way up to general destroyed and altered records to cover up My Lai and similar incidents, without anyone beyond Lieutenant William Calley being punished for it.

Hersh's work now attracted attention all around the world. In addition to the European newspapers that had from the very first published his Dispatch News Service stories, the Soviet Union authorized serialization of Hersh's *New Yorker* articles in one of its newspapers. The North Vietnamese government also issued two separate invitations for Hersh to visit Hanoi to report on what the war had done to that capital and on how it was treating American prisoners of war. *New Yorker* editor William Shawn discussed "doing something for them from Hanoi," Hersh said, "and the foreign editor of the *New York Times* asked if I could do some stuff for them on the trip, so I went. I wound up doing six or seven pieces for the *Times* from Hanoi. When I got back I was going to do something long on how American prisoners were being treated—this must have been after they had been tortured because they were being treated better—but that was when Hanoi began its offensive. They didn't tell me they were going to do that. It would have been in poor taste to do how the prisoners were being treated when the North Vietnamese were attacking. I was too ignorant, so I decided not to do anything."

Hersh was then also mulling over a discussion he had with Abe Rosenthal, the managing editor of the *New York Times*, about going to work in the *Times*'s Washington bureau. "I wrote to Rosenthal about a job before the Hanoi trip and he said to talk when I got back," Hersh recalled. "Shawn, whom I really respected, said it would be a good idea for me to work for the *Times* to become more well rounded as a journalist. When Abe called me after I got back in the country, I decided to accept a job there. I was warned by a lot of my friends and people like David Halberstam, who left the *Times*, that I shouldn't go, that the *Times* wasn't the right place for me. They gave me only six months. But I knew that was bullshit. I knew I wouldn't be winging it at the *Times*. I was basically a cautious, conservative, good reporter, and I knew I could live up to the standards at the *Times*."

The *New York Times*'s Washington bureau had done relatively little sustained investigative reporting before Hersh came, although the paper had occasionally published investigative articles on such traditional New York muckraking targets as organized crime and police corruption. Its reporting of most institutions of government during the turmoil of the 1960s remained largely unskeptical. And its Washington bureau, in particular, had gained a reputation among journalists for suppressing some out-of-the-ordinary stories, such as advance knowledge of the preparations being made for the ill-fated Bay of Pigs invasion of Castro's Cuba.

But during the later years of the Vietnam war, skepticism about the American government's explanations of just what was going on there began to creep into the columns of the *Times* through the Pulitzer Prize-winning dispatches of Halberstam from Vietnam, some of the stories Neil Sheehan wrote from the Pentagon, and Hersh's own stories picked up from the Associated Press. Finally, Sheehan brought the *Times* the Pentagon Papers he obtained from Daniel Ellsberg, and the newspaper decided to publish them in the face of determined government opposition to what the Pentagon considered a grave violation of national security secrecy. At the *New York Times*, where he worked in the Washington bureau, Tom Wicker later said, "The Pentagon Papers made the big difference."

Hersh brought to the *Times* his name and Pulitzer Prize, his contacts in the Pentagon and on Capitol Hill, his unusual determination to get the ungettable story—and the Peers report. On June 4, 1972, Hersh revealed in a front-page story in the *Times*'s Sunday edition (always the edition with the biggest circulation) that the report had accused two Army generals, Major General Samuel

W. Koster and Brigadier General George H. Young, Jr., with forty-three acts of misconduct in trying to cover up the My Lai massacre. Hersh reported that no criminal charges were brought against either general, although both were formally censured and Koster was demoted to brigadier general. Accompanying Hersh's story was almost a full newspaper page of excerpts from the still-secret Peers report itself. In the next few weeks came the story of General Lavelle's secret bombing of North Vietnam, after which Hersh told a reporter for *Newsweek*: "I'm tired of writing about Vietnam. Professionally, I think it's a dead end. There are a lot of other issues in America."

As it happened, the event that would become the next great national issue—the Watergate burglary—had occurred just a few days before Hersh's *Newsweek* interview. During the next several months the *New York Times* Washington bureau fell far behind the *Washington Post*'s Woodward and Bernstein in pursuing that story, partly because many of the bureau's reporters and editors simply did not perceive its seriousness. Every now and then, however, *Times* managing editor Abe Rosenthal in New York would react to a big Woodward and Bernstein story by ordering the Washington bureau to get Hersh onto the story. Finally, it did.

"If you ask me whether I think I could have cracked Watergate myself if I had been on it from the beginning like Woodward and Bernstein were," Hersh later told me, pausing for just a moment to smile slightly in recognition of how smug it might sound, "I'd have to say 'yes.'"

The way Bob Woodward remembered it, "Hersh kept refusing to work on Watergate because he knew we were too far ahead, and he couldn't catch up." But Woodward admitted that Hersh did catch up and helped provide an important turning point in the coverage early in 1973 after Nixon's resounding reelection and a long period of inactivity for Woodward and Bernstein had left the story dormant. "There was a vacuum after the election," Woodward said, "when Carl and I really weren't concentrating. We had taken some time off, and were working on our book and traveling around making speeches. Hersh moved right into the vacuum."

Hersh did so with a bit of a flim-flam that his critics have said is too typical of his style. Somehow, although he has repeatedly denied it, he saw a copy of a book outline being circulated at Random House, Hersh's publisher at the time, by free-lancer Andrew St. George, a spy buff and adventurer. St. George had met Watergate burglar Frank Sturgis back when Sturgis was a CIA operative inside Cuba and St. George was writing from there. Sturgis and St. George were going to collaborate on an insider's story of Watergate once the January 1973 trial of the Watergate burglars was over. But Hersh found out about the outline, went to St. George and, according to St. George, implied he would print everything that was in it if St. George did not put him in touch with Sturgis for a background interview. "St. George's mistake was leading me to Sturgis," recalled Hersh, who nevertheless denied doing anything improper. With details from Sturgis, which were later confirmed by news sources Hersh had gained among both the Watergate prosecutors in the U.S. Attorney's office in Washington and the lawyers for the burglary defendants, Hersh was able to write a story saying that the burglars and their families were being regularly paid $400 and more each by someone unknown and that John Mitchell was being kept informed of their activities. Until Sturgis "told me about the money they were getting," Hersh later said, "it did not occur to me or anyone else to change our focus from what they did before and during the break-in to what happened afterward—the cover-up."

The possibility had occurred to Woodward and Bernstein, who were told by some of the same sources Hersh had used to confirm Sturgis's story that the four Cubans involved in the Watergate burglary were being offered future executive clemency and financial security if they would plead guilty at their trial and keep their mouths shut. Editors at the *Post*, however, were worried that the trial judge, John J. Sirica, might take action against the reporters or the newspaper for printing such a story in the midst of the trial. Uncertain about whether they should go ahead, they agreed to think about it for a day.

Meanwhile, editors at the *Times* had ordered Hersh to cut back a five-part series he had proposed on the Sturgis-St. George revelations to one long story. Then, after St. George called managing editor Rosenthal to complain about Hersh's reporting tactics, another week passed while Hersh confirmed the story with Watergate prosecution and defense sources his editors trusted. On Saturday, January 6, Hersh's story got the go-ahead for Sunday's *Times*, where it appeared at the top of page one under a large headline. Woodward and Bernstein's story followed. The competition between them and Hersh, which helped speed the unraveling of Watergate, had begun.

Hersh had not been very happy with the *Times*'s editors' drastic cutting and rewriting of the Sturgis story, however. "A month and a half's work was turned over to group editing," Hersh said later. "Everybody wanted to be in on the action. So they wrote a composite lead that took the news out of it. They made it read 'New evidence has been uncovered by the *New York Times*. . . .' Then the next paragraph said, 'That new evidence shows. . . .'"

So Hersh tried one of the tricks of his wire-service days. On the Friday night before the Sunday, January 7, story, Hersh waited until after the New York editors who had been working on the story had all left for the weekend and then wrote a new lead of several paragraphs from his home in Washington. He simply telephoned it to a night editor in New York. "I went back to my old lead saying, 'At least four of the five men arrested in the Watergate raid are still being paid by persons as yet unnamed, according to sources close to the case,'" Hersh recalled two years later, remembering the exact words. "Nobody said anything about it, and it went right into the paper that way.

"Finally, the *Times* had its own Watergate sources. I went back to them and got our own piece of the (Donald) Segretti story. I was the first reporter to write that Dwight Chapin (who had been President Nixon's appointments secretary) paid Segretti through (Herbert) Kalmbach, Nixon's lawyer. And I got Chapin's resignation. A guy in the White House called me and said he just got out of a meeting in which it was said that Chapin was gone, although he hadn't officially resigned yet, and was out job-hunting. Zeigler denied it on the record, but I wrote the story, and Chapin left officially the next day. People were coming to *me* now."

When Watergate burglar James McCord broke his silence and began telling what he knew to federal prosecutors and the staff of the Senate Watergate Committee behind closed doors, Hersh raced Woodward and Bernstein to sources in both places to find out what McCord was saying. The resulting stories, which said that McCord was implicating high Nixon campaign officials in Watergate, were attributed to unnamed "sources close to the case," and Hersh's efforts to get them published achieved mixed results. "I got into the paper a story about McCord naming (Kenneth) Parkinson (an attorney for the Committee to Re-elect the President) as having channeled hush money payments to the burglars," Hersh said, "but they held a story about McCord also naming Mitchell and (Jeb Stuart) Magruder.

"Two days later Woodward and Bernstein did the Mitchell and Magruder story and got it on the front page of the *Post*. Then it was okay for me to go ahead. After that, standards changed at the *Times*, and it was Katie bar the door. I'd meet in the mornings with Clifton Daniel (the new *Times* bureau chief) about what I was doing, but I didn't really tell him much. I told Abe Rosenthal who my sources

were, but I used other names in the meetings in Daniel's office.
Otherwise they would have been all over town."

As the competition between Hersh and Woodward and Bernstein
grew keener, David Obst, who had become Woodward and
Bernstein's agent for *All the President's Men*, decided in April 1973,
to bring them together with his old client Hersh. "Obst told us we just
had to meet this guy," Woodward recalled "and he got us together in a
Chinese restaurant." In *All the President's Men*, Woodward and
Bernstein described that first meeting in a way that left Hersh still
angry many months after the book had been published.

Hersh, 36, horn-rimmed and somewhat pudgy, showed up for dinner
in old tennis shoes, a frayed pinstriped shirt that might have been his
best in his college freshman year, and rumpled bleached khakis.
He was unlike any reporter they had ever met. He did not hesitate to
call Henry Kissinger a war criminal in public and was openly
attracted and repelled by the power of the *New York Times*. . . .

"Bernstein should talk about how somebody dresses," Hersh
protested to me, "and do I look pudgy to you? I'm much more of an
athlete than either one of them. And that remark about Kissinger
being a war criminal—What they didn't say in the book was that we
were all sitting around getting high and putting down everybody. I
didn't see them put in the book what they were saying about Ben
Bradlee (the editor of the *Washington Post*) that night. Damn cheap-
shot artists."

But just as Hersh was alternately attracted and repelled by the
Times, and both defended its "standards" and castigated its general
lack of skepticism, he had the same kind of mixed feelings about
Woodward and Bernstein. Each of the rivals respected the
breakthrough stories by the opposition, while occasionally complaining about the other's reporting methods. Hersh and Woodward,
however, became particularly fascinated with each other.

"I had an indoor tennis court reserved for every Tuesday night
from ten to midnight at the Arlington 'Y,' and I invited Hersh to play
with me," Woodward recalled. "We began playing regularly. Hersh
was a very competitive player and usually beat me. Funny thing, all
the time we played there, Hersh never volunteered to share the cost of
the court, even though he came week after week.

"This was happening during the height of our competitive
reporting of Watergate during the spring and summer of 1973. We'd
go to a pizza place in Arlington after the games and talk for an hour

or two about what was going on. We'd share anecdotes and humor of the situation we were in the middle of, but we never traded hard information. Hersh would tell how Chuck Colson (then a White House lawyer) would leak CIA-type stories to Hersh, trying to trade on his interest in national-security stuff to get him off Watergate, but Hersh decided never to bite. Sometimes, without actually asking, Hersh would try to steer the conversation in a way that might get me to reveal some of our sources, but I wouldn't play. He tried to milk me in a manipulative but good-natured way. It was tricky sometimes, but fun—absolute fun."

Woodward also believed that Hersh sometimes bullied sources and targets of Watergate stories. "Hersh would put in a daily call for weeks to the White House for Gordon Strachan (a Haldeman aide whom Hersh suspected of being one of the keys to the Watergate puzzle). He'd always get a secretary, to whom Hersh would always give the same message: 'Just you tell Strachan to watch the *New York Times* tomorrow!' "

One Watergate prosecution source contacted by both reporters, Woodward said, was a good friend of Hersh's and one of his most important sources. "Hersh played him like a violin," Woodward said. "He pushed him around and got him indignant and then the guy would talk." Although Hersh said the source was only one of many he had, and was not particularly relied on, the source himself acknowledged being called frequently by Hersh. He denied to me, however, that Hersh ever bullied or took advantage of him. "Oh, he'd tell me that I was full of shit and didn't know what was really going on in the case," the source said. "But that was part of our trading information. He was telling me something about what he had found out elsewhere that I needed to know. I had good trust and rapport with Sy. He would agree to go off the record with me or hold something out of a story or exchange information. He knew tomorrow was another day. Woodward and Bernstein weren't like that."

Also unlike Woodward and Bernstein, Hersh wrote stories explicitly presenting the original Watergate prosecutors' point of view when they were being strongly criticized for wrongly arguing (during the January 1973 trial of the Watergate burglars) that the conspiracy went no higher. This paid off for Hersh later that spring when he was shown a memorandum in which the prosecutors outlined what they had found out about the entire Watergate cover-up and recommended the indictment of a host of White House and Nixon campaign officials—including Haldeman, John Ehrlichman,

"If they knock down a story, I believe them unless I find hard evidence elsewhere."

Mitchell, Magruder, and John W. Dean, III. Hersh wrote the story, and from the names of prospective defendants to the detailed description of what they were accused of doing, it was almost exactly matched by the Watergate cover-up indictment produced by the Watergate Special Prosecutor's office, which later took over the case.

But Hersh also was occasionally misled in his relationship with the prosecutors. He wrote on May 9, 1973, that government investigators had concluded that John Dean, Nixon's White House counsel, had no evidence that could directly implicate President Nixon in the Watergate cover-up. It later appeared that the prosecutors had sought to plant the untrue story to prevent the Senate Watergate Committee from granting Dean partial immunity in exchange for his testimony before the committee.

"That story wasn't completely wrong," Hersh stubbornly insisted to me. "It never said that Dean *never* would implicate Nixon. It just said that he hadn't yet in his interviews with the prosecutors."

"There was a lot of pressure on Hersh, and he became pretty excited," Bob Woodward recalled. "When we beat him the people would have a fit at the *Times*. They'd call him up late at night to get him to confirm our story and do better. When we were in Florida writing our book and got from out of the blue the story about how Nixon bugged his own brother, Donald, to make certain he wasn't up to anything embarrassing, Hersh called and yelled at me, 'You fucker, you fucker!' "

Woodward believes, however, that except for their heated competition, Hersh never regarded Watergate as more than "a diversion from his real task." Hersh, said Woodward, "is an old-line radical in a way. He is interested more in the abuse of really big power, concentrated power, in the military and international capitalism. That's why he got so deep into the national-security stuff like the wiretaps and the plumbers."

Hersh pursued the story of the White House plumbers unit and its wiretapping of newspaper reporters and others as more than a single piece in the Watergate puzzle, working especially hard on the relationship of Henry Kissinger to the plumbers' activities. Hersh's zeal in going after Kissinger produced several scoops for him on the wiretapping story. The most significant was a report that Kissinger was involved in authorizing FBI wiretaps of his own aides to trace leaks to newsmen. *Post* editors held up a Woodward and Bernstein story under pressure from Kissinger, but Hersh received approval to write that President Nixon himself had authorized the wiretaps and Kissinger had supplied the FBI with the names of aides to be placed under surveillance.

Hersh spent many weeks reporting and writing stories first leaked by the Nixon White House itself that Naval officers on the national security staff of Henry Kissinger had been sending copies of National Security Council and other Kissinger documents to Admiral Thomas H. Moorer, chairman of the Joint Chiefs of Staff. Said Hersh, "I think it was a really important power struggle between Kissinger and Moorer and was maybe involved with the passing of secret Vietnam bombing orders from Kissinger's office."

Despite his constant pursuit of Kissinger, Hersh told me that some of his best sources were "important people close to Kissinger." He said they, too, continued to talk to him, because they found most of what he wrote accurate and because he held back on stories when they insisted the information was wrong. "If they knock down a story," Hersh said, "I believe them unless I find hard evidence elsewhere."

Hersh also was fascinated with the CIA and the rest of the Washington "intelligence community," which, like Henry Kissinger, had seemed to be a center of untouchable power and great mystery. From sources in Congress he got the story of the CIA's secret efforts to bring about the overthrow of Salvador Allende in Chile. He climaxed a series of follow-up stories with an essay in the Sunday *Times* "News of the Week in Review" section in which he argued for an end to the CIA's clandestine subversion of foreign governments. He cited a long list of covert CIA activities abroad, which he said he had gathered from previously published accounts and his own research.

This material was spotted by Washington free-lance writer John Marks, co-author with former CIA agent Victor Marchetti of the best-selling *The CIA and the Cult of Intelligence*, as part of an enviable dossier Hersh had built on the U.S. intelligence establishment since 1973 for a proposed book. "Hersh has been sitting for years on what would be spectacular stories about American intelligence operations," said Marks. "But Sy stopped work on the book, because he figured there can't be another best-seller in that field since ours made it so recently.

"Sy really needs to be unique. That's why he was never *really* happy on the Watergate story, because he was never number one to outsiders, even though he beat Woodward and Bernstein on several occasions. You have a big ego problem when you're the world's greatest investigative reporter."

Hersh nevertheless was still digging into the intelligence community whenever he got a chance. He read all the books he could find on the subject and talked to people with a first-hand knowledge of the CIA's activities. Among those activities were the CIA's secret, illegal spying on American dissidents during the years of antiwar demonstrations and black power politics. Hersh heard about dossiers kept by the CIA on thousands of Americans, unauthorized wiretappings, illegal inspections of mail, and even burglaries. From someone with high-level knowledge of the CIA—someone who has remained Hersh's secret at this writing despite speculation in Washington that it might have been James Schlesinger or William Colby—Hersh received the confirmation of his sketchy information that convinced editors at the *Times* that they should run a story he had written, which began:

The Central Intelligence Agency, directly violating its charter, conducted a massive illegal domestic intelligence operation during the Nixon Administration against the antiwar movement and other dissident groups in the United States, according to well-placed government sources.

Although the December 22, 1974, article appeared under an unusual four-column headline at the top of the *Times*'s front page and filled three-fourths of the inside page on which it was continued, it contained relatively few specific details to back up its principal allegations. Several follow-up stories by Hersh added nothing really new, and competing reporters disparaged Hersh's original story as unusual overreaching of the facts by the *Times*. But public disclosures by CIA director Colby in January 1975, and the report of the Rockefeller commission on the CIA in June, substantiated everything Hersh wrote, leading to further investigations and a reevaluation in Washington of the role of the CIA in American society. Hersh himself argued in the *Times* that the Rockefeller commission's recommendations for reform of the CIA did not go nearly far enough.

It also turned out that Hersh had been the first reporter to discover that the CIA, using a sophisticated salvage ship provided by Howard Hughes, had tried to raise a sunken Soviet nuclear submarine from the floor of the Pacific Ocean. Hersh who had first learned of the bizarre project while it was still going on in 1973, was then gathering material for his proposed book on the CIA, as well as a possible *Times* series on national security issues. The continuing demands of Watergate allowed Hersh to work on the submarine tip only sporadically, however, until one of his inquiries brought an unexpected call from CIA director Colby. In a forty-minute interview in February 1974 Colby gave Hersh more details on the project but also persuaded him to postpone writing about it, in the interest of national security, because the mission had not yet been successfully completed. Hersh agreed not to resume researching the story until he talked to Colby first.

Meanwhile, other reporters in Washington heard about the submarine salvage mission, and in February 1975 the *Los Angeles Times* published a sketchy and partly inaccurate story that put the sunken submarine in the Atlantic rather than the Pacific Ocean. Although the story was moved off the *Times*'s front page between editions, after Colby apparently called and told them that it could jeopardize further salvage efforts, Hersh, among other reporters, noticed the story. "I hit my head and said, 'Dumbbell,' " recalled Hersh, who then telephoned Colby to tell him their agreement could no longer be maintained. Hersh tied up loose ends in his reporting and turned in a long story on the submarine salvage mission to *Times* managing editor Abe Rosenthal. Again Colby got the story put aside. The busy CIA director also called a number of other newspapers, news magazines, and television networks to stop their efforts to report the story, citing national security in each instance. However, columnist Jack Anderson, who heard about the story in March 1975, decided to put it on his radio program despite Colby's plea. Anderson first warned Hersh, who he knew had the most complete story. "Everywhere we went, Hersh had already been there," Anderson said later. Once Anderson went on the air, Rosenthal allowed Hersh's story to be published in the next day's *Times*, on the front page under another unusually large five-column headline.

The *Times* obviously had come to trust Hersh and feel comfortable both with giving his unorthodox stories unusually prominent display and in tolerating his unusual style and work habits. Hersh, who has suffered a psychological letdown after each of his big stories, often disappeared from the *Times*'s pages for weeks or months between projects, letting most of the follow-up reporting fall to other correspondents in the Washington bureau. "They don't seem to mind around here that I'm not writing stories," he said. "They leave me alone and still pay me. They figure I'm working on something when they see me here at my desk reading a book. It's beautiful. It's the investigative reporter mystique."

By the middle of 1975, for instance, coverage of the many ongoing investigations of the CIA was being handled by a new investigative reporter in the *Times*'s Washington bureau, Nicholas Horrock, who was hired away from *Newsweek*. Hersh worked at the bureau on and off while his wife attended medical school in New York. He took time to relax and read before going back to writing occasionally for the *Times* and pursuing the possibility of finally writing the book on national security and the intelligence community. Presumably, Hersh's own exposé of the CIA's domestic spying had helped create a new market for it.

"I'm in a situation where I'd like to make more money," Hersh said in a long, taped two-part interview in *Rolling Stone* magazine, itself a sign of his growing celebrity. "It's a very crass materialistic thing to say, but it's a fact. I wouldn't mind making a million dollars on a book. Having Robert Redford play me wouldn't bother me at all."

Hersh was obsessed with the remarkable personal success of Woodward and Bernstein following Watergate and resentful that it did not come sooner to himself. Bob Woodward remembered arranging for Hersh to meet Robert Redford when the actor was in Washington once. "Hersh went to have breakfast with Redford in his hotel room," Woodward recalled, "and seemed almost to ignore him. Hersh himself talked frenetically the whole time. He came in talking, talked all during breakfast and then suddenly rose from the table, still talking, and walked out of the room, stopping only to yell over his shoulder to Redford, 'See ya.' "

While he was at the zenith of his importance and independence in the *New York Times*'s Washington bureau, Hersh acted like the cock of the roost there, fairly swaggering as he received the growing number of reporters who wanted to interview *him*. He proudly displayed from a collection he kept in his desk drawer the many letters he has received from readers praising him for "doing a great service for the country."

But he still couldn't seem to step completely out of the shadow of rivals Woodward and Bernstein, and it gnawed at him. During an interview on an autumn Thursday in 1974, Hersh interrupted his visitor to look in the *Times*'s mail boxes for his copy of the next

Sunday's *New York Times Book Review* section. "I check this right away every week," Hersh said as he opened the *Book Review* to the second-last page, where the best-sellers are listed. "There it is," he said with lingering resentment in his voice. "It's still number one." He was pointing to *All the President's Men*, which that week had made its twenty-third consecutive appearance on the *Times*'s best-seller list.

"I keep thinking of all the money Woodward and Bernstein got. But then that's what helped create the mystique about investigative reporting. I can't really complain. It's put money in my pocket, too."

3: The New Breed

Deep inside Philadelphia's labyrinthine Victorian city hall, where the criminal courts are located, two *Philadelphia Inquirer* reporters spent the autumn of 1972 going through records of 10,000 criminal indictments, police complaints, warrants, arrest sheets, bail applications, and court hearings, 20,000 pages of courtroom testimony, and 1000 miscellaneous psychiatric evaluations, probation reports, and hospital and prison data. Out of all this material, they culled the completed cases of 1034 criminal defendants charged with murder, rape, robbery, or aggravated assault, and they methodically noted from these records 42 different pieces of information about each defendant and his case. This information was then coded onto 9618 IBM cards and put into a computer.

From the resulting 4000 pages of computer printouts, plus their own visits to the criminal courtrooms in city hall and lengthy interviews with defendants, crime victims, prosecutors, defense lawyers, judges, and other court personnel, the two reporters— Donald L. Barlett and James B. Steele—fashioned an abundantly detailed portrait of local criminal courts "in far worse shape— practicing subtle, wide-ranging forms of discrimination and routinely dispensing unequal justice—than even their harshest critics would have guessed." These findings were presented to readers of the *Philadelphia Inquirer* in February 1973 in a week-long 25,000-word series of articles, supplemented by graphic charts and tables drawn from the computer-analyzed data.

Barlett and Steele told of judges who worked three-day weeks, courthouse patronage workers who misplaced hundreds of case files, and prosecutors who seldom prepared their cases before going to court. With dramatic case histories and convincing statistics, the reporters showed how persons with similar backgrounds facing similar criminal charges received widely varying treatment in Philadelphia's courts. Violent habitual criminals often went free, while many defendants convicted of lesser crimes went to prison.

Black defendants were found guilty more often than white defendants in similar circumstances, and blacks were more often convicted when the victim was white than when both the accused and the victim were black. Defendants under thirty years of age were more often convicted than those over thirty. Defendants convicted of crimes committed inside places of business received harsher sentences than those convicted of committing crimes inside homes. And one of every four persons charged with a serious crime who was later acquitted, or had the charges against him dropped, nevertheless spent the intervening months in jail because he could not post bail.

Barlett and Steele pointed out significant conflicts between their findings and the annual reports, press conference statements, and speeches of Philadelphia's politically ambitious district attorney, Arlen Specter. Specter had declared that his staff of prosecutors pressed to bring cases to trial; Barlett and Steele found that far fewer trials were held in Philadelphia than in comparable jurisdictions because Specter's prosecutors disposed of a majority of their cases by dropping the charges against the defendant or bargaining with him to plead guilty to a lesser charge. Specter had claimed that the average wait for a trial for those defendants who insisted on one had decreased to four months; Barlett and Steele found that the average delay had increased to well over six months and was growing. Specter blamed local judges for the lenient sentencing of habitual offenders; Barlett and Steele found that Specter's own assistants had regularly recommended short sentences or probation for many defendants to attract guilty pleas.

Arlen Specter was defeated in the next election. In the meantime Barlett and Steele won the Heywood Broun Award, for exposing injustice through unusually enterprising reporting, and the Sidney Hillman Foundation Award, for authoritatively presenting an important social problem. The reporters also received admiring letters from many Philadelphia judges and lawyers, although most of these correspondents asked that their names not be connected with their comments. Requests for reprints of the articles were still coming in two years later from court officials, civic groups, and colleges and universities throughout the country. The articles became a classic work in a highly specialized field. No insider—lawyer, judge, or academic researcher—had ever produced a study so well documented or so clear and compelling in its presentation.

Philadelphia's criminal court system is not the only complex subject Barlett and Steele have turned inside out for the *Philadelphia Inquirer*. After searching the city's land records in 1971, the then newly formed team became the first reporters to expose widespread fraud in the Federal Housing Administration's three-year-old subsidy program for the renovation and sale of slum houses to the poor. Two years later, after analyzing oil corporation records at the Securities and Exchange Commission in Washington, inspecting the oil fields of Texas and Oklahoma, checking offshore drilling leases in the Gulf of Mexico, and examining oil tanker shipping records at Lloyd's of London, Barlett and Steele concluded that the 1973 "oil crisis" was more the consequence of oil company manipulations of supply than of excessive American demand or the Arab oil embargo.

In April 1974, after going through Internal Revenue Service reports, internal IRS studies, 20,000 federal tax liens filed in cities from Philadelphia to Los Angeles, 30,000 pages of court records in two dozen jurisdictions, and countless other documents, Barlett and Steele showed how IRS enforcement methods favored wealthy tax evaders and allowed billions of tax dollars to go uncollected year after year—revelations that won them a Pulitzer Prize. And in November 1974, after comparing State Department claims and records with what they found on their own inspection trips to South America and Southeast Asia, Barlett and Steele proved that much US foreign aid—"the most massive relief effort in the history of man"—had bypassed the poor and instead further enriched the wealthy and the powerful in recipient nations.

The journalism of Donald Barlett and James Steele represents a significant step beyond traditional muckraking. Rather than depending on clandestine meetings with mysterious anonymous sources and purloined secret documents, it relies on what is already available somewhere on the crowded public record. Instead of just reporting still unproven accusations and focusing on individual corruption, it reveals with expert analysis and thorough documentation what has systematically gone wrong with the powerful, complex institutions that affect so much of life today. The best of this work, in addition to giving the rest of us our first clear look at such shortcomings, reaches far enough beneath the skin of those institutions to enlighten even those who run them, thus improving the chances for change.

In recent years there have appeared a surprisingly large number of this new breed of muckraker—to use the term most broadly. Like Barlett and Steele, most of these reporters are between thirty and forty years of age and have not become nearly so well known to the general public as the more traditional muckrakers of our time. Those of this newer breed tend to be less flamboyant or frenetic than other investigative reporters. They slip quietly into government agency record repositories and courthouse file rooms for days, weeks, or months of patient research. Without daily deadlines to work toward, most reporters would find such research unbearably tedious and frustrating. But those of the new breed are fascinated by the mysteries of records, excited by the challenge of mastering the highly specialized information they contain, and can lose themselves in the essentially scholarly pursuit of piecing together bits of information to reveal a significant story.

The *Wall Street Journal* has for years been an incubator for this new breed of muckraker. Its reporters regularly search records wherever they can find them, in and even outside the country, to uncover hidden scandals and institutional malfunctions in business and government. The *Journal's* regulatory agency specialist in Washington, Louis M. Kohlmeier, won a Pulitzer Prize years ago by finding in Federal Communications Commission records for the Johnson City, Texas, broadcast stations evidence of the great wealth Lyndon Johnson and his family accumulated while he was serving in public office. Stanley Penn, operating out of the *Journal's* main newsroom in New York, spent five years periodically reading new filings in a single civil case in federal court there to piece together a complicated Libyan oil concession swindle involving American businessmen.

Jerry Landauer, perhaps the *Journal's* best-known investigative reporter, went through voluminous federal and state coal-mining records to find and prove the existence of massive irregularities in the United Mine Workers union pension fund. His stories helped bring about the eventual reform in the union's leadership. "I went to the Labor Department first," he explained. "They list every mining company that contributes to the UMW pension fund. It's all on the record, so you know how much came from each company. They are supposed to pay forty cents a ton. So I took that information and went to state records. Every state publishes the annual output of each mining company in the state. Then I knew how much they should have paid into the pension fund and, with Labor records, I knew how much they did pay." Landauer found huge discrepancies. "The amount of stuff on the public record in Washington is just incredible," he said later. "We don't properly exploit it."

Ronald Kessler, a younger reporter who went from the *Wall Street Journal* to the *Washington Post,* has mastered accounting and other complicated kinds of record-keeping to unlock the secrets of a variety of previously impenetrable institutions. By studying the government's own computer printouts of hundreds of leases of private Washington area office buildings contracted by the U.S. General Services Administration, Kessler found that the federal agency was giving favored treatment to certain building owners, including some with close business ties to the federal officials awarding the leases. By auditing internal accounting records of Washington hospitals, Kessler discovered how patients' bills were systematically inflated to cover overcharging by staff doctors and technicians, conflicts of interest in the awarding of overly lucrative contracts for supporting services, and the manipulation of the hospitals' bank accounts to benefit banks at which hospital trustees were directors. By analyzing U.S. Postal Service records and inspecting mail-handling facilities throughout the country, Kessler was able to show that the new public corporation was spending considerably more money to deliver the mail more slowly and less efficiently than the old Post Office Department. His series of articles was followed by similar although less exhaustive examinations of the new postal service by other newspaper and television reporters and the beginnings of reconsideration of the whole idea by Congress. "I went through records, documents, statistics—three or four filing cabinets full," Kessler said of his postal inquiry. "I read all the (congressional) testimony that had ever been given on the subject. Eventually, I knew more about the place than anyone who worked there."

The new records of political campaign contributions that became available to reporters in the 1970s have been a gold mine for others of the new breed who, pocket calculators in hand, were willing to spend long hours going over thousands of figures to find contributions of unusual significance. By correlating what could be found in these records with those of Securities and Exchange Commission investigative files and other sources, some reporters discovered disguised, illegal campaign contributions from vested interests. James Polk, then a free-lancer working for the *Washington Star* with a grant from the Fund for Investigative Journalism in Washington, found a secret $250,000 cash contribution financier Robert Vesco made to the Nixon campaign. The payment stemmed from the time Vesco was trying to persuade the Nixon administration to stop an SEC investigation of the financier's tangled stock dealings. Brooks Jackson, the top reporter on an Associated Press investigative team in Washington, found a number of special interest and corporate campaign contributions, many illegal, which had been funneled to key congressmen in positions to return the favor. In particular, Jackson traced the massive secret corporate contributions the dairy industry made to influential politicians and the Nixon campaign through dummy fund-raising committees, while seeking government action to raise milk prices.

Another reporter on the AP team, Jean Heller, specialized in monitoring the federal government's daily information on how it was spending taxpayers' money. While reading the *Commerce Business Daily,* a Department of Commerce listing of contracts awarded by the government, Heller noticed in 1969 an agreement by the Navy to pay the Techfab Division of Alsco, Inc., $13.9 million for rocket launchers. Heller, who remembered that Techfab was under investigation by a federal grand jury in Washington, spent the next year regularly checking federal procurement and court records on the Techfab contract. Finally, in February 1970, she revealed in a long Associated Press exclusive that the Navy had been bilked into paying millions of dollars for fake invoices rather than rocket launchers, and that the ill-gotten profits had been routed to secret Swiss bank accounts.

Later that year Heller looked through the numerous consultant contracts awarded by the U.S. Office of Economic Opportunity and discovered that a large number of them had gone to a few relatively new consulting firms located in Washington office buildings just across or down the street from OEO. Checking on the owners and employees of these firms she found that many of them had recently left jobs inside the agency. In all Heller totaled up nearly $12 million worth of OEO consultant contracts for fiscal 1970 that went to just sixteen nearby consulting firms founded and staffed by former OEO officials. She estimated that an average of one of every four of these contracts had gone to such firms since the "war on poverty" began in the mid-1960s.

When Heller helped cover the Republican National Convention in Miami in 1972, she ran into another AP reporter, who passed on a tip about a public health experiment in Alabama in which syphilis patients were said to be dying. The reporter gave Heller some correspondence with the US Public Health Service's Center for Disease Control in Atlanta that referred to a "Tuskegee study" of syphilis in Tuskegee, Alabama. After returning to Washington, Heller searched for and found PHS records for the study and followed up with repeated telephone calls to the Center for Disease Control in Atlanta. "I already knew so much by the time I called," she

"The challenge is to gather, marshal, and organize vast amounts of data already in the public domain and see what it adds up to."

remembered later, "that it was easy for me to get details from their records over the phone. It all took just seven days."

On July 25, 1972, the front pages of newspapers all over the country featured Heller's story revealing that for forty years the Public Health Service had used hundreds of unsuspecting, mostly poor, uneducated black men suffering from syphilis as "human guinea pigs" to test what the disease did to the human body. For the purposes of the study, the men were not treated for the disease, and Heller found that between 28 and 100 had been allowed to die. Her Tuskegee stories won several national journalism awards, brought an end to the Tuskegee study, and opened a still-continuing national debate over the rights of human subjects of scientific studies. Heller herself later became a Washington correspondent for several newspapers and has continued her investigative reporting.

"The challenge is to gather, marshal, and organize vast amounts of data already in the public domain and see what it adds up to," explained Jim Steele, a slim, stylish, easy-talking thirty-one-year-old with thick black hair, as he and Donald Barlett sat in their cluttered little office hidden away on the thirteenth floor of the *Inquirer* tower in downtown Philadelphia. "Inside sources can't always do that for you," Steele said. "They're too involved. And they aren't always necessary, except for investigations of things like Watergate and the CIA, because there is usually already a lot on the public record. You just have to know where and how to find it."

"It's not that we don't have sources, too," interjected Donald Barlett. A shorter, fleshier, more sedately dressed, balding man of nearly forty who wore horn-rimmed glasses, Barlett is generally much more reticent than Steele, except when he feels it necessary to make an important point. "We just have a different kind of source," Barlett said. "We have authorities on different subjects all over the country. We call on them for expertise, and they call us with information they think we might be interested in."

"After we've got all the information we can find and have come to some tentative conclusions," Steele added, "we try them out on these expert sources, including the people we might be looking into. You need both to do this kind of work—sources and records."

"I don't think of it as investigative reporting," Barlett said with a frown of disapproval at the suggestion of that term. "I think that phrase is redundant anyway. We don't do investigative reporting in the sense of going after corruption. I don't believe you always have to expose corruption. What we do is really in-depth reporting. We try to find and get across a certain amount of important information that people didn't have before."

"We're not after indictments or immediate results necessarily as the measure of what we're doing," Steele said. "If that were the case, we'd have to stay away from a lot of subjects that we know would never lead to that kind of action. What makes us feel good are the letters from people asking for reprints and thanking us for what they learned from our stuff—like the woman who read our foreign aid series and then saw in *Newsweek* that we had done other things, too. So she asked for those reprints."

Before teaming up with Barlett at the *Inquirer*, Steele had been an "urban affairs" writer of the kind in vogue during the 1960s, analyzing housing, urban planning, and labor problems. He had grown up in Kansas City and paid his own way through the local branch of the University of Missouri by working as a reporter for the *Kansas City Times*, the morning sister paper of the better-known afternoon *Star*. Like Barlett, Steele had decided in high school that he wanted to be a newspaperman. A family friend who worked at the *Star* helped him get a job as a copyboy at the *Times*, and within six months Steele became a reporter. He was just eighteen years old.

"It was a good training newspaper," Steele recalled. "It was the kind of place where they gave you a copy of Fowler's *(Modern English Usage)* as a present when you graduated from copyboy to reporter. I was schooled in the use of records to verify facts for stories like obituaries. I was taught respect for facts and shown how they could be found in records of all kinds."

Steele covered suburban governments, courts, school boards, and the local urban renewal agency before becoming a night rewrite specialist for the morning paper. When a big story broke, such as an occasional tornado, Steele wove together information gathered by a number of other reporters on the scene. It was a time when newspaper editors were trying to develop specialists, as news became more complicated, so Steele, when he was not busy rewriting, involved himself in labor reporting.

This work led to an opportunity for a labor union job involving congressional lobbying in the capital. He took it to see Washington and how things worked there, Steele said, "knowing the whole time that I would eventually get back into journalism." During his two years in the capital, he became particularly interested in urban affairs legislation and learned in detail just where information could be found in the federal bureaucracy.

Steele also found and enjoyed art, theater, and good dining in Washington, where he lived with his wife in a downtown apartment. It was a pattern they followed when they later moved to Philadelphia and took up residence near Rittenhouse Square, in a neighborhood of handsome historic buildings within walking distance of most theaters, movie houses, restaurants, and other urban attractions. Steele made clear that he and his wife, an editor of textbooks for J. B. Lippincott in Philadelphia, preferred the cosmopolitan life.

Barlett grew up in Johnstown, Pennsylvania, and quit college after one year at Penn State. After beginning work as a reporter in Reading, Pennsylvania, he bounced from job to job with no clear road map for his future, eventually settling outside Philadelphia in the distant countryside of Bucks County, Pennsylvania, with his wife, a nurse, and one child. Along the way, Barlett had served in the Army as a counterintelligence agent. Either from that experience or from his small-town upbringing, he retains the blunt, taciturn demeanor usually associated with investigators. Although he warmed up during conversation to become quietly friendly, Barlett generally gave terse answers to questions put directly to him and let Steele do most of the talking, while he listened impassively. "Steele has an infinite capacity to get along with people," Barlett volunteered at one point, "while I often just want to say that they're all a bunch of jerks and walk away."

Also unlike Steele, Barlett had been, before alighting at the *Inquirer,* a traditional scandal-hunting investigative reporter. From Reading, Pennsylvania, he had gone to the Akron Ohio *Beacon-Journal,* where he covered courts and the city hall, and was introduced to investigative reporting by being asked occasionally, "When you finish everything, can you look into this?" Next Barlett moved to the *Cleveland Plain Dealer,* where he investigated the local sheriff's department and probate court and worked under cover for six months in the Lima state mental hospital before writing about deplorable conditions there.

He then returned to Reading with the intention of settling down as an editor, isolated from the complexities of the outside world, but he was bored after five months and moved to the *Chicago Daily News.*

Once again, Barlett specialized in uncovering local corruption, but he found that editors in Chicago would occasionally suggest that he was hitting too close to friends of the directors of Field Enterprises, owner of the *Daily News.* "They'd ask me," Barlett remembered, "'Why don't you look at this from a different angle?'" So it was back to the *Cleveland Plain Dealer.* From there Barlett decided to go to a Knight newspaper, because the chain's editors seemed to encourage more aggressive investigative reporting. He was about to choose the *Free Press* in Detroit, when he heard that Knight had just bought the *Inquirer* and was hiring there. As it happened, Jim Steele had just been told the same thing, and the two men started work in Philadelphia on the same day.

Knight Newspapers, Inc., bought the morning *Philadelphia Inquirer* and an afternoon tabloid, the *Daily News,* from Philadelphia millionaire Walter Annenberg on January 1, 1970. The *Inquirer* was to join the Miami *Herald* and the Detroit *Free Press* as a showcase newspaper of the Knight chain. However, under Annenberg, who was less interested in journalism than in money and power, the *Inquirer's* staff and plant had been allowed to run down badly. Although the good, gray *Evening Bulletin,* a locally owned independent newspaper, had been steadily losing circulation for a decade, the *Inquirer* had remained second in both subscribers and professional standards. "Eight-column banners and inaccurate and often slanted reporting were *Inquirer* trademarks," a former *Bulletin* reporter, Eugene L. Meyer, wrote in the *Columbia Journalism Review* in 1971. Annenberg used the newspaper to help his friends and political allies and to hurt or make nonpersons of his enemies. "Annenberg simply kept news about people he didn't like out of the paper," Meyer wrote. Those on Annenberg's blacklist ranged from the president of the University of Pennsylvania to the owner of Philadelphia's professional basketball team. Even accounts of the basketball team's games disappeared from the *Inquirer.*

Investigative reporting under Annenberg consisted only of finding and publishing unflattering facts and rumors about those of his enemies who had not been blacked out entirely. That changed abruptly, however, when the new owners sent a young independent editor to take over the paper. Within a month the new *Inquirer* documented the "other side" to the police version of the fatal shooting of a black teenager by Philadelphia patrolmen, raising serious questions about how the incident had been handled by then police commissioner Frank L. Rizzo, an Annenberg friend. Investigative reports soon followed on narcotics traffic in the city, conditions at the public general hospital, the manipulations of a large-scale real estate speculator, and conflicts of interest of members of the local Bicentennial commission and of the state board that set milk prices. Some of these targets were a little too easy to hit, but the new editors were making their point. There were no more sacred cows or enemies lists at the *Inquirer,* which would now be much more skeptical about everything.

Steele said he had been hired by the new editors "with the understanding that I would be allowed to do in-depth stuff on urban affairs," and he began by writing neighborhood profiles and examining Philadelphia's urban renewal projects. He found and wrote that the city's oldest project, the first in the country to be funded by the federal government after passage of the 1949 enabling legislation, was still not finished because of bureaucratic mismanagement and worse, leaving empty a large area of the city's downtown where old buildings had long ago been demolished. Barlett, meanwhile, was one of the new reporters who had investigated local narcotics traffic and had also written about phony business bankruptcies staged by local racketeers.

"Barlett was a phantom around the office," Steele recalled. "I never really met him until the executive editor asked us to look around Philadelphia for evidence of abuses in the FHA 235 program for the renovation and sale of old houses to low-income families. Philadelphia had been cited in a report by Wright Patman's banking committee in Congress. We spent a few days looking at local real estate records to see what was there. We suggested to the editor that it would take a long time but that the research would be fruitful, so he let us go ahead.

"We found right away a tremendous foreclosure problem," Steele said. "George Romney was rapidly becoming the largest property owner in Philadelphia, according to the land records. What was happening was that the people who bought these houses with FHA-guaranteed, low-interest loans were finding that they had been left in bad shape by the real estate speculators who sold them. So when things got too bad, or they couldn't keep up their payments on the loan, the family just left, like they always had in rental housing. The loan was foreclosed, and nobody else would buy the house, so it wound up in the hands of the Department of Housing and Urban Development, because of the government guarantee of the loan. Romney was then HUD Secretary, so we kept finding houses deeded over to HUD in his name after foreclosure.

"Then we soon figured out the rest. The speculator had bought the run-down house cheap, held it for a month or two, and then sold it at a good price with the government-guaranteed loan to a low-income buyer. The family buying it would live there a year or two and then leave. Philadelphia was filling up with abandoned houses like that, more than in any other city except maybe New York or Detroit.

"It took us six to eight weeks before we were ready to write our first story. We had to go through deeds and mortgages to see what the speculators were doing and who bought houses from them. We went out to see the houses and interview the families living in them. We had to decide how many houses we had to see before we would have enough back-up stuff to prove our thesis. This is a fundamental decision in this kind of work. What do you have, and what do you need to prove it? How many interviews and examples do you need?

"You have to be systematic and review your assumptions as you go along. We took one big speculator in Philadelphia and set a goal of how many of his buyers we'd have to see, and we stuck to that even though the first houses we went into were so terrible we knew then that we were right.

"We thought we'd be finished with the subject in three months," Steele said, "but each story generated tips for another story, and we were at it for a year all told. We got into the mortgage companies that made the government-guaranteed loans through the speculators— these were the people who made it all possible. We'd write about how horrible these houses were and about how the speculators selling them were getting trips to California and Europe from the mortgage companies for every so many mortgages they got placed. The mortgage companies got interest subsidies from the government and then all the loan money back when the house was abandoned and the government had paid off on its guarantee. We published pictures of these people leaving on their paid trips, with everybody hiding their faces behind their coats."

One subject then led to another for the oddly matched team. During their FHA investigation in 1971, for which Barlett and Steele won the George Polk Memorial and Sigma Delta Chi Distinguished Service in Journalism awards, they heard about conflicts of interest in the city's urban renewal authority. "And when some of the people we were writing about wound up in court," Steele said, "we began to notice some strange things coming out of the district attorney's office. He and Rizzo kept complaining about lenient judges and other problems, so we decided to find out what was really going on in the criminal courts. We wanted to know exactly what the dispositions of the cases were."

In September 1972 Barlett and Steele began what became a seven-month study of Philadelphia's criminal courts. They arbitrarily selected the cases of all persons indicted for murder and for rape during 1971 whose cases were completed by August 1972, all persons indicted for robbery during a nine-month period of 1971 whose cases were disposed of by August 1972, and all persons indicted for aggravated assault during a two-month period of 1971 whose cases were closed by August 1972. In this way they wound up with 62 percent of all defendants indicted for rape in 1971, 52 percent of the murder defendants, 44 percent of the robbery defendants, and 16 percent of those accused of aggravated assault.

The reporters went through the more than 19,000 indictments returned by Philadelphia grand juries during 1971 to find all the defendants who fit their criteria—1034 in all. They made lists of the defendants' names and case numbers and then searched for every police, court, prison, or other document that could supply them with any information about each defendant and his case—about 100,000 pieces of information. They devised their own standard form for recording, for each defendant, his name, address, age, race, prior record, circumstances of his arrest and indictment, whether or not he was released on bail, the final disposition of his case by a prosecutor, judge, or jury, the identities and races of the judges, and the identity, address, age, race, and relationship to the defendant of the victim of the crime.

"We use forms a lot to organize our information," Steele explained. "In the FHA study, we used a standard FHA mortgage form and filled out a copy for each example we researched. For the court study and much of our work since then, we've made our own forms. The challenge we faced in the court study was to categorize such an enormous amount of information. We spent four months in that little room in city hall filling out these forms. Then we suggested the use of a computer to analyze the information to see which factors appeared to determine the outcome of each case.

"We made a decision to hold the series down to dispositions of cases and how they were arrived at. We could have had the computer

programmed to do other things if we had wanted to change gears—
like when and where certain crimes were most likely to happen. We
joked about charting robberies by the victims' and robbers'
horoscopes."

"The important thing," Barlett added, "was that we got all the time
we needed. The *Inquirer* also paid thousands of dollars for the
computer work alone on the court series. This is what sets the Knight
organization apart from the other places I've worked. We get the time
and everything else we need, and they never interfere. No one has ever
killed a story in my five years here. After the FHA series was
published, we found out that it had cost the *Inquirer* considerable
money in lost advertising. Real estate brokers and mortgage bankers
had threatened to pull their ads if the stories ran, but we never heard
about it. The paper just went ahead and published them, and the ads
were pulled. We only found out about it later from some of the real
estate people themselves. They were surprised that it didn't stop the
stories."

"After the court series," Jim Steele recalled, "we noticed the
increasing national drift of the newspaper and decided to try a
national subject next. We talked to Gene Roberts (the executive
editor) and considered a lot of ideas. Oil came to the top."

It was then the middle of 1973, and there had been a heating oil
shortage the previous winter in the Midwest. With summer had come
the first reports of gasoline shortages affecting vacationing motorists,
accompanied by higher prices at the gas pumps. Meanwhile, the
major oil companies had begun an advertising campaign to convince
Americans that they consumed too much oil and gasoline and would
have to cut down.

Barlett and Steele began their quest for a better explanation of
what had happened by going to the Securities and Exchange
Commission's files in Washington to look through the annual reports
of major oil companies. Individually, each report told them relatively
little. But when Barlett and Steele began charting information from
ten consecutive years of annual reports for each American-owned
multinational oil firm, they began to discern a significant trend: The
five largest oil companies had greatly expanded their sales of
petroleum to foreign markets at the expense of the United States.
Mobil, for example, had shifted from selling 54 percent of its
petroleum products, including gasoline, inside the United States in
1963 to selling only 42 percent of its 1972 output in the United States,
with the rest going to new customers in Europe and Asia.

"You don't get conned, if you know the facts before you start asking questions."

"At the same time American oil companies with worldwide operations are telling their customers in the United States to cut back on their consumption of oil products," Barlett and Steele later wrote, "the companies are urging their customers in Europe and Asia to buy more oil products . . . The American taxpayer is subsidizing the sale of petroleum products across Europe and Asia through a variety of tax allowances and benefits granted to American oil companies. The cost to the American taxpayers can be measured in billions of dollars over the last ten years."

By examining shipping records at Lloyd's of London, the reporters found that even during the Arab embargo, oil tanker sailings to the West from Middle East ports actually increased. By searching through major American and European newspapers, they found that a week before the Standard Oil Co. of Indiana explained in U.S. advertisements that it was rationing its supply of gasoline to outlets in the United States because "demand has outstripped this country's crude oil supply . . . and foreign crude availability isn't up to this country's needs right now," the same multinational giant urged in an ad in the *Financial Times* of London, that British industrialists buy more of its oil because "Standard Oil Co. (Indiana) . . . has an enviable supply of established crude resources." After confronting a senior vice president of Texaco with similar evidence of his company's contradictory marketing practices, Barlett and Steele elicited from him the explanation that "the same shortages do not exist elsewhere." They then found in federal records that among the reasons for this discrepancy was a joint effort by the oil multinationals and the U.S. government in earlier years to keep domestic oil product prices up by restricting oil imports.

Their three-part series on oil in the *Inquirer* attracted wide attention as the first documented explanation of how the early stages of the eventually worldwide "oil crisis"—before the oil-producing countries drastically raised their royalty rates—was in large part the result of deliberate policies by the multinational oil firms, abetted by the U.S. government, to manipulate the supply of crude oil. Once Barlett and Steele had shown the way, the rest of the media and committees in Congress began their own investigations. What others found only substantiated the conclusions the two *Inquirer* reporters had already presented, making even more impressive their mastery of such a complex subject in a few months' time.

Painstakingly thorough preparation for a new subject was especially beneficial to Barlett and Steele in their investigation of how American foreign aid money was really spent overseas. They studied thick congressional staff reports and hearing transcripts and State Department records on U.S. foreign aid, plus those kept by the World Bank, the Export-Import Bank, International Finance Corporation, Asian Development Bank, Overseas Private Investment Corporation, and other conduits for individual foreign aid expenditures Barlett and Steele decided to audit at random. Everywhere they went, they found that few officials expected the two reporters to be nearly so knowledgeable. "You don't get conned, if you know the facts before you start asking questions," Barlett pointed out.

"At the State Department," Steele remembered, "we asked for their files on two or three specific Asian housing projects financed with American aid money. After a couple of days they called us over, and we were taken to a huge conference room with a long table piled high—in four or five tall stacks—with files of all kinds. I can only guess what they were up to, but maybe they figured we would be discouraged and confused by all that paper and would never find what we came for. They clearly expected us to keep at it for only a short time because some guy kept looking in to ask how we were doing.

"Anyway, we surprised them by staying for three or four days, coming back the first thing each morning and staying until late in the afternoon, going through all the files. We knew what we were doing, and we found a gold mine of information in those files, way beyond what we were originally after."

For each individual foreign aid project, Barlett and Steele put together a neatly typed, plastic-tabbed file folder of the information collected from the State Department and various aid agencies. Along with their typed notes, each folder contained copies of official records pertaining to the project—the amount of money spent on it, the location and purpose of the project, and reports of what was to be accomplished with the money. Barlett and Steele had assembled the complete official version of what had happened to one slice of the foreign aid pie, plus enough information for one of the reporters to check up on the government's account by visiting the project site himself.

Armed with their briefing books, Barlett and Steele must have appeared to be diplomats or traveling business executives as they flew off to Peru and Colombia in South America and Thailand and South Korea in Asia. In Lima, Bogota, and Seoul, they found that money intended for the construction of housing for the poor had instead been used to subsidize luxurious homes and apartments for professional families in the upper 10 percent of each city's income brackets. In Bangkok Barlett found American aid money had been siphoned off and pocketed by Thai and American developers, in place of low-cost housing. Barlett surprised the director of the State Department's Agency for International Development office in Thailand with what he knew and elicited an admission that AID did little to monitor such projects to see that its money was being spent as originally intended.

Elsewhere in Thailand Barlett found U.S. aid money used to inflate the worth of an industrial paper manufacturing company and enrich its stockholders, most of whom were wealthy Thai and American businessmen. In South Korea he found that AID was subsidizing sweatshop factories exploiting local labor at less than subsistence wages. He also found that one American construction company had received millions of U.S. aid dollars for several projects in both Asian countries that produced little or no new employment or economic gains for the people of these countries.

"What was really exciting," Steele later recalled, "was finding things you didn't expect to find when the itinerary was being planned. In Peru, for instance, I found out that because of the nationalization of some American business holdings there, foreign aid credits were being quietly cut off, just like they were in Chile before the fall of Allende. Nobody told me this was happening, but I found in the records in Peru that the U.S. money began to dry up after the generals started taking over companies. So I began asking questions."

Donald Barlett believes this kind of exhaustive examination of a single subject about which the general public understands relatively little "is where newspaper circulation is going to be ten years from now." He sees what he and Steele have done as the logical next step from the muckraking of Lincoln Steffens or Woodward and Bernstein to a deeper examination of our society's institutions to discover why they do not seem to work better. Because they are not chasing specific villains and are not limited by whatever subject seems to be presently in vogue, Barlett and Steele expect to be able to continue their work, and maintain their enthusiasm for it, indefinitely.

"We'll stay together as a team," Barlett added. Despite their great differences in personality, he and Steele have worked closely together, sharing a professional intimacy that includes wordless communication through meaningful glances and shared jokes that have to be explained to outsiders, although they seldom see each other away from work. "We each need someone to bounce things off," Barlett explained. "Give and take on what you find is important in evaluating it. We also keep each other from becoming personally involved in what we're reporting."

"Personal involvement can be very bad," Steele said. "It can lead to bad mistakes in judgment. We try not to get outraged. We don't see ourselves as righting wrongs, but merely looking at complicated public issues for patterns that haven't been seen before."

Their isolation in a cramped, cluttered room several floors above the *Inquirer* newsroom is self-imposed. "Newspaper offices are gossipy places," Steele said, "and we don't want everybody to know what we're working on before we write it." Although the two reporters apologized for the condition of their office, most of their information from previous projects had been neatly filed away in cabinets that consumed much of the room's floor space. A question about any of the series of articles they have written for the *Inquirer* sent Steele directly to one of the tightly packed drawers for just the right file to document his answer.

"We don't weed anything out," Barlett explained. "And the only real disagreement Jim and I have ever had was over where we should put the new filing cabinets we need. We can't decide whether we should stack them up to the ceiling."

They work as independently as newspaper reporters possibly could. In general, they come into contact with an editor only when deciding what subject to look into and then again, months later, when they turn in their articles for final editing. And they deal only with editors at the top. For a time, their assignments came exclusively from the executive editor. Then there was some confusion over whether they should be edited by the metropolitan or national editor. Finally, they were turned over to Steve Lovelady, a young bearded assistant managing editor of the *Inquirer* who in 1974 was put in charge of special news projects, including whatever Barlett and Steele were working on.

Barlett and Steele properly appreciate the unusual freedom, opportunities to travel, and open-ended work schedule their privileged status has provided them. "When people ask me after each project we finish if I'm getting tired of this kind of work," Barlett said with a rare smile, "I say, 'Are you kidding? How could I get tired of this?'"

Steele insisted, however, that the real pleasure of their work comes from the process itself. "Spending months on a subject and having it all come together at the end is extremely rewarding. No matter how much you know, there is always more to find out."

Barlett, an investigator by temperament, also enjoys the hunt for information that no other reporter had previously unearthed. "We're always finding records we didn't know existed and information we didn't expect to find, including lots of stuff we have never had any reason to use. When we were going through the records of natural gas pipeline companies for the oil series, we discovered they kept public records of all the legal fees those companies pay, because they're regulated by the federal government. And for the big El Paso natural gas company we found records showing they had paid a lot in fees to a New York law firm by the name of Nixon, Mudge, Rose, and whomever—you know, the firm that Richard Nixon and John Mitchell were in."

"There are always more records and more in them to find out," Jim Steele said with a certainty of mission one would expect of a scientist searching for a cure for cancer. "The work is never done."

4: Stalking a Senator

Mike Baxter first saw Jim Savage the day Baxter arrived in Miami from Lincoln, Nebraska, where he had been recruited from the University of Nebraska's journalism school by an editor at the *Miami Herald.* "I was still wearing my Nebraska farm boy blue jeans on my first day in town," Baxter remembered, "when another *Herald* reporter took me to the Fountainbleau Hotel to see what Miami was really like. As we went into the lobby he pointed out Savage, who was sort of hiding behind a pillar in his drip-dry Miami suit. He was waiting to grab Frank Sinatra and question him or something for an investigation Savage was doing for the *Herald* about the Mafia and the Fountainbleau."

But Baxter never really got to know Savage during the next several years, as their careers at the *Herald* took divergent paths. Jim Savage, five years older than Baxter, was one of several investigative reporters who helped earn the newspaper a national reputation during the 1960s for vigorous muckraking of southern Florida's modern frontier boom-town scandals. He and others exposed local organized crime activities, unjust courts, and corrupt municipal and county officials. They helped to put a number of wrong-doers in prison and, in the case of veteran police and court reporter Gene Miller, helped free from death row several others who had been wrongfully convicted.

Baxter, meanwhile, became a metropolitan staff reporter whose smooth writing style brought him mostly feature-story assignments and a two-year stint on the staff of the *Herald*'s glossy Sunday magazine, *Tropic.* "I was pretty much a feature writer," Baxter recalled, "and I looked upon Savage as pretty much a Mafia writer. I guess I had about as much interest in most of his Mafia stories as he must have had in my features."

But in 1971, about four years after Baxter arrived in Miami, "professional rivalry" between the *Herald,* the "flagship" of the Knight newspaper fleet, and the other two major Knight dailies, the *Detroit Free Press* and the *Philadelphia Inquirer,* brought Baxter and Savage together as an investigative reporting team on the trail of local builders, bankers, bureaucrats, and, ultimately, a U.S. senator. "Both the *Free Press* and the *Inquirer* had done big FHA investigations," Baxter remembered. "Our editor had them spread out in his office. He wanted us to find out what was going on with FHA in Miami."

In Detroit and Philadelphia inner-city real estate dealers had bribed Federal Housing Administration officials to approve sales of run-down slum houses to unknowing low-income families under a new FHA housing program. In a typical case found by reporters a dealer in Detroit bought a delapidated slum house for $4000 and bribed an FHA official to falsely certify that it had been extensively renovated. The official then approved an FHA-guaranteed and subsidized bank loan to a woman on welfare, who bought the house for $12,600. The dealer got that money immediately, so when the woman was later unable to keep up her payments on the loan and abandoned the house, which was falling down anyway, the government had to reimburse the bank and take possession of a house that could not be resold. Stories in the *Free Press* and *Inquirer* reporting that thousands of such transactions had taken place in the two cities led to a congressional investigation of that particular FHA program.

In Miami's Dade County, however, as in other fast-developing urban areas, more complicated FHA subsidy programs were being exploited by developers who claimed to be building new houses and apartments for low-income families. The federal government both guaranteed and subsidized the construction loans to the developers and paid part of the rent or home mortgage interest of the families moving into the houses and apartments. In a variety of sophisticated ways Florida developers and FHA officials had conspired to illegally obtain federal guarantees and subsidies for poorly constructed homes and apartments that the developers then milked for exhorbitant profits. But these abuses were much more difficult to understand and expose.

When the *Herald's* metropolitan editor, Steve Rogers, decided to investigate FHA activities in Miami, Mike Baxter—an angular, boyish-looking six-footer, who was then still only twenty-seven years old—had written "a few minor stories" about FHA housing projects there. "It turned out that I had written about FHA most recently, when we got our first tip," Baxter said. "It did not produce a really big story, but it opened the door on the FHA in Miami for us. Rogers got Jim Savage and me together and threw us into the breach."

That first tip came out of the *Herald* itself, buried in the real estate section of the fat, 318-page Sunday edition of September 29, 1971. It was "in a weekly column that a local real estate abstractor wrote for us listing recent transactions," Jim Savage later remembered. "One of our editors saw it down inside the column—a $100,000 mortgage loan made on unusually generous terms to William F. Pelski, enabling him to buy an expensive new home."

Pelski was director of the regional FHA office in Miami. The former mayor of a small nearby coastal town, he worked in Richard Nixon's 1968 presidential election campaign in Florida and was rewarded, on the nomination of Florida's Republican U.S. senator, Edward J. Gurney, with the Miami FHA job. Baxter and Savage looked into the $100,000 loan and discovered it was made to Pelski by a local mortgage banker and developer who had applied to Pelski for FHA approval for a federally subsidized housing project. His application, which had been rejected earlier, was reconsidered and approved by Pelski, even though the developer did not have clear title to the land on which the subsidized apartments were to be built.

Although the $100,000 loan story attracted comparatively little attention, it did produce the next, much more important tip. Another builder whose own application for FHA assistance had been repeatedly denied by the Miami office complained to a *Herald* editor that two other developers seemed to be getting favored treatment from FHA. One of them, John J. Priestes of Miami, the builder-informant said, was getting the lion's share of subsidy money for new single-family homes to be sold to low-income families. This tip, without the name of the builder-informant, who did not want to further jeopardize his own future dealings with FHA, was passed along to Baxter and Savage.

They asked around among Miami real estate people about Priestes, but no builder they contacted could remember hearing his name. They also failed to find Priestes in the *Herald*'s library of clippings. "He was listed in a Miami cross-reference directory as a proprietor of a hole-in-the-wall hearing aid dealership," Baxter said, which made Priestes only more of an enigma. But it was still too early to seek out and question the mysterious Priestes, Savage decided, because they knew so little about him. They would be at too great a disadvantage if he simply lied to them, and if he denied the anonymous tipster's allegation, the two reporters would be unable to muster evidence to support it.

"We had no evidence of any crime when we began our

investigation," Savage told me. "We had to learn first how the FHA was supposed to operate before we could substantiate our instinctive suspicions and show that Pelski and Priestes were violating the law. The most difficult aspect of the investigation for me was this initial necessity to fight our way through the bureaucratic regulations and records of FHA to prove our case. "

The necessary tedious research did not stop Baxter, though, who figured out just what records they needed. Then the two reporters went to the Miami FHA office and asked to see the list of all the builders who had received approval from that office for federally subsidized, single-family home construction under section 235 of the National Housing Act of 1968. (Section 235 authorized the subsidies for the construction and sales of single-family houses to low-income families, while another section, 236, authorized subsidies for the construction and rental of apartments for such families.) Despite the specificity of their request, however, Baxter and Savage were told by Pelski's deputy, Louis Baine, "I'm sorry, gentlemen, but it's impossible."

There followed several weeks, during which "our lawyers debated with their lawyers," Savage said. "We had entered a period that was extremely frustrating for me." Savage had grown accustomed in his Mafia-hunting to receiving cooperation, albeit usually piecemeal and anonymous, from federal prosecutors and investigators who believed an effective way to fight organized crime was through unfavorable publicity. But there simply were no helpful government sources to tap for this FHA investigation.

Instead, lawyers for the *Herald* drew up a court suit claiming that under the federal Freedom of Information Act, the FHA records Baxter and Savage were seeking should be made available so that the public could know how its tax money was being spent. Under threat of this suit, Pelski finally released the list. "I was extremely disappointed," Baxter said. "Those records indicated that John Priestes was building only 40 of the 1400 federally subsidized houses in Dade County. I thought we had a good tip. I thought we had Priestes, and he hardly showed up on those records."

Savage found the long list of builders, corporations, and FHA commitments "just so much gobbledygook that didn't add up to anything." He and Baxter went back to Pelski and his top subordinates to ask them questions, "but their answers completely threw us off the track. They talked in the double-talk of industry jargon and kept insisting there was nothing to our suspicions about favoritism for Priestes. They kept saying we just didn't understand

"It can be boring work, going through the records day after day . . ."

their operation. People in the industry told us it took something like five years to find out how the FHA operates anyway, and they were deliberately misleading us on top of that. We found some people in the local real estate industry who gave us good advice about what we might be on to, but still there were many days we came out of that FHA office after being turned around so many times that I had doubts. I thought maybe we were just wrong. But Mike had fewer doubts than I did."

Baxter became convinced, as their real estate contacts had told them, that Priestes was somehow hidden in several places on that FHA list in the disguises of several unfamiliar corporations. "I had nothing to do for a couple of weeks while Savage worked on some leftover Mafia stories," Baxter recalled, "so I went down to the courthouse to find out in the records who these corporations were, what lawyers call 'piercing the corporate veil.'

"The corporate records led me to land transaction and mortgage records. I had never been in these records before. Our real estate writer showed me what books to use and how to use them. It's amazing how many reporters don't know how to use records like these. They think it's some kind of mystical thing. But it only took me a few minutes to figure out what to do.

"It can be boring work, going through the records day after day, writing down the names and details of corporations, land sales, and mortgages that don't mean anything at first. I also had to learn more about the 235 and 236 housing programs and the complicated FHA red tape. You acquire all this technical expertise you know you'll never use again. I learned that investigative reporting can be tiring and boring this way much of the time. I've seen reporters come to the *Herald* since then to do investigative reporting only to decide they don't really like it because it's so boring."

Baxter, however, became caught up in his sleuthing through the courthouse records. He began finding real estate corporations that Priestes was on record as controlling, although none of these corporations turned up on the FHA list of subsidy commitments. At the same time, he found that many of the corporations on the FHA list did not turn up in the telephone book, other city directories, or the courthouse corporation records.

These mysterious companies did appear from time to time in the land records, however. They bought land for the projects that the FHA office had approved subsidies for and contracted mortgages for the federally guaranteed and subsidized housing construction loans. The names signed as officers of these corporations were unfamiliar, but Baxter noticed that the notaries used by all the mysterious corporations were the same. They were also the same notaries who appeared on deeds made by the known Priestes corporations. Baxter found that these corporations also often bought the land for their FHA-approved projects from known Priestes corporations. And they all used the same "qualifiers"—people licensed to build under a peculiar Florida law that allows development corporations to "rent" qualifiers and their licenses for construction projects.

"These mysterious corporations had gotten FHA commitments for twenty, forty, and even sixty subsidized units in a single day, according to the FHA list," Baxter said, "while the biggest-well-known Miami builder on the list had been allocated only twenty-three units altogether." These corporations were really controlled by Priestes, Baxter figured, and used as fronts for building sites and FHA commitments without anyone but the complicit FHA officials knowing that Priestes was getting more than his share of the subsidy money. Baxter and Savage tried this theory out on their sources and some functionaries they had made contact with in the Miami FHA office. Several said it sounded plausible.

"After a while, every time I found another corporation on the FHA list or in the land records that I could not find in the telephone book I figured it was another Priestes front," Baxter said. "And after I found three or four indications that it was a Priestes front, we would call the telephone number for the known Priestes companies and ask if the 'X-Y-Z Corporation' were really Priestes, and sometimes we'd catch them, and they'd say 'Yes.' And a few of them began to tell us a little more."

But Pelski continued to deny everything, and his aides still gave confusing explanations about why Baxter's assumptions were mistaken. It was time, Savage decided, to see John Priestes.

"I did most of the records work," Baxter said, "and Jim concentrated on the interviews. Jim taught me all about the art of interviewing. He was the best I've ever seen, including other reporters, lawyers, you name it. He's first-generation Irish on both sides and has that blarney. He was soft spoken and disarming in our interviews. He had a way of getting people to talk when they really wanted to throw us out."

"You have to prepare well for interviews with subjects who are targets of an investigation," said Savage. "You have to know much more than your subject thinks you know. The first interview is usually just to get him on the record about what you're working on. You try not to tip your hand while getting the subject to talk freely. You want him on the record with his lies; it will be useful to show that they're lies later. That's what we had done with Pelski, and then much later we were able to confront him and our readers with his lies."

Baxter and Savage did not let on to John Priestes, a short, stocky man who had been a semipro baseball player, what the real reason was they had come to his office to ask questions that first time. "We told him we just wanted to know more about how the 235 program was working in Miami," Baxter said. "We asked him a bunch of naive-sounding questions. If there were any doubts in our minds before we talked to him, we came away convinced by his answers that all those corporations were Priestes fronts.

"We asked him, for instance, about the Ellarud Corporation, which had turned up on the FHA commitment list. We asked Priestes, wasn't Ellarud one of the big FHA developers in the Miami area? He professed not to know much about it. He said he had heard a company by that name was building some 235 houses somewhere.

"But I knew that the same construction company that built for Priestes corporations was doing the building for Ellarud. I knew that the notary usually used by Priestes on deeds and mortgages was the notary on deeds and mortgages for the Ellarud projects. And I knew that Ellarud stood for Priestes's Aunt Ella and Uncle Rudy, who had come down from Pittsburgh. So I knew he was not coming clean."

While recounting that first Priestes interview for me more than two years later, Baxter chose his words carefully and used his somewhat incongruous, well-controlled television newsman's baritone to great effect in dramatizing the breakthrough he helped make possible. Trapping the clever Priestes had thrilled him. It had justified those long hours in the county courthouse record books. Like a journalistic Sherlock Holmes he had collected a miscellany of arcane pieces of information and shaped them into a suddenly convincing picture. It was the turning point that convinced Baxter he had become an investigative reporter.

It had not been laid out for him in the courthouse records. He had only collected clues and tantalizing coincidences there. The rest had come from calling and calling, along with Savage, everyone they could find who worked anywhere for Priestes or had worked for him in the past, as well as present and former lower-level employees of the Miami FHA office and others in the real estate development industry in Dade County. None of them had spelled it all out either. Instead, a few more stray clues from interviews here and a key admission or two there had to be combined with bits and pieces of information from the courthouse records to solve riddles like the Ellarud Corporation. There had been no magic to it, just hard, frequently frustrating work.

Within just a few more weeks Baxter and Savage were able to document that a dozen corporations on the FHA list of subsidy allocations were fronts for Priestes and that he had actually received half of the section 235 single-family home construction commitments made by the Miami FHA office. The story ran on the front page of the *Herald* in February 1972, sending a tidal shock wave through the Miami real estate community.

Priestes had refused a request to have his picture taken, so Baxter and Savage arranged for a *Herald* photographer to catch him by surprise emerging from a local restaurant, wearing a striped polo shirt. "Priestes hated that picture we got of him," Savage recalled. "When he realized that we were going to continue writing about him and keep using that picture because we had no other, he walked right into the newspaper office one day to have a new photograph of himself taken."

Savage and Baxter had come to share both the continuing search through land records, local directories, and FHA documents, and the scatter-gun interviewing they conducted to nail down the true identities of Priestes's front corporations, though each developed sources that would talk only to one of them.

Savage became obsessed with chasing down one particular corporation, the "Richard Green Construction Company." According to the FHA list, that corporation had been allocated subsidy money for the construction of forty-nine houses under the section 235 program. And Savage found that forty-three of the houses had indeed been built and sold with federally guaranteed and subsidized loans to lower-income families. But when Savage looked for the company itself, he found it had no location. And when he tried to find Richard Green, he began to doubt that any such person existed.

"It was strange at first," Savage said, "because the signature of Richard Green appeared on all the deeds and mortgages of the houses in that project and on FHA records. Pelski and his aides at the FHA office in Miami told me that they even remembered Green coming in and signing the necessary forms in person.

"But then I found a newspaper ad from when the Richard Green Construction Company was marketing its new houses. I found a telephone number in it and dialed the number. It turned out to be Priestes's office. I asked to talk to Richard Green, but they said he wasn't in. Then, later, a man called me back and claimed he was Richard Green, although he could not intelligently answer questions about himself and his own company. He quickly began sounding funny and hung up.

"I kept after everyone connected with the Richard Green Company's financial transactions and finally found a mortgage broker who admitted that he had signed Richard Green's name to some documents. It was kind of dumb of him to admit it. He said it often happened, that brokers or someone else handling a transaction would sign the name of somebody else who was too busy when the deal was already approved. But as soon as he admitted that, I knew we had a story about the falsifying of official documents, the fact that there was no address for the Richard Green Company, and that it's telephone number was the same as that of Priestes.

"We ran that story the day after the first Priestes story appeared. Later we learned that there definitely was no such person as Richard Green and that the Richard Green Construction Company was a phantom invented by Priestes and Pelski in complete collusion to hide FHA commitments that were actually being made to Priestes. It was Priestes who had built and sold those houses, and everyone, including Pelski, had lied and lied about it.

"Because of those two stories," Savage said, "there had to be a federal investigation of Priestes and Pelski." And because the stories noted that Pelski had been personally selected for the Miami FHA job by Senator Gurney, it was Gurney himself, in a press release issued by his office a week later, who call for a "thorough and speedy speedy investigation" by the U.S. Department of Housing and Urban Development, FHA's parent agency.

As Savage and Baxter later wrote, the HUD investigation was "speedy and shallow." An internal HUD report they obtained much later showed that no criminal prosecution was recommended, despite the illegal forging of documents. Priestes, who "literally wined and dined HUD's trio of investigators," according to a later account by Baxter and Savage, suffered only a belated, quietly carried-out suspension from the FHA approval list. He was soon at work passing around money during the 1972 election campaign and thereafter in an attempt to get himself reinstated, but Baxter and Savage did not know it at the time. Nor did they yet know that he had paid Florida political figures for his favors from Miami's FHA office.

Shortly after the first two Priestes stories appeared in February 1972, however, Baxter and Savage got another important tip, which gave them their first indication that there might be more of a connection between John Priestes, William Pelski, and Senator Edward Gurney than Gurney's outwardly routine sponsorship of Pelski's appointment as the Miami FHA director. That tip came in a call and subsequent interview with a respected Gainesville, Florida, builder, Philip Emmer. "We first learned from Emmer," Savage said, "that there was a young man named Larry Williams traveling around Florida collecting under-the-table 'contributions' for Gurney from FHA builders."

Emmer told Savage and Baxter that he had applied for FHA subsidy money from the Jacksonville regional office, which was headed by Forrest Howell, who also had been recommended for his job by Gurney after the 1968 Nixon victory. After his FHA subsidy application had been stalled for months, Emmer said, he had received a telephone call in February 1971 from Howell, telling him a man named Larry Williams was coming to see him. When Williams arrived, Emmer said, he asked Emmer for a $5000 cash contribution to help defray the expenses of Senator Gurney's field office in Orlando. Emmer told the reporters Williams asked him for $2000 immediately and said he would collect the other $3000 after Emmer had received approval of his FHA subsidy applications. According to Emmer, "Williams said, 'I want $5000 in cash so the public and the newspapers won't be writing about it, because you know it's very embarrassing for you businessmen to see these things in the newspapers.'"

It would make a great story, but Emmer said it had to be kept off the record. If his name were used in the newspaper, for example, he told Savage and Baxter, his business might be ruined, especially as far as FHA was concerned. He said he had called because he had seen the Priestes stories and wondered if the same kind of transaction had taken place in those cases. And he hoped that the two reporters could somehow write about the shakedown by using another case.

Emmer had already given up on the federal government, to which he first complained in confidence in 1971, shortly after Emmer had refused to pay Williams any money. HUD and the FBI both investigated the incident, but the Justice Department determined after a review of the FBI reports that it had no case against anyone. FHA did, in the meantime, approve Emmer's application for a subsidized project to be built in Pensacola.

Emmer's application for another project in southern Dade County was rejected by Pelski's Miami FHA office, however, after Pelski, according to Emmer, told him that the priority for subsidized projects would be placed elsewhere in southern Florida. It was a decision, Pelski said, that Gurney "and his aide Larry Williams" concurred in. "I got the message and I was shocked," Emmer told Savage and Baxter, "I was stunned. I said I now understand the game, and I assumed we are not going to get this thing."

Baxter and Savage went to builder after builder in south Florida to get another account of a shakedown by Williams, but they found nothing more than a few vague accounts of solicitations by Williams for political campaign contributions for Republicans, possibly including Gurney. Those were not surprising because Williams, a former salesman who in 1972 described himself as a public relations and advertising consultant and real estate investor, had been the Florida Republican party's state finance director from 1968 until January 1971. Baxter and Savage argued repeatedly with Emmer for permission to use his name and case, but he kept refusing.

"Although it now occurred to us that we might be on the trail of a United States senator," Baxter later recalled, "We were still far from certain. Williams might not have been working for Gurney at all. Emmer might have overreacted to a normal fund-raising approach. Or Gurney simply might not have known what Williams was up to."

Baxter and Savage continued to examine the entire FHA housing subsidy program in southern Florida, searching out other builders with FHA-approved projects, finding out how they won FHA approval and what they had built. They also kept checking the various subsidized housing projects John Priestes had built under the many names of his front corporations. In one of those neighborhoods of cheaply built houses Baxter and Savage made their next big breakthrough.

In July 1972 a woman who had recently moved into a Priestes

house complained to the two reporters that the walls throughout her new home were suddenly cracking. It was not fair, she told them, that she had to make monthly payments on a house that had not been built better than that. She also mentioned in passing that she had not made any down payment on the house. The FHA program required that a down payment be made by all buyers, even though it might be much smaller than that needed for most home purchases. This gave buyers some financial stake in their homes, no matter how small, and forced the developer to build the house well enough so that prospective buyers would want to make that initial investment.

"I knew it was illegal for a developer with an FHA loan to not require that a down payment be made," Savage remembered. "It happened that a friend of my mother was in the real estate business and had been indicted for that. It was a violation of federal law."

Baxter and Savage found that none of the woman's neighbors had made down payments either. "Now Priestes was in real trouble, and he knew it as soon as he realized we were asking around about this new story," Savage said. "Priestes went out to these people's homes at night and threatened them so that they would change their minds about what they had told us."

In fact, the first woman Baxter and Savage had talked to called them to deny everything she had said. But after they continued asking questions of other people, she called back to say that she had told the truth the first time after all, that Priestes had paid her and some of her neighbors to change their stories. Baxter and Savage wrote all about it in a long front-page article in that Sunday's *Herald*.

On Monday FBI agents showed up in the Priestes subdivision to interview the residents about not being required to make down payments and about Priestes's attempts to prevent them from telling anyone about it. The agents came away with several incriminating statements and five new $100 bills that had been distributed by Priestes in his attempt to keep the homebuyers quiet.

Thus began the third federal investigation of possibly illegal activity connected with the FHA subsidy programs in south Florida. It was the second of those investigations to be started in response to a story by Baxter and Savage, and it was the first that appeared likely to produce results. An FBI-Internal Revenue Service investigative task force was formed following a special request by Miami congressman Dante Fascell, a Democrat whose constituency included nearly a thousand families who had bought homes from Priestes under the FHA subsidy program. The task force began checking Priestes's income tax returns and investigating him for everything from violation of FHA regulations to obstruction of justice.

Now Priestes and many of the people who worked for him became panicky. As a few more people became convinced that it might ease their consciences to tell at least a little of what they knew, the two reporters discovered that Priestes was frantically begging some of his associates to lie to the federal grand jury that was considering evidence from the FBI-IRS task force. It didn't work. Hopelessly trapped, Priestes began negotiating a deal with the government: He would trade his guilty plea and testimony about payoffs he made to politicians and government officials, including Pelski, for leniency by the federal prosecutors.

How did Savage and Baxter feel, now that their reporting, after nearly a year of frustration, was finally having some effect? "It was encouraging," Savage told me much later, "when it became clear that federal grand juries were confirming our stories and a number of those involved were getting ready to enter guilty pleas. It had always disturbed me that there were public officials and businessmen who were corrupt and that reporters normally covering them on one beat or another never seemed to write about that. I enjoyed being the one who cut through that first level most reporters stopped at, so that I could learn about the hidden activities that went on at the public expense. Accomplishing that always gave me a thrill. And having the power of the *Miami Herald* behind me usually meant that some action would be taken on what I helped uncover."

Savage, who had come to work at the *Herald* in 1963 as a general assignment reporter in its one-man bureau in Titusville, Florida, near Cape Canaveral, had been first introduced to investigative reporting after moving to the Fort Lauderdale bureau in 1965. There he met Hank Messick, who specialized in discovering from law enforcement sources what the local grand jury was investigating and then matching or surpassing its secret work with stories in the *Herald*. Savage watched and later helped with some of the reporting, as Messick uncovered wrongdoing in the sheriff's offices of Broward (Fort Lauderdale) and Dade Counties, matching strides with local prosecutors until their almost joint newspaper and court investigations produced indictments.

In 1967 Savage went with Messick to the *Boston Herald-Traveler* to join an investigative reporting team headed by Nicholas Gage, whom Savage knew from his college days at Boston University. The team broke up only months after it was formed, however, when the newspaper killed stories that hit too close to some of the businessmen

"I enjoyed being the one who cut through that first level most reporters stopped at . . ."

on its board of directors. Gage went to the *Wall Street Journal* (and later to the *New York Times*); Messick went to Fort Lauderdale, where he has since been writing books about organized crime. Savage went back to the *Miami Herald*.

In the FHA investigation he conducted with Baxter, Savage told me, his determination for the first time was matched by the anger he felt about what had happened to the victims of the network of kickbacks, influence peddling, and violation of FHA regulations and federal laws that he and Baxter were uncovering. "The poor people these programs were supposed to be serving were getting the worst kind of houses out of this," Savage said. "Instead of going into their houses, the money was going to government officials, politicians, and into the builders' pockets. We went out and saw the houses. The roofs were falling in, and walls were buckling—on brand-new houses. And the buyers had no recourse. They called the FHA office to complain, but nothing was ever done. They were told to put it in writing. So they'd write letters and get back only mimeographed replies. It made me damned angry."

It required that outrage and a strong curiosity, fueled by the hunch that more important people than just Priestes and Pelski were involved in the FHA influence-peddling, to push for another big breakthrough. "There were no friendly FBI agents or police agents available to provide background," Savage reminded me. "In fact, in several instances after our stories initiated an official investigation, we were told that government agents were specifically instructed not to talk to us because of fears that prospective criminal defendants might later accuse the government of giving us confidential information. The investigators first learned some stuff by reading us. So there was no pipeline from the official investigation, no magic source."

But Savage and Baxter were able to make some headway by going after those under investigation and people who worked or had worked for them. "We had to convince some people who were themselves under suspicion that it was to their advantage to talk to us," Savage said. Most of these sources would only reveal tiny tidbits of information or, more often, only confirm for the two reporters information or theories they obtained elsewhere. "We had some surprising results with some of the targets of the investigation," Savage said. "We'd piece together information to come up with theories and then try them out. We'd bluff them into thinking we knew more than we did. Sometimes we'd hit pay dirt and then try out that theory on another source."

Often even the process of confirming information was carried out in a kind of code, Savage said, because some sources refused to answer any questions directly. "They would only respond obliquely by giving us hints if they thought we knew something. It was dangerous for us because we were not always sure what we knew. We'd come back to Steve Rogers (their editor) with what we thought was a story, and he'd ask a bunch of questions about it that we couldn't answer yet. So we didn't have a story."

In trying to check out developer Philip Emmer's allegations that young Larry Williams was shaking down Florida builders on behalf of Senator Gurney, Savage and Baxter "interviewed everybody we could think of who ever worked for Gurney," according to Savage. "Our Washington bureau man helped by referring to us people he heard of who had left Gurney's staff and might talk."

One of those former employees finally did, and what she told them turned out to be just enough to keep Baxter and Savage on the story. Pat Kotler, formerly an assistant press secretary for Gurney in his Capitol Hill office, said that back in 1971, when Philip Emmer told the FBI that Larry Williams had tried to shake him down, Williams had sent a complete report of his interview with the FBI on a telecopier from Gurney's Orlando, Florida, office to the senator's office in Washington. She said she had been watching the telecopier on the Washington end when William's report, marked "Larry Williams—Testimony to the FBI," began rolling out.

"It was an unusual piece of information," Mrs. Kotler told Baxter and Savage. "It put our office into a bit of turmoil." When Gurney's administrative assistant, Jim Groot, realized she was reading the report as it appeared on the machine, Mrs. Kotler said, he "raised hell." "'Did you read this?' he asked me," Mrs. Kotler said. "'This is strictly confidential; you are not to mention this to anyone at any time.'"

In the report, Mrs. Kotler said, Williams was "just telling them what went on, what he did. And he admitted going to Forrest Howell's office (at the Jacksonville FHA) and sitting down with him and getting lists of contractors who were either getting, or up for, FHA contracts. And then he would go and visit the contractors and ask for contributions.

"My memory is acute" on what the report said, Mrs. Kotler told the two reporters. "That's essentially what it boiled down to. That's what I read. It shocked me. It seemed to me blatant to admit it. My reaction was, aha, that's how it's done."

She also told Baxter and Savage that she met Williams once in Gurney's office in Washington. Groot made the introductions. "I was told he was an employee," Mrs. Kotler said, "a staff member."

More certain than ever that they were on the right path, Baxter and Savage talked to more FHA builders in Florida. Several said that Williams told them "he worked for Senator Gurney in some office in Florida" and made overtures to them that seemed like offers of "political influence." None told of a shakedown attempt by Williams that was as specific in detail and clear in intent, however, as the incident described by Philip Emmer back in February 1972.

It was now the summer of 1973. For the sixth time the reporters called Emmer and argued strenuously for permission to use his name and story. This time—perhaps because the federal investigation of Priestes appeared to be more serious and determined than the Justice Department's brush-off of Emmer's original complaint, and perhaps because he had nothing more to lose with the FHA program that was now in turmoil in Florida anyway—Emmer said yes.

Baxter and Savage put his story of the shakedown attempt and Mrs. Kotler's account of William's FBI interview into a long presentation of Larry Williams's activities in Gurney's name that was spread across all eight columns at the top of page one and filled an entire page inside the Sunday edition of the *Miami Herald* on July 8, 1973. The headline said, " 'Gurney Worker Asked Cash for FHA Deal'—Gainesville Builder Says He Would Not Pay."

The response was immediate. Forrest Howell, the Jacksonville FHA office director, acknowledged talking with Emmer about his stalled FHA subsidy application. Larry Williams admitted soliciting a political contribution from Emmer. But both men said Emmer must have somehow misinterpreted these conversations. Senator Gurney issued a long statement, published verbatim by the *Herald*, in which he acknowledged knowing Williams as a Florida Republican fund-raiser and volunteer, admitted hearing of allegations that Williams had used his name "in an attempt to raise political funds," and even confirmed that his Senate staff had been informed of the contents of Williams's interview with the FBI back in 1971. But Gurney insisted in the statement that he had subsequently told Williams himself "that under no circumstances was he to use my name or the name of my office in the conduct of his business or political activities."

Now other builders felt freer to talk, and Baxter and Savage were able to obtain and publish several other detailed accounts of Williams offering them opportunities to buy influence with the FHA for money he told the builders he was collecting for Gurney. Williams, the two reporters found out, began rising at 4 a.m. on Sundays—the days when Baxter and Savage usually broke major new stories—to buy the first copy of the *Herald* available in Orlando, where he lived in a huge, expensive, white-columned home near the Orlando country club. Publicly, Williams denied working for Gurney, and the senator's office stood by Gurney's written statement disassociating himself from whatever it was that Williams had been doing.

For Gurney, the handsome, curly-haired, deep-voiced migrant from Maine, the Baxter-Savage stories during the summer of 1973 had come at a particularly inopportune time. He was then enjoying his first real national prominence as a member of the Senate Watergate Committee, appearing daily on coast-to-coast television as a solemn advocate of strict observance of the letter of the law, proper judicial conduct, and pursuit of the exact truth. As President Nixon's strongest defender on the committee, Gurney had taken Nixon's chief accuser, former White House Counsel John W. Dean, III, to task for inconsistencies in his testimony and his diversion of Nixon campaign funds to pay for his honeymoon. As Washington gradually became aware of the stories about Gurney emanating from Miami, he and his staff began to worry about their effect on his Watergate Committee image.

Gurney himself abruptly changed his public opinion of investiga-tive newspaper reporting. On May 17, 1973, at the opening of the the Watergate hearings, he expressed confidence that Watergate would be "cleaned up," thanks to his committee, the courts, and investigative reporters. But by October 13, when he addressed a Republican women's club in Sarasota, Florida, he had concluded that the press had had "a Roman orgy with Watergate... The power of the press, totally unchecked, unregulated and often misused, is capable of great mischief." In his few unguarded asides to other reporters, he repeatedly referred to Baxter and Savage as "hatchet men."

"But we never got to talk to Gurney himself, except once briefly," Baxter said. "He never would talk to us. He dealt with our stories with press releases or silence. The one exception was when he came to our newsroom one day on other business, to see our political writer about some routine story. So I went over and kind of surprised him. I got to ask just one question: 'Is it true that your office used influence to get HUD approval for one particular apartment project (Emmer's) in Jacksonville?' He denied it categorically and quickly walked away."

In September 1973 Baxter and Savage reported that Priestes had just told the Florida grand jury that in March 1971 he had carried a brown sack filled with $30,000 in cash aboard a Miami houseboat to pay William F. Pelski, the Miami FHA director, *and* Larry Williams for FHA subsidy commitments for a Priestes housing project. Priestes said he was paying $500 per house for FHA loan guarantees and subsidies for the construction of sixty houses. Altogether, on a number of occasions, he testified, he paid Pelski and Williams $175,000 for such FHA commitments. He told the grand jury it was the only way he could stay in business as a builder. His testimony led to Pelski's later conviction and 18-month prison sentence.

Now the connection between Priestes and Emmer had finally been made. According to their separate testimony, Larry Williams had approached them each for payoffs to get FHA commitments—Priestes in FHA's Miami region and Emmer for both Miami and Jacksonville projects. Williams could no longer lie about what he had really been up to when he criss-crossed Florida visiting FHA developers.

According to Baxter and Savage, Senator Gurney's lieutenants went to Williams and tried to stop him from succumbing to the pressure the federal prosecutors would now put on him to admit fully what he had done and implicate higher-ups to win leniency. "They urged him to lie to the grand jury," Baxter and Savage reported later. "They also made overtures about an extended, expense-paid vacation in South America.

"Instead, Williams agreed to plead guilty to two charges, in return for immunity from further prosecution. He confirmed to the prosecutors what the *Herald* had written, despite Williams's original denials: Larry Williams worked for Ed Gurney." Williams told the prosecutors he collected more than $300,000 from Florida FHA builders for "a secret Gurney Boosters Fund" to help pay the expenses of running Gurney's Florida offices, among other things.

Baxter and Savage soon reported, after piecing together more information extracted from and confirmed by people very close to those involved, that the money collected by Williams had been stored in five places: three bank accounts and a safety deposit box "for Gurney's use" in the Commerical Bank of Winter Park, Florida, of which Gurney was a director. Some of the money had been passed in cash-filled envelopes directly to Gurney's administrative assistant, Jim Groot, who "placed the money in the safe in Gurney's inner office" on Capitol Hill.

The stories about Gurney's "slush fund" began to make headlines in Washington during the autumn of 1973 and plunged Gurney's staff into confusion. "At one political strategy meeting," Baxter and Savage later reported, "Gurney aides laughed aloud at the analogies between Watergate and their own slush fund scandal," including the involvement of Miamians in both. His aides had debated during the summer whether Gurney should "belatedly report the slush fund cash as (political) contributions," Baxter and Savage reported, but they "believed 'the *Herald* could only do a couple of slush fund stories . . . and then it'd die away.'

"The suggestion they report the cash was finally scuttled when one ranking aide warned that reporters covering the Watergate hearings would seize on the irony. 'Every time he (Gurney) asked H. R. Haldeman a question, Carl Stern (of NBC) or somebody would be saying, "Ed Gurney, who just revealed his own secret fund, just asked Haldeman about (Herb) Kalmbach's secret fund,"' the aide said."

Finally, on November 19, 1973, Gurney acknowledged through a press spokesman that the Justice Department was investigating allegations that Florida builders had made cash contributions to him through Williams to get preferential treatment from Florida FHA offices. But the spokesman said Gurney denied the allegations and all knowledge of responsibility for Williams's business and political activities.

Then, in December, Baxter and Savage reported that one of the Winter Park bank accounts into which the money collected by Williams had gone was that of a corporation called Oxnard, Inc.— and that Oxnard's owners and officers were Larry Williams, Edward Gurney, and Gurney's administrative assistant, Jim Groot. Oxnard used money collected by Williams from Florida FHA builders to buy an option on some land in St. Petersburg and to pay "for lawn care at Gurney's home in Winter Park," according to Baxter and Savage in another Sunday front-page story in the *Herald*.

That prompted Gurney for the first time to answer their stories in person. He held a crowded televised press conference in Florida on December 6, doing his best, the two reporters later said, to avoid being questioned by Baxter and Savage themselves. Gurney again denied knowledge of any shakedowns of Florida FHA builders by Larry Williams, but he admitted meeting with Williams and others early in 1971 to discuss establishing an "Ed Gurney Boosters Fund" for campaign and office expenses. Gurney said he thought no final decision had been made, however, and he was surprised to find in 1972 that Williams had already collected $100,000. That money had not yet been reported to anyone as political contributions, Gurney said, because his reelection campaign had not yet started.

None of the money had actually been turned over to him, Gurney said, except for $16,000 that had been given to his Winter Park office and used for office expenses without his knowledge. He said he did not know of any money kept in his office safe, that he did not even have the combination to it, and that when he finally asked his aides to open it they reported that it contained no money. Finally, Gurney said, the only money that he knew of being invested in Oxnard, Inc., was $10,000 of his own that he said he had never gotten back.

Early in 1974 stories began appearing in Washington newspapers that Gurney, Florida's first Republican senator since Reconstruction days, was in deep political trouble back home, and several prospective candidates were getting ready to challenge him in the Florida primary later in the year. In the spring a county jury in Florida indicted Gurney for violating state campaign finance laws, but the indictment was quickly thrown out in court and was dismissed by everyone close to the Gurney investigation as inconsequential headline-hunting by a local prosecutor. The Florida law involved was vague and seldom enforced, and Gurney's failure to report the money Williams had collected was the least of the sins for which he was being actively investigated by federal prosecutors in Jacksonville.

Just what the federal investigators had in mind became clearer in April, when Baxter and Savage reported that Williams told federal investigators under oath that Gurney had agreed to accept a developer's offer of a rent-free, ocean-front condominium apartment in Vero Beach, in return for Gurney's approval of Williams's intercession with local FHA officials on behalf of the developer. Williams—who was by then serving a one-year prison term after pleading guilty to charges of channeling illegal payments to an FHA official and attempting income tax evasion—said that Gurney told him, "fine," when the apartment transaction was presented.

In July 1974 the federal grand jury in Jacksonville cited the apartment transaction in two of eleven counts of bribery, conspiracy, and lying to a grand jury for which it indicted Edward J. Gurney, who became only the sixth senator in United States history—and the first in fifty years—to be indicted while in office. He was accused of conspiring with Williams and several others—including his former administrative assistant Jim Groot; his former campaign manager George Anderson, who also had been president of the Commercial Bank of Winter Park; the former chairman of the Florida Republican Party; and two Florida FHA officials (but not Forrest Howell, who had been the Jacksonville office director)—to extract at least $233,160 from Florida developers with subsidy applications pending before FHA. Gurney also was accused of lying to the grand jury when he said in testimony, as he had publicly, that he had never authorized what Williams had done. The grand jury charged that Gurney had discussed the scheme at length in several meetings with Groot, Williams, and others, many of which were held during the summer of 1973 at the time of the Senate Watergate Committee hearings.

The indictment, which likely would never have been brought against Gurney without the investigative reporting of Baxter and Savage, forced the senator to abandon running for reelection in November 1974. But he fared better when the case came to trial during the summer of 1975.

Taking the stand in his own defense, Gurney reiterated that he did not know what Williams was up to until being told in June 1972. This was eighteen months after Williams's extortion of Florida builders had begun and many months before it ended, according to other testimony at Gurney's trial. Gurney said he had "a very poor memory" and could not remember meetings before that date at which prosecution witnesses said Gurney approved Williams's hiring and authorized his fund-raising scheme. Gurney did not dispute testimony that Williams's activities were discussed at several meetings Gurney had with his staff after June 1972, but he admitted only that he had not been quick or forceful enough in investigating whether Williams had done anything illegal.

Several jurors told reporters afterwards that the prosecution had not presented sufficient evidence to counter defense assertions that Gurney had been "conned" by Williams. As a result, they found Gurney innocent of five charges: bribery, receiving unlawful compensation, and lying on three occasions to the federal grand jury.

The trial jury failed to reach a verdict on another perjury count and the key charge of conspiracy. One juror, Harold Franklin, with whom several others agreed in interviews with reporters, said he voted for acquittal on the five charges, because "the prosecution put on a very poor case in proving guilt beyond a reasonable doubt." But Franklin added that he, and eight of the others, voted for conviction on the conspiracy charge because the defense acknowledged that Gurney was aware of what Williams had done after June 1972, and that, Franklin reasoned, "is when he began more or less a cover-up." In December 1975 the U.S. Justice Department decided to retry Gurney, who was already deeply in debt to his lawyers, on the conspiracy and remaining perjury charges.

Long before the 1975 trial, however, Baxter and Savage had moved on to other things. Savage had even left the *Miami Herald* on a long leave of absence spent at Stanford University in California. As is so often the case with investigative reporters, the chase had ended for them with the last of their investigative stories, leaving to the courts pursuit of the Gurney case to its final conclusion and to the other reporters the task of covering that part of the story. Baxter and Savage steadfastly refused to discuss whether they thought Gurney— or the several other defendants convicted in the case—should have been found guilty or innocent of violating the law.

Their job, Baxter said, was only to "show something improper had been done"; setting things right was up to others. "I'm still not conscious of having gone after Gurney," he added. "*New Times* magazine asked me to write something about 'the story' and Gurney, but I said no. To me, it wasn't one story, but 100 stories" about homebuyers being cheated, FHA programs abused, taxpayers' money wasted, builders extorted for illegal campaign contributions, and the power of a U.S. senator's office abused by *someone*. "I really don't know anything about Ed Gurney himself," Baxter insisted. "I only spoke to him that one time in the newsroom."

Of course, Baxter is evading the issue. Although they had not originally intended it to be that way, their stories wound up pointing to Edward Gurney just as surely as the Watergate stories pointed to Richard Nixon. Their stories ruined Gurney's political career, hurt his personal reputation, virtually bankrupted him financially, and threatened his freedom. While remaining personally distant from him, as most investigative reporters are from their targets, Mike Baxter and Jim Savage became, in another dimension of reality, intimately caught up with Edward Gurney. However his legal problems might end, they had shared in determining his fate.

5: Muckrakers, Inc.

It was autumn 1969, and Jack Anderson was in the Capitol Hill office of an old acquaintance, Representative Robert Giaimo, a six-term Democrat from Connecticut. With Anderson, who had recently taken over the syndicated "Washington Merry-Go-Round" column following the death of Drew Pearson, was Les Whitten, an unfamiliar, deceptively boyish-looking investigative reporter who had just filled Anderson's old job as the column's number-two reporter. The two men were investigating a tip by an admitted Mafia money courier: that Giaimo was a close friend and business associate of a gambler, money-lender, and restaurant owner identified by Justice Department investigators as being "very high up" in organized crime in Connecticut. But they disguised their purpose with a "good guy-bad guy" technique that would have been familiar to anyone who had watched enough police melodramas in the movies or on television.

Acting like the Capitol Hill lobbyist he had come to resemble—with his fleshy face, growing paunch, and fawning manner—Anderson began the meeting by complimenting the congressman on his political popularity in Connecticut and even asking him if he had considered running for governor. "Jack convinced Giaimo that he thought he could get elected governor," Whitten later recalled with relish. "Can you imagine? Giaimo ate it up."

As Anderson and Giaimo continued to chat, Whitten broke in to ask why the congressman was socializing and doing business with people in the Mafia. Giaimo reacted angrily, and Anderson, too, appeared to be annoyed, saying, "Now Les, there must be an explanation for that." But Whitten continued with hostile questions about Giaimo's relationship with the Connecticut gambler and a Washington, D.C., fireworks merchant reputedly financed by the Mafia. "Take it easy, Les," Anderson kept repeating, as he appeared to become increasingly impatient with Whitten's treatment of

Giaimo. Finally, Anderson roared, "Shut up, Les, and let the congressman explain!"

"Jack acted like he was about to fire me on the spot," Whitten said later.

Giaimo denied everything. However, as Whitten kept citing information from his sources that contradicted the congressman, Giaimo admitted that he knew the Connecticut gambler, but not that the man had anything to do with the Mafia. When Anderson observed that there wasn't anything wrong with seeing an old friend now and then, no matter who he was, Giaimo went a little further. He said of the gambler: "He's a good friend. He's a good guy."

Whitten persisted with pointed questions about certain favors that Giaimo, according to Whitten's sources, had performed for the gambler's Mafia friends. Anderson, now seemingly perplexed, told Giaimo that Whitten's sources may not have had everything exactly right. "You must have records to support what you say," Anderson suggested to the congressman. "We can show Les that he's wrong about this."

"Jack got Giaimo to say I could look through all his records right then and there," Whitten recalled. "Giaimo told his secretary to let me go into his files and look at whatever I wanted. I made copies of everything I needed, using Giaimo's own office copying machine. It was all there—the business connections and correspondence proving most of what I had been told. Afterwards, Jack shook the congressman's hand, and we walked on down the corridor of the House office building. After we got around a corner, Jack broke into a wide grin and said, 'I can't believe this!'"

The material from Giaimo's files documented that he had been a partner with the Connecticut gambler and Mafia money-lender in an apartment house investment, that Giaimo's law firm had represented the gambler when he pleaded guilty to income tax evasion, and that Giaimo had been a frequent guest at the man's home and on his yacht. It also proved that he had repeatedly interceded with the Selective Service and U.S. Army authorities to try to keep out of military service two young men connected with the Connecticut gambler. One of these men was the money courier who had contacted Whitten and provided him with some of the information he confronted Giaimo with, in what Whitten and Anderson called their "Mutt and Jeff routine" in the congressman's office.

Giaimo later issued a public statement calling Anderson's columns about him "nothing more than character assassination," and he denied that he knew of any ties between his Connecticut gambler friend and the Mafia. He also telephoned Anderson to say that he now knew just what had been done to him during his interview with Anderson and Whitten and to complain that the columns had not disclosed where they had gotten their documents. "Giaimo said the least we could have done," Anderson remembered "was to have said in the columns that we got those records from him instead of from a confidential source."

Nothing came of those columns. Nothing in them was refuted, but the Justice Department never saw fit to take any action against the congressman based on what was contained in the documents from his files, some of which Anderson had turned over to Justice. Anderson and Whitten maintained that they really liked Giaimo, who was variously described in the columns they wrote about him as "affable," "likeable," "congenial," and a "towering, darkly handsome man."

The Giaimo affair served, however, to help enliven the column during its critical months of marketplace testing after the death of Drew Pearson. The column not only survived this period, but prospered, as Anderson filled it with more significant revelations that established him in his own right as one of the naton's most influential muckraking reporters. Anderson was the first to report U.S. efforts to undermine the late President Salvador Allende in Chile, and to publish classified documents that revealed the United States' secret backing of Pakistan in the 1971 India-Pakistan war. Anderson uncovered the Federal Bureau of Investigation's secret dossiers on public officials and entertainers who criticized the government and was the first to report, years before the full facts became known during a 1975 congressional investigation, that the Central Intelligence Agency had plotted to assassinate Cuban Premier Fidel Castro. Anderson also obtained the controversial Dita Beard memo that led to the discovery of the International Telephone and Telegraph Corporation's curious relationship with the Nixon administration, and he was the first to document in detail how President Nixon had used government money to lavishly outfit his San Clemente, California, and Key Biscayne, Florida, homes.

Woodward and Bernstein may have become larger folk heroes and Seymour Hersh's revelations of atrocities and secret bombing raids during the war in Vietnam may have had a greater effect on altering U.S. policy, but Jack Anderson worked further out on the frontier of investigative reporting many years longer than any journalist who has come to prominence during the new era of muckraking popularity. For two decades as Drew Pearson's chief investigative reporter, Anderson uncovered incriminating information from Capitol Hill that pushed several corrupt politicians out of Congress, including former Senator Thomas Dodd of Connecticut. When other investigative reporters or their editors were slow to pursue and publish particularly sensitive or potentially controversial stories, Anderson went boldly ahead. He was the first to raise doubts about Senator Edward M. Kennedy's account of his Chappaquiddick accident, to report that Attorney General Robert F. Kennedy knew of FBI wiretaps of the conversations of the late Reverend Martin Luther King, Jr., and to reveal that the CIA had spent an estimated $350 million attempting to salvage a sunken Soviet Union submarine in the Pacific Ocean.

Thus, even after muckraking had gained new national acceptance, Anderson's column remained the cutting edge of American investigative reporting. He and his staff continued to find and publish stories no one else could or would get. The column's daily revelations have run the gamut from trivial complaints and titillations to startling outrages—from some government agency's wasteful disposal of trash to billion-dollar defense contract overspending, from details of Jacqueline Kennedy Onassis's share of her late husband's fortune to the financial corruption of U.S. senators, a Vice President, and a President, from a single government employee's mistreatment by the system to Henry Kissinger's calculated deception of the American people on the possible involvement of the United States in a military confrontation with the Soviet Union. So much wrongdoing has been packed into each seven-day week of Anderson columns that some of his most important scoops—including the taxpayer-financed refurbishing of Richard Nixon's western and southern "White Houses" and the CIA's plots to assassinate Castro— have gone almost unnoticed until other reporters picked up and expanded on them in stories that then became front-page news.

"Ours is the ice-breaking role," Anderson told me. "There is still not enough investigative reporting, and I always fear there will be a retrenchment by editors and then there will be even less. We have the responsibility of being the watchdogs for the public and the rest of the press."

Anderson has built his operation into a veritable "Muckrakers, Inc." A loosely organized staff of six reporters—including Anderson and Whitten, who began sharing the column's by-line in 1975—plus an office manager, receptionist, and four to six unpaid intern reporters produce seven columns each week for daily newspapers, another column for weekly clients, a six-nights-a-week radio

"Ours is the ice-breaking role . . . "

program, a weekly televison commentary, regular contributions to *Parade* magazine, and several Anderson books, of which the next is to be *The Confessions of a Muckraker.* In 1975 the column appeared in nearly 1000 newspapers, with perhaps 60 or 70 million readers, and the radio program, with completely fresh material, had been syndicated independently to more than 100 radio stations. In addition, Anderson made one out-of-town public lecture each week, which provided him with most of his personal annual income of over $100,000. All of the income from the column and its adjunct radio and television programs, Anderson said, paid for salaries of his staff and other overhead expenses.

Since 1974 Anderson has housed the operation on an entire floor of a restored red stone-and-brick Victorian mansion on Sixteenth Street, six blocks north of the White House. The mansion, with its corner turrets and imposing stone steps, finely carved wood trim and huge office fireplaces inside, is eerily reminiscent of the stately surroundings favored by the powerful Washington lawyers and lobbyists Anderson has often derided in print and public speeches but with whom he has sometimes hobnobbed—to use one of his own favorite expressions.

The morale at "Muckrakers, Inc.," has always been strikingly high, despite or perhaps partly because of the prodigious work load facing a still relatively small reporting operation. The task of seeking out fresh scandals has been aided somewhat by a daily influx of 200 to 300 letters and countless telephone calls, many bringing valuable tips. A good number of the tips come from regular sources carefully cultivated over the years by Anderson and each of his reporters. The informants are always assured anonymity, even if it means filling a particular column with extraneous or possibly misleading informa-tion to camouflage them. They also are profusely praised and thanked for their assistance. "Very, very helpful," a bubbling Anderson told one caller who had just given him a good tip. "Hey, you're great. Thanks a million." The enthusiasm for a good story is infectious in Anderson's offices. "You really do feel that there is a sort of missionary quality about laying low the people most journalists don't have the guts to go after," said Les Whitten. "I felt reborn when I came to work for Jack, like someone converting late in life to Catholicism."

Anderson has been somewhat more generous with both recognition and money for his staff than his predecessor, Drew Pearson, had been. Salaries have ranged from the traditional starting pay of about $13,000 (which Pearson paid Anderson for twenty years) to the more than $30,000 Les Whitten was paid by Anderson in 1975. And he has credited "associates" on the columns for which particular staff members did most of the reporting, publicly praising them for especially sensational stories. Anderson's reporters have also been encouraged to write free-lance articles for other publications with the backing of Anderson's name and the assistance of his nationwide contacts. Most important, each man on Anderson's staff has been free to pursue to the end any story that comes his way, knowing that Anderson will most likely publish it, no matter what the risks may be, if the reporter can document its accuracy.

As hard as his extraordinarily devoted and energetic staff has worked, however, "Muckrakers, Inc.," has depended mightily on Anderson himself. His high-level government sources have produced the column's most important inside information and secret documents. He has continued to write a large share of the daily newspaper columns himself and to review, edit, and often rewrite most of the columns other members of his staff assembled. He also has taped the radio and television programs and has regularly crisscrossed the country lecturing and promoting the column at every stop. From leg work to writing to editing to huckstering, Anderson could have and often has done it all.

Jack Anderson had been in apprenticeship to Drew Pearson for twenty-two years before Pearson's death in 1969. Although Anderson came to share top billing with Pearson during later years, he remained the hard-working second banana to the charismatic, socially well-connected, and politically powerful Pearson. The columnist shared only a small fraction of his large income with Anderson, yet the junior partner often had to keep the entire enterprise going almost single-handedly while Pearson held forth as a salon pundit in Washington and traveled all over the world. Anderson got into the habit of working very long hours and at least part of all seven days of every week, laboring at night and on weekends in his suburban Maryland home. Anderson nevertheless remained steadfastly loyal to Pearson, enjoying the autonomy he had in his reporting and valuing Pearson's courage in publishing stories no other Washington journalist would touch for fear of ostracism or libel suits.

The well-educated, well-traveled son of a Swarthmore College professor who also was a Chautauqua circuit impresario, Pearson's early career included lecturing in his father's Chautauqua show. He then flitted from job to job as college geography teacher, itinerant foreign correspondent, and finally Washington correspondent for the *Baltimore Sun*. When in 1932 Pearson and another Washington reporter, Robert S. Allen, were discovered to be the authors of two unsigned, best-selling books of gossip and scandal, *Washington Merry-Go-Round* and *More Merry-Go-Round,* they were fired by their newspapers. So the two decided to start the "Washington Merry-Go-Round" column, which was picked up by the Scripps-Howard's United Features syndicate. Pearson began broadcasting a radio version of the column in 1940, and by 1942, when Allen dropped out of the venture, the columnists had built their circulation from an original six newspaper clients to more than 350 newspapers. When Pearson died of a heart attack in September 1969 at the age of seventy-one, the column was appearing in more than 650 newspapers, almost twice as many outlets as any other newspaper column had at the time, and a Louis Harris poll had just shown Pearson to be the best-known columnist in the United States.

The columns themselves combined punchy, colloquially phrased reports of Washington scandals—peopled by the town's "bigwigs," "brasshats," "poohbahs," and "gumshoes"—with Pearson's preachy personal commentary on political issues and foreign policy. He helped make himself a world figure by trading insults with U.S. presidents, dashing abroad to cover international conferences and interview foreign leaders, and organizing humanitarian campaigns like the 1947 Friendship Train, which traversed the United States collecting ten trainloads of food for the hungry of postwar France and Italy. In Washington Pearson wielded enormous power with the praise and blame he bestowed on politicians in a column read daily by millions of voters throughout the country. He used the power to lobby vigorously in the column, over radio, and on Capitol Hill in person on behalf of pet causes and political favorites and against those persons and issues he strongly opposed.

"Drew was an idealist who believed in following through on his stories," Jack Anderson said. "He'd write about issues and then try to control their outcome in Congress. A couple of times each year, he'd asked me to go up there and line up votes for him, something I strongly opposed but had to do for him. Pearson was not fundamentally an investigative reporter. He was more an idealist and crusader. He was less concerned with accuracy than crusades and would sometimes omit certain facts from the column, if he thought it to be in the best interests of the country."

In this way, Pearson sometimes misused his great influence. He was an intensely partisan Democrat who always seemed to find more fault with Republicans, although he also exposed enough wrongdoing by Democrats to convince many readers that all Washington politicians were on the take, sleeping in the wrong beds, or simply incompetent. At the same time Pearson marshaled public opinion in favor of much of the New Deal, but against Franklin D. Roosevelt's plan to pack the Supreme Court. He came out early as one of the staunchest opponents of Senator Joseph McCarthy's witch-hunting demagoguery and advocated an end to American isolationism and the beginning of peaceful coexistence with the Soviet Union long before either position became fashionable.

Typical of the scandals Pearson exposed in his column were his 1948 revelations of the kickbacks Congressman J. Parnell Thomas of New Jersey was taking from House of Representatives employees in return for protecting their jobs. Helen Campbell, Thomas's executive assistant of many years, was offended by the senator's badly concealed romantic liaison with a young secretary in the office. After following Thomas to the secretary's home one night and finding his car still there the next morning, its radiator cold, she went to Pearson immediately with documentation of Thomas's kickback arrangements. Pearson's subsequent columns on Thomas prompted a federal investigation that eventually put the congressman in prison.

Nearly twenty years later, as Pearson was nearing seventy and Jack Anderson was doing the lion's share of real digging for the column, Anderson obtained a much larger group of internal documents from another congressional administrative assistant. Although Senator Thomas Dodd of Connecticut had been spoken of as a contender for higher office, Anderson had been investigating reports that Dodd drank heavily on the job and performed questionable favors for his campaign contributors and clients of his Connecticut law firm. When Anderson heard of discontent on Dodd's Senate office staff, he called

James Boyd, Dodd's administrative assistant, told him what he had heard, and suggested that if Boyd ever wanted to tell anyone about it, he would be most welcome in Anderson's office.

After Dodd's reelection in 1964, Boyd and other Dodd staff workers became suspicious about what had happened to half of the $500,000 that had been raised for the campaign. Only $250,000 could be accounted for in legitimate electioneering expenses. As they began looking through office records and correspondence they found voluminous documentation that Dodd had banked for his personal use money from campaign fund-raising events, as well as other questionable payments he received from corporations and individuals seeking favors in Washington. He also had accepted numerous flights on private corporate aircraft and a free grand tour of the Orient paid for by a shipping company. In return for the tens of thousands of dollars he received from businessmen, Dodd tried to use his influence in Washington to win government contracts, business loans, and even ambassadorships for his benefactors. After months of collecting evidence of such activities, Boyd finally went to see Jack Anderson.

Anderson immediately won Boyd's confidence and convinced him to carry thousands of documents from Dodd's files to Anderson's home, where he and Boyd went over them night after night, weekend after weekend, for nearly a year, piecing an estimated 7000 pieces of information into a coherent, provable pattern of wrongdoing. Anderson wrote column after column that dribbled out the evidence against Dodd a little at a time, so that it would be digestible for the readers. But after about twenty columns and little reaction from the rest of the media, newspaper editors grew impatient with the steady diet of Dodd's foibles, while Dodd himself answered with public statements of outrage and an FBI investigation of Anderson's informants that only an ex-FBI agent like Dodd could have instigated so quickly.

Pearson, who usually allowed Anderson considerable independence, cut off the Dodd columns for a time to appease subscribers and weather the storm. But the old warrior lifted the embargo and charged back into battle after Anderson, Boyd, and his co-conspirators inside Dodd's office visited Pearson at his Maryland farm to make an emotional appeal for resumption of the campaign. Pearson even contributed a few files he himself had been keeping on Dodd. In all, more than 100 Drew Pearson-Jack Anderson "Merry-Go-Round" columns were published on Dodd—all but two of them written by Anderson—and a disgraced Dodd was censured by the

Senate. For Pearson it was a fitting last hurrah. For Anderson it was an important victory that impressed Washington insiders who knew of his key role in the Dodd investigation. Already in his mid-forties, Anderson was finally emerging from Pearson's long shadow.

Anderson had been only twenty-four, and Drew Pearson already fifty, when Anderson came to work for the column in 1947. Born in California, Anderson was taken by his Mormon parents to Salt Lake City while he was a young child. There at age fifteen Anderson was editing the Boy Scout page of the *Deseret News,* and soon the teenager was contributing news stories to the paper and logging more column inches than were many of its full-time reporters. By the time he was eighteen, Anderson was a salaried city reporter for the *Salt Lake City Tribune.* Then a year later, he interrupted his career by undertaking obligatory two-year service as a Mormon missionary, seeking converts in the South.

Anderson, who believes much of his muckraking motivation derived from "the basic Mormon teaching that there is a fundamental struggle between force and freedom—and that the good guys are on the side of freedom," found his missionary experience important for his development. "Imagine," he later remembered, "there I was, nineteen years old, and people were telling me everything—their fears, their sins, their marital problems. Oh, I learned a lot." He also picked up his flamboyant and sometimes overbearing evangelist's public-speaking style, which he often used to restate his philosophy of exposing and expelling wrongdoers in government.

"The incestual relationship between government and big business thrives in the dark," Anderson declared in a typical sermonlike address to a group of fellow Mormons a few years ago. "When those responsible for it get caught in the sunlight, they are like fish out of water. They flip and they flop. They backtrack. They trip over the tongues." His booming voice rose even higher and his index finger jabbed sharply in the air as he admonished his audience: "Are we going to tolerate this? Are we going to let them corrupt us? They are not your masters. They are your servants. *You* have the final decision. *You* have the final vote!"

After serving briefly as a cadet officer in the Merchant Marine during part of World War II, Anderson went to China as a civilian war correspondent for the *Deseret News* and other Mormon papers. He was with a band of nationalist Chinese guerrillas behind Japanese lines, when he was drafted by the Army and assigned first to training duty and then to the Shanghai edition of *Stars and Stripes.* World

War II ended while he was still in China, and Anderson became bored
with his Army duties, so he found a way to cover the new conflict in
China between the nationalist forces of Chiang Kai-shek and the
communist insurgency lead by Chou En-lai and Mao Tse-tung. "I
struck up a deal with Spencer Moosa, the bureau chief for the
Associated Press, who was covering the nationalists," Anderson
recalled. "Moosa had an AP contingency fund of $150 a month,
which he paid me to moonlight for him covering the communists. I
came to know Chou En-lai well."

Anderson also began planning for his future. He wanted to work in
Washington, he said, because "it was the news center of the Western
world," but he had been there only once—on a Boy Scout trip from
Salt Lake City. American correspondents he met during the war told
him that one good way to learn about the capital was to work on
Drew Pearson's staff as a reporter for his column. "They said it was
the best way to get to know the town," Anderson recalled, "because
Pearson had the best sources in Washington."

So as soon as he was discharged from the Army, Anderson went
straight to Washington and Pearson, who had just fired a member of
his staff who had secretly joined the American Communist party.
Anderson could have the job, but not if he wanted to work just long
enough "to learn the ropes in Washington," Pearson said. He was not
operating a journalism school, and Anderson would have to commit
himself to stay at least three years. "At the end of that time I stayed
on," Anderson said, "because I was enjoying it too much to leave.
Drew gave me total freedom to roam, *and* he printed what I came up
with. I learned the satisfaction of getting tough stories into print
before anyone else."

Anderson quickly became Pearson's most trusted and productive
reporter. While Pearson cultivated Presidents and entertained
Washington's best-known figures at his elegant Georgetown home
and 800-acre Maryland farm, Anderson walked the corridors of
government agencies and congressional office buildings, befriending
junior senators, congressmen and their staff members, White House
aides, and countless middle-level bureaucrats who really ran the
government and came into possession of most of its secrets. Using
Pearson's name as an entrée, Anderson became a fixture in the
reception room just off the Senate floor, sending messages into the
chamber to ask this or that senator if he could speak with him for a
minute. Acting on a hunch or a tip, Anderson engaged the senator in
what seemed to be a knowing insider's conversation on the subject,
listening carefully for important information Anderson needed to

confirm or fill out a story. Anderson freely acted the part of the sycophant playing court to his source. He praised congressmen he might later embarrass in the column, ostensibly urging them to use the column for publicity to tell their side of the story in some controversy.

Whenever a source was displeased with what finally appeared in the column, Anderson blamed Pearson. With rising indigntion he recounted how Pearson had refused his entreaties to go easy on the source or his interests. Stick with me, Anderson told the source, and we'll do better next time. Similarly, Pearson blamed Anderson when his sources were upset. In conspiratorial Washington this charade convinced a surprisingly large number of officials.

Anderson ran errands for Pearson, checking out the details of tips Pearson had received from cronies and helping to line up and count votes in Congress on issues Pearson was lobbying for or against. But on his own Anderson discovered some of the column's most celebrated stories. It was Pearson who found out that businessman Bernard Goldfine, seeking favors in Washington, had given a vicuna coat to Sherman Adams, President Eisenhower's top White House aide. But it was Anderson who uncovered evidence of wrongdoing by the "five percenters" of the Truman administration, by the "kickback congressmen" of the late 1940s and early 1950s, and by Congressman Adam Clayton Powell and Senator Thomas Dodd during the 1960s.

All this time Anderson was being paid only $250 a week for his work on the column. "I never really asked for more money," Anderson said. "Drew and I never discussed salary. He just paid me what he paid me. But I was concerned about my career. I saw that Drew got $50,000 from the *Saturday Evening Post* for a series of articles I helped him prepare. I realized I could have done it all and earned that money if I had had more recognition on my own. I was concerned about always being in Drew's shadow.

"So I made arrangements with *Parade* magazine (a Sunday supplement distributed by many newspapers) to become its Washington editor with a good salary and my own by-line. When I told Drew, he thought it over and promised me that I would inherit the column if I stayed on. I agreed to that and went back to *Parade* and told them what happened. They and Drew let me work out a deal, so that I would write articles for them regularly with a minimum guaranteed payment that was still higher than my salary from the column."

Thus fortified financially, Anderson continued working long hours for the column during the week and wrote articles for *Parade* on the weekends. He first won national attention with a series for the magazine on the misdeeds of various congressmen and senators in the late 1950s. After that, Pearson let Anderson share the by-line on the "Merry-Go-Round" column and appear with him on the radio program, where Anderson's booming evangelist's delivery proved quite effective. With the Dodd columns, for which other Washington journalists gave Anderson the credit due him, and publication of the highly successful *The Case Against Congress,* over the names of both Pearson and Anderson, the junior partner finally had the recognition as well as the experience to take over the column and its subsidiary operations when Pearson died.

Anderson still had a large rebuilding job to keep the column going successfully. First he had to replace the rest of Pearson's staff, most of whom had slacked off considerably when they found out that Anderson, rather than one of them, would inherit the column. One by one, they were eased out and replaced. He selected Opal Ginn, who had helped him for *Parade,* to become his secretary and office chief of staff. A large, gregarious woman who wanted everyone to call her simply "Opal," she delighted in shocking the men of the office with her sometimes rough language and fondness for the Bloody Marys she kept mixed every day. She also screened all of Anderson's calls and mail, handled his schedule, managed the column's distribution, and generally became her teetotaling boss's protector. To replace himself in the column's number-two job, Anderson chose Les Whitten, who left the declining Hearst Deadline Service when it could no longer could put his stories into enough newspapers. Brit Hume, a young, lanky, patrician-looking reporter from the *Baltimore Sun,* talked his way onto the staff with his brash bravado and the talent evident in a muckraking book he had written on the then corrupt leadership of the United Mine Workers Union. And Joe Spear, a quiet, industrious native of Maryland's isolated Eastern Shore, was hired to help with the column and take over the work for *Parade* magazine. Later, James Boyd, former administrative aide for Senator Dodd, became the *Parade* writer and the collaborator on an Anderson book. The other two full-time members of Anderson's staff, Jack Cloherty and Bob Owens, were hired after Hume left in late 1972. They have done most of the reporting and writing for the radio and television programs.

Anderson's next biggest problem was improving the column's reputation for accuracy. He did not write the personal commentary or "think pieces" Pearson had sprinkled throughout the columns, and

"Losing a story now and then is a risk worth taking for accuracy."

he checked his facts more carefully. "Drew was terrible on details," Anderson said. "He found that if he checked with everybody, the word would get around, and he'd lose his big scoop. I thought that was a wrong reason. Losing a story now and then is a risk worth taking for accuracy." Anderson also said he never threatened sources with defamation, if they refused to come across with information, as many Washington officials had complained during Pearson's tenure. Anderson continually reminded his staff that such conduct would constitute a firing offense and added, "if there is anyone in Washington who says I ever used the column to blackjack information, I'd like to meet him and take a lie-detector test with him."

The column's credibility had been called into question just before Pearson's death because of two items: Pearson had been unable to furnish proof for his charge that President Nixon had tried to manipulate the Apollo moon-flight ceremonies for his personal political gain; Anderson had stirred up a great controversy with a similarly undocumented column challenging Senator Edward M. Kennedy's version of the Chappaquiddick auto accident that killed Mary Jo Kopechne. Anderson wrote that Kennedy had been taking the young woman for a moonlight swim, and that after the car he was driving went off a bridge, Kennedy first persuaded his cousin, Joseph Gargan, to take the blame. Critics attacked Anderson's reconstruction of the incident as consisting more of conjecture than fact, though Anderson insisted that his account had been pieced together from interviews with Kennedy's own friends and investigating officials.

He was able to get the information about Chappaquiddick, Anderson said years later, through use of the same "circle technique" of interviewing that Woodward and Bernstein used in piecing together the Watergate story. "You get one small piece of information from one of the small circle of people with first-hand knowledge," Anderson explained. "Then you go to another guy with that one fact and get him to elaborate on it. You have to act as though you know the whole story and you are only trying to confirm what happened next. Then the person you're interviewing will think someone else broke and told you everything, so he feels freer to talk. Sometimes you might call a person and tell him something outrageous about what you might know. Then, in the process of denying that, he'll volunteer an important new fact." Years after the incident, large doubts remained about what really did happen at Chappaquiddick, and there was still no evidence to support or contradict Anderson's version.

Anderson's mission after Pearson's death was to find better documented but sufficiently juicy items to keep the column's newspaper subscribers satisfied. Stories like the one about Congressman Giaimo's friendship with the Connecticut gambler helped, but Anderson was looking especially for what Brit Hume called "stories so big they couldn't be ignored, which would call attention to the column and make it plain that Jack Anderson and those who worked for him were serious about investigative reporting and capable of doing it well."

Then, in March 1970, one of Anderson's sources told him that George Murphy, the former Hollywood song-and-dance man, was receiving an annual cash retainer, a rent-free apartment in Washington, and use of company credit cards from the Technicolor Company while serving as junior U.S. senator from California. Hume, who had just come to work for Anderson, was in his office listening as Anderson called Murphy to confirm the information. Anderson answered Murphy's denial like an old friend trying to help the senator out of a jam: "Well, Senator, I think you should know that I've been talking to the Senate Ethics Committee. I don't want to say anything to give away my source, but I understand you have gotten clearance from them for this. I understand it involves $20,000 in consultant fees, rent on your Washington apartment, and use of some of the company's credit cards. Now, for all I know, this is perfectly proper, but I thought it my duty to at least look into it. Now, Senator, you and I have been friends for a long time. I don't think you want to be quoted as denying this whole thing. So, because we've been friends, I'll forget what you said before and give you another chance, in fairness."

To Hume's amazement Murphy then admitted everything, as Anderson hurriedly scribbled notes on the back of an envelope. Hume thought that Anderson had cleverly tricked Murphy by pretending he knew more about the matter than he did and by invoking the name of the Senate Ethics Committee, which Hume knew as "the most tight-lipped operation in town." But through Ben Fern, the committee's chief counsel, Anderson discovered that the committee had actually approved Murphy's arrangement with Technicolor, as questionable as it may have been. To get the details of the arrangement from Murphy, however, Anderson had used another of his favorite interviewing techniques. He began the conversation by asking Murphy general questions about business arrangements with Technicolor. Then, after Murphy made the expected denial, Anderson surprised him with the details he already knew. "I always try to begin by asking a question to which I already know the answer," Anderson explained. "As the guy starts talking, I say, 'Now wait a minute, court testimony indicates . . . 'I have a document that says . . .' That throws him off stride."

Anderson also hinted that he might not publish anything at all about the Technicolor arrangement, at least not any time soon. "You say there was no conflict, and I've always known you to be honest, so I'm inclined to take your word for it," Anderson told the senator, according to both his and Hume's recollections of the conversation. "I'm not sure what I'm going to do with this information, but I do want to look into it a bit further before I make a decision. I hope you will do me the favor of not saying anything about it until I've had a few more days to work on it." Anderson wanted to stop Murphy from issuing an explanatory public statement about the matter before Anderson's exclusive story could be distributed across the country, which would take three or four days. An uncertain Murphy did nothing, and the column created a sensation in California a few days later, forcing the *Los Angeles Times,* which had dropped the column after Drew Pearson's death, to scramble to catch up with the fifty California newspapers that carried it.

Stories like George Murphy's arrangement with Technicolor had been the column's stock-in-trade during the Pearson-Anderson years. They consisted essentially of good word-of-mouth tips confirmed through resourceful, if sometimes duplicitous, inter-viewing by Pearson, Anderson, or someone else on the staff. What ultimately characterized Anderson's solo tenure, however, were the extraordinary number of top-secret documents and transcripts that found their way into the column after he took it over. Almost every week there were references to or excerpts from State Department cables, military intelligence reports, CIA data, transcripts of closed hearings and committee meetings in Congress, internal memos from the White House, a variety of other classified government agency documents, and even transcripts of the secret proceedings of the federal grand jury investigating Watergate. Anderson seldom missed a chance to point out in the column that a document being quoted had come to him with "top secret" or "eyes only" stamped on it, or that top officials were being quoted on exactly what they had said in a tightly guarded, closed national security meeting inside the White House. In this way the column gained a new respect in Washington, where political gossip is cheap but classified documents are the coin of the realm, and attained a new authority for readers across the country, who were being taken inside the secret precincts of the capital.

He also played on Washington's many policy rivalries. From Pentagon friends in the Army he could get secret reports documenting wasteful spending by the Air Force. From Navy sources he could get intelligence reports on the Russian Navy that his sources hoped would stir public opinion in support of larger expenditures for new U.S. ships. From foreign policy hard-liners in the Pentagon, the State Department, or Congress Anderson could get voluminous intelligence reports, diplomatic cables, and secret government studies that appeared to be evidence of threats to American security abroad. From other sources, even inside the Pentagon, who were fearful of foolish U.S. military action, Anderson could get other documents indicating that these same threats had been exaggerated.

In the case of the Gulf of Tonkin incident in 1964, for example, Anderson was shown cable traffic from U.S. ships in the gulf indicating that North Vietnamese PT boats may not have intended to attack at all and in fact had fired only warning shots in confusion over the purpose of a U.S. destroyer in the area. The second reported attack, Anderson was told, may only have been the result of a misleading radar reading. All this was included in an Anderson report that some top military officers thought President Johnson may have been "trigger-happy" and were worried that he overreacted in the Gulf of Tonkin incident. That column created the only public doubts, as short-lived as they were at the time, about the wisdom of the congressional resolution supporting President Johnson's retaliatory air attacks against North Vietnam.

"Although it may still come as a surprise to many people," Anderson told me, "very few of our sources are disgruntled employees out to get their bosses or to do harm to the country. We usually find such people unreliable anyway. We also do not pay for information, except for occasionally paying free-lance reporters to find a story for us, and we do not pay for documents.

"I was the first reporter to find out that Spiro Agnew had been taking kickbacks from government contractors, but I couldn't print the story because I would not pay for some documents we were offered to prove it. After first hearing about the kickbacks from two separate sources who offered no documentation, I called Agnew's press secretary. I took the frontal approach with him and explained in detail what I had and asked if Agnew wanted to respond. I had hoped that Agnew would try to explain the money somehow, like by claiming that the payments were campaign contributions. Then I would have a story based on his explanation.

"But Agnew wouldn't fall for it. He denied receiving any money in any form. I was stuck. My sources were confidential, so if I wrote a column it would be Agnew's word against anonymous sources. Then somebody came to us with purported documentary evidence they wanted to sell. I must admit that the temptation was great. But I turned it down."

His typical sources of classified documents, Anderson said, "are loyal to the country and believe in the system. They just believe that their real duty is to the whole country and not just people who happen to be temporarily sitting in positions of authority, like Nixon or Kissinger. They believe it is in the national interest for the American people to know certain things, and I encourage that attitude. Sometimes they come to me with something they think should be out, but more often I get in touch with them regularly and ask what's going on.

"I cultivated most of these sources back in the days when I was working for Drew, when I was more anonymous. In working the various government agencies, I went right into the offices where people were working in key policy areas. Sometimes, they would tell me I had to go to the public information office, but many other times I was able to sit down and chat with them. After a while I would begin telling them my philosophy about the people's right to know certain things."

Referring to one particular government source who had been especially helpful to him, Anderson described a process of evangelic conversion that must have been accomplished in much the same way that a younger Jack Anderson operated as a Mormon missionary. "If I had asked for secret papers the first time I met him," Anderson explained, "he would have thrown me out of his office. But I got to know him. He developed confidence in my motives. He agreed that the document he had was overclassified. He talked a little. Then he read the document to me. Eventually, he let me see it, and finally he gave it to me. Every source has to be baptized slowly."

It was just such a source, "cultivated over many years," Anderson said, who delivered to him the documents that revealed how the United States was secretly supporting Pakistan in the 1971 war with India over territory that became Bangladesh. Publicly, both President Nixon and his foreign affairs adviser, Henry Kissinger, declared that the United States would not involve itself in the conflict in any way. "We are neutral," Nixon told a group of congressional leaders at a White House briefing. "We are not taking sides." When Washington reporters asked Kissinger about rumors that the White House really favored Pakiston, he called them "inaccurate."

About this time Anderson received a call from his source, who had first-hand knowledge about what Nixon and Kissinger really were doing about that war. In strategy discussions with top government officials inside the White House, the source said, Nixon and Kissinger decidedly supported Pakistan and expressed strong prejudices against India. "Sometimes, Kissinger acts like a wild man," the source said. "His animus toward India seems irrational." Anderson's source was quite worried that the American people were being deceived about a tense international conflict that could involve the United States and China, which also backed Pakistan, in a military confrontation with India and its patron, the Soviet Union.

"Every President is entitled to secrecy in matters of national security," Anderson later wrote in his book, *The Anderson Papers,* "but this privilege does not allow him to deliberately mislead the American people. When I was persuaded that America was being misled, I asked my source for the documentary evidence that would also convince the public." He arranged to meet the source several times in "crowded places where secret papers, in brown Manila envelopes, could be passed quickly and inconspicuously."

Anderson's source had no hesitation about turning over these classified documents to the newspaper columnist. "I really believe his whole purpose was to inform the American people," Anderson told me. "I had helped condition him to take that view. He actually tended to admire Kissinger, but he thought he was very wrong in this case."

Among the hundreds of pages of top-secret papers on the India-Pakistan conflict that Anderson received were diplomatic cables between Washington and its ambassadors in both warring nations, State Department "situation reports" containing summaries of CIA information from secret agents inside India, and, most important of all, transcripts of the secret White House meetings of the Washington Special Action Group (WSAG) created by Nixon as a crisis management team of the National Security Council. Chaired by Kissinger, WSAG included top-level representatives of the Joint Chiefs of Staff, the State and Defense departments, and the CIA. Quoting the President, Kissinger issued orders at these meetings to the military and the diplomatic corps to "tilt" toward Pakistan in their behind-the-scenes maneuvering connected with the war. There were also suggestions in the WSAG transcripts that a U.S. military task force should be sent to the Bay of Bengal, where a Russian presence was already being established.

Anderson was still trying to decide what to do with the documents when his source, using their prearranged telephone signal, asked for a meeting at a drugstore near Anderson's office, just two blocks from the White House. "He was anxious as he pretended to be picking over Christmas items at a drugstore counter next to me," Anderson recalled. "The President had approved the plan to send a powerful flotilla into the Bay of Bengal, he whispered tersely. I walked out of the drugstore and wrote my first column on the secret American involvement."

It was a cautious column that began with a eulogy to Drew Pearson on his birthday and followed with the news that "in the back rooms of the White House" Kissinger had passed the word that the United States would like to see Pakistan defeat India. Kissinger "has contended," Anderson wrote, "that we cannot permit Pakistan to be overwhelmed while the Russians supply aid to India, that our allies will lose faith in us if we don't honor our commitment to Pakistan, that our whole national security structure could be jeopardized if we let Pakistan down."

The next day Anderson wrote that "a dangerous confrontation is developing between Soviet and American naval forces in the Bay of Bengal" and quoted from the transcripts of the December 3 and 4 White House meetings of the WSAG, including a remark by Kissinger that he was "getting hell every half hour from the President" about the need to be more supportive of Pakistan. Two days later, after Kissinger again told reporters that the United States was not anti-India, Anderson wrote that "behind the guarded doors of the White House Situation Room, however, Kissinger sings a different tune." Anderson quoted from the secret WSAG meeting transcripts once more, but in none of the three columns did he indicate that such documents were the source of his information about these "meetings behind closed doors," nor did he identify the other documents he had. In two other columns he included the information from the diplomatic cables he had been given, again without revealing his source of information.

But even after all five columns had been published, the last of them on December 21, 1971, there was little reaction from the press or the public. Nobody noticed what Anderson was really doing, and the story, he said, "was too good to go unnoticed." So he decided simply to start all over again, rewriting the columns to make clear that he had top-secret documents in his possession and specifying what they were. Beginning on December 30, the second series of columns on the India-Pakistan conflict appeared, filled with quotes from and complete descriptions of the WSAG transcripts, diplomatic cables, and intelligence reports he had in his possession.

This time the columns attracted attention. The *New York Times* published a front-page story about what the columns revealed; the Associated Press and the NBC "Nightly News" then picked up the story. And after *New York Times* columnist Tom Wicker praised Anderson in a column headlined "The Anderson Papers," reporters and television crews besieged Anderson's offices for interviews.

"Then Kissinger made a big mistake," Anderson recalled. "He accused me publicly of quoting him out of context in the columns. So I impulsively said, 'Let's provide him with the context.'" Anderson gave several key documents to the *Washington Post*, which could write about them more quickly and quote them at greater length than Anderson could. Dozens of other newspapers that carried Anderson's column now requested their own copies of the documents. In between giving interviews to other reporters, Anderson and his staff methodically sanitized the documents—obliterating all markings that revealed Anderson's source and all information that Anderson believed to be legitimate national security secrets—and made copies for everyone. In succeeding weeks they gradually released copies of more of the documents, keeping the story, and Anderson's name, on the front pages of newspapers all over the country.

Although the war had already ended with the fall of East Pakistan, Anderson believes his revelation of the documents' contents may well have stopped Nixon and Kissinger from deeply involving the United States in a dangerous military defense of Pakistan. What is more certain is that the documents helped Anderson to emerge fully from Drew Pearson's shadow. *Time* and *Newsweek* published sympathetic profiles of him, both in Janaury 1972, when the documents were front-page news, and again that spring, when Anderson won a

Pulitzer Prize for national reporting. The column picked up scores of new newspaper clients, and Anderson negotiated a $100,000 advance on royalties from Random House for the *The Anderson Papers*.

From then on the column enjoyed a new respectability in Washington. It seemed to break more big stories first, and the atmosphere inside "Muckrakers, Inc.," became electric. Experienced young reporters showed up at the door begging to work there without pay, just to find out how it was done. Other investigative reporters in Washington watched the column for leads. Government officials braced themselves for the worst when told that Jack Anderson was calling.

Nobody enjoyed all this more than Les Whitten, who in his mid-forties remained an incurable romantic who loved the excitement and moral crusading of his work with Anderson. Whitten recounted to me with boyish enthusiasm his interrogations of congressmen, secret meetings with bureaucrats and confidential sources, tense interviews with Mafia informants while riding around in their gangland Cadillacs, and his arrest by FBI agents on a downtown Washington sidewalk while carrying a carton of stolen U.S. Bureau of Indian Affairs papers. "It proves you can still have fun reporting after the age of forty-five," Whitten said. "It's really a sexy way to make a living."

Whitten, a wiry, energetic man with the rakishly handsome face of a movie matinee idol, had the manners, taste, and command of foreign languages associated with the Europeans he had lived among for several years in several different countries. During the 1950s he had first sniffed around young communist groups in Europe and then gone to work, unknowingly at first, for the CIA as a news writer for Radio Free Europe. There Whitten developed a fascination for intrigue that blossomed in his fertile imagination into several novels of mystery, black magic, sex, and scandal.

Born in Florida, Whitten grew up in Washington, where his father represented electrical manufacturers seeking federal government contracts. "My father spent a lot of his time on exclusive golf courses where you are followed around by black people in uniform carrying clubs, balls, and refreshments," Whitten said. "He played in foursomes with high Army and Navy officers, and that's when he got most of his work done. He never did anything wrong. It was just all part of the game."

At his father's urging Whitten enrolled in engineering at Lehigh University but hated it and enlisted in the Army in 1946. He eventually earned a degree in English and journalism, and after

"It's really a sexy way to make a living."

adventuring in Mexico and working his way up from messenger boy to director at NBC in New York, he suddenly set off for Europe. "I realized TV was a whore's game, an endless line of guys kissing each other's asses," Whitten said. He wandered among the intellectual left in Europe but soon became disillusioned by what he saw of communism there. "There was something funny about the Reds," he recalled. "They seemed forbidding, narrow-minded, and humorless."

Whitten went to work for Radio Free Europe in Munich, beginning again as a messenger and becoming its chief of news back in New York. It took Whitten years to discover that the CIA ran the operation, "because we had people on the staff from the far left to the far right. It was a great newsroom, staffed with professionals, and we told the truth so far as I know."

Whitten eventually moved to the old International News Service and its successor, United Press International, before getting a job at the *Washington Post* on the strength of his clippings and his response to what was then a standard question for *Post* applicants: What were the last three books you read? "A biography of Clement Atlee, Proust's *Cities in the Plain,* and a collection of poetry," truthfully answered Whitten, who was assigned to the municipal court beat, where he first began functioning as an investigative reporter. On being sent to the court, he said he was told by an editor: "Ain't nobody going to take care of them poor niggers down there if you don't." "That was in effect a tremendous charge given me to write about the inequities and problems of an unfair and racist system. I did as many as nine stories a day and clipped them all for my scrapbook." In the court's file room he found stories of injustices and local scandals. "A dulcet calm set in as I crossed the hot (courthouse) square, passed the ancient horse chestnut tree and went to the file room," Whitten wrote poetically years later. "No editors could find me there, in that cool, dry and somehow virginal repository of human secrets. I was alone, a kid again alone in his quiet place, in the file room with the stories of 'con men and Wall Street cash and collateral turned to ashes . . . in the dust, in the cool tombs.'"

Whitten left the *Post* in 1963 to work for the Hearst Headline Service, which offered him a relatively large salary and freedom to follow anywhere any story he came upon. Although he covered the nuclear test ban treaty debate in Washington, the invasion of the Dominican Republic, the funerals of John and Robert Kennedy, and the investigation of U.S. Senate aide Bobby Baker for corruption, Whitten specialized in the investigative reporting of what he called "pocket exclusives—small, hot stories you could develop in a day with a good tip and a few phone calls." One grew out of a tip that insurance executive Don Reynolds, a witness in the congressional investigation of Bobby Baker, had given an expensive stereo set to President Lyndon Johnson, who had been Baker's mentor when Johnson was Senate majority leader. "I made just three telephone calls," Whitten said: "to a congressional source for documents confirming the tip, to Reynolds himself, who also confirmed it, and to the White House for comment. And, *boom,* I had a sensational story." It was the first story to involve Johnson in the Baker scandal.

After six years with Hearst, Whitten got "itchy" again, particularly after the demise of the *New York World Journal Tribune* left the syndicate without a big-city newspaper client. Whitten found that some of his best investigative stories were simply not reaching the public or other reporters and thus were having little impact in Washington. "I needed more exposure," Whitten said. "You want the respect of your peers, the guys who are hard-assed investigative reporters, when you bust one over their heads." So shortly after Drew Pearson died, Whitten went to see Jack Anderson. He was hired at a salary of $20,000, more than Anderson ever was paid by Pearson during the twenty-two years he worked for him.

"I knew as soon as I started working for the column that I had found my home," Whitten said. "Jack gave me complete freedom and was fearless about printing everything that checked out. We made a good marriage. Jack's sources, some of whom he inherited from Pearson, turned out to be pretty high up in the government. Mine were still on middle and lower staff levels, including a lot of old friends from my police and court coverage days."

As Anderson had been during his years with Pearson, Whitten became the column's workhorse. With seemingly limitless energy, often working on several investigations at the same time, he covered everything from government waste to consumer protection, from organized crime to the wrongdoing of still more congressmen. In a rerun of the J. Parnell Thomas episode of two decades earlier, an employee of Representative Irv Whalley, a Republican from Pennsylvania, came to Anderson and Whitten with a sworn affidavit accusing Whalley of forcing him and other employees to pay the congressmen kickbacks. A subsequent federal investigation of the allegations, reported by Whitten in the column, ended with a guilty plea from Whalley, who left Congress. In this case the column's source plainly was a disgruntled employee seeking revenge. Whalley's embittered aide even urged Whitten to use his name, so that Whalley would know "who did it to him."

More frequently, Whitten, like Anderson, has received information from government employees who are unhappy about a certain agency's policies. When they are unable to change these policies inside the system, the bureaucrats decide, usually after agonizing contemplation, to let the public know what is going on, hoping to bring about some change that way. Whitten's well-known liberal political views seemed to draw a new group of such dissidents to the column. In Laos, for example, Whitten was introduced by a dissident American to Laotian villagers who told him of destructive American bombing raids that the U.S. government had denied. As Whitten's receptivity to such stories became widely known, he was put in touch with a Washington bureaucrat in a very high-level position with an even more shocking story to tell about American activities in Southeast Asia.

This official had access to classified documents dealing with "Operation Phoenix," a secret CIA program of systematic assassination of Viet Cong leaders in Vietnam. He was both shocked by the "Phoenix" program itself and unhappy with the CIA for other undisclosed reasons, and he had considered taking his information to the *Washington Post* or the *New York Times* because of the influence they had in Washington. Instead, a close friend urged him to talk with Whitten. The two men met for lunch at a local Greek restaurant, where Whitten impressed the bureaucrat with his sincerity, responsibility, and determination to hold the U.S. government accountable for adventures like "Operation Phoenix." The bureaucrat had brought with him longhand copies he had made of "Phoenix" documents. "At first he wanted to give me only one sheaf or two or three," Whitten recalled, "but over stuffed grape leaves and retsina he agreed to give me all of them. We went casually to a Xerox in his office and ran off all ninety-nine pages."

Whitten's most celebrated haul of government documents resulted from the takeover of the Bureau of Indian Affairs building in

Washington by a coalition of Indian activist groups in November 1972. When they ended their siege, the Indians took with them several boxes of documents, discovered in file cabinets in the building, that detailed the government's neglect and mishandling of Indian problems. One of the leaders of the Indian militants, Hank Adams, an Assiniboin-Sioux, got in touch with Whitten, whom he knew had inquired about obtaining some of the documents as the basis for columns about the mistreatment of the Indians. There then ensued a cloak-and-dagger scenario of airplane flights around the country, secret meetings, and tests of Whitten's reliability that he later remembered with considerable satisfaction as his most exciting reporting experience.

Whitten was first instructed to fly to Phoenix, where he was taken to meet several Indian leaders in a motel. Fearing that the room and even their automobiles might be bugged by the FBI, which had begun a nationwide hunt for the missing papers, the Indians took Whitten to a bowling alley, then a coffee house, and finally a parking lot to discuss giving him access to the papers. Other reporters had offered money for the documents, according to Anderson and Whitten, but they never considered paying for them. They relied instead on Whitten's being able to convince the Indians of his sincerity. It worked. Two of them flew with Whitten to Minneapolis, where he was questioned by one of the group's top leaders about his ability to interpret the contents of a few sample documents. Whitten passed the test and was given boxes of documents to read and take notes on in a motel room guarded by an armed Indian security man seated in a chair against the locked door. Out of those papers came dozens of columns about "how the white man's government had bilked the Indians," which Anderson and Whitten entitled the "Trail of Broken Treaties Papers."

The columns drew the attention of the FBI, which was still searching for the documents. Hanks Adams, meanwhile, had already returned a number of other items taken from the BIA building— paintings, office equipment, and other documents—to an FBI agent in Washington. Unknown to Adams, the FBI had his apartment under constant surveillance and had placed an undercover agent among the inner circle of Indian leaders often present with Adams in the apartment.

In late January Adams was sent more stolen documents from Indian leaders elsewhere in the country. He was to give them to the counsel for a House subcommittee on Indian affairs, who wanted to see them before they got into the hands of the FBI. Adams called

Whitten, too, to ask if he wanted to see them before they were returned. Whitten found Adams's description of the documents uninteresting but decided there would be a good story in their return, so he drove over to the Indian's apartment. Whitten offered to help Adams carry the heavy cartons out and because an associate of Adams who was supposed to transport the documents did not show up—he later turned out to be the undercover agent—Whitten also offered to let Adams use his car.

Whitten was loading one of the boxes into his auto, when "the FBI came swarming out of neighboring cars and doorways like ants from a rotten log." He instinctively took his notebook and pencil from his pocket and began taking notes, but they were grabbed from him and he was handcuffed and placed under arrest for "receiving and possessing stolen property for the purpose of converting it to his own use," a felony punishable by up to ten years in prison and a $10,000 fine. Whitten was jailed for five hours, before being released without bail to await the outcome of the case.

"For two weeks," Whitten later wrote, "felony charges hung over our lives, like noxious smoke. During that time, it was suggested that I link Hank to criminal acts and the smog over me would quickly lift. But to grab this subtle suggestion was unthinkable: it was not true; Hank was my friend; finally, to betray a source was to write finis to reporting. The fraudulent case, as it turned out, fell of its own weight."

After Justice Department officials quietly admitted their chagrin about the whole affair, a federal grand jury threw the case out. Anderson was still so angry about what happened to Whitten, however, and the fact that the FBI used his arrest to justify subpoenaing telephone company records of his and Whitten's long-distance calls to their sources, that he used the column and his personal influence on Capitol Hill to lobby hard against confirmation of L. Patrick Gray as FBI director. As acting director, Gray had approved the agents' actions in the Indian papers case and defended them at his confirmation hearing. In the column and in conversations with senators on the Judiciary Committee Anderson raised questions about Gray's competence and his handling of the FBI's investigation of Watergate that eventually helped lead to Gray's disastrous admission, unexpected even by Anderson, that at the suggestion of the White House he had destroyed some documents confiscated by the FBI from Howard Hunt's White House safe after the Watergate burglary arrests. Gray was disgraced, and his nomination was withdrawn. "That is one of the few times I have used the column like that since Drew died," Anderson told me. "I acted impulsively out of anger at what they did to Les."

Revenge of another kind figured in Anderson's virulent opposition in 1972 to Senate confirmation of Richard Kleindienst as U.S. Attorney General. This time Anderson was defending the column against attacks on its credibility. He had learned from Pearson that nothing was potentially more dangerous to the column, and that the best defense against such attacks was to strike at the jugular of its critics. Kleindienst just happened to be in the middle of such a struggle between Anderson and one of his reporters, Brit Hume, against the Nixon administration, which concerned the administration's relationship with the multinational International Telephone and Telegraph Corporation.

Anderson had obtained a copy of a memo purportedly written by Dita Beard, a Washington lobbyist for the corporation, that linked an ITT offer of $400,000 to help stage the 1972 Republican national convention in San Diego with a favorable settlement of the government's suit against ITT. In an extraordinary interview with Dita Beard, Hume had gotten her to admit writing the memo. Kleindienst, who as acting Attorney General was accused of having knowledge of the ITT arrangement while ITT was the defendant in an antitrust suit brought by Justice, was thus put on the spot at the time of his Senate confirmation hearings. The White House, ITT, and congressional defenders of Kleindienst tried to dismiss the charge as outrageous. They also tried to prove that the memo was a forgery by forcing Dita Beard to change her story and attacking her reliability at a time when she was critically ill. Kleindienst's confirmation hearings were to be a showcase for these attempts to put a quick end to the whole affair.

"Thus, a vast effort undertaken by three of the most powerful institutions in America was under way to discredit a story that had a real potential for reform and, in the process, to destroy my reputation as a newspaperman," Anderson wrote somewhat melodramatically in *The Anderson Papers*. "Normally, when I have filed a story I am done with it. I don't try to promote it in the press or to manipulate reactions. Partly this is because we must always be at work on the next story if we are to publish every day and partly it is because I feel a reporter should stay a reporter and not deteriorate into back-room mover and shaper of events. But in this instance I deviated from the passive role. So much organized pressure was being exerted to sweep the Dita Beard memo under the rug that counterpressure had to be applied by someone."

"We evolved a plan of counterattack," Anderson recalled. Hume went after and obtained more ITT documents, which Anderson decided to share with other investigative reporters in Washington, thereby putting a pack of hounds on ITT's trail. Anderson also convinced Senate Judiciary Committee chairman James Eastland to call him and Hume as witnesses against Kliendienst at his confirmation hearings. By prearrangement, in a variation of his "good guy-bad guy" reporting routine, Anderson instructed Hume to calmly defend his reporting under hostile questioning from Kliendienst's defenders on the committee, while Anderson roundly attacked Kliendienst, the Nixon administration, and ITT witnesses as liars and obfuscators. Anderson followed up his denunciations at the witness table with even more intemperate statements in interviews with newspaper, radio, and television reporters after each day's hearing ended. At length he provoked blustery Republican Senator Roman Hruska into sputtering: "Conventions all over America are bought all the time by business communities, and everyone in this room knows it."

Anderson had purposely made himself "a disrupting influence" at the Kliendienst hearings—"someone to contradict the smooth, coordinated alibis," he later wrote, "someone to shout, 'Liar,' and to remind the public of the evasions and contradictions the committee majority was swallowing, someone to bait pro-ITT senators for their condonation of scandal, someone to whom conscientious senators could address questions that would elicit information they wanted publicized, someone to keep the hearings going, to foul up the whitewash machinery and to give chance and circumstances the opportunity to create the chaos that sometimes causes even the best-staged hearings to slip out of control and run amok."

Kliendienst survived the chaotic hearings and was confirmed by the Senate. Although they lost that battle, however, Anderson and Hume eventually won the war. Evidence that the Special Watergate Prosecutor's office turned up later showed that Kliendienst had testified falsely at some points during the hearings, and he was forced to plead guilty to a misdemeanor charge. As far as ITT was concerned, other documents obtained by Hume and published in the column in 1972, long before Seymour Hersh's more definitive accounts, revealed that ITT and the CIA had conspired to undermine the leftist Chilean government of Salvador Allende by buying votes in

Chile and trying to disrupt its economy. Some of the documents obtained by Hume showed that the corporation had involved the U.S. ambassador in Chile in ultimately unsuccessful negotiations to finance the Chilean government's purchase of ITT's assets there through the use of U.S.-backed Chilean bonds. This would have meant that American taxpayers were, in effect, compensating ITT for its loss.

Anderson and Hume concluded that their counterattack not only vindicated the column but also individually benefited each of them. "The ITT affair was the best thing that ever happened to my career," Hume later wrote in *Inside Story*. "Now I was well known throughout the news business and even known to some outside it. Magazines were interested in my free-lance work, and my agent reported expressions of interest from book editors. My lecture agent was booking more dates than I could keep and still fulfill my duties with the column." Hume became such a hot property that he eventually left Anderson's employ to devote full time to lecturing, free-lance writing, and television work. For his part, Anderson pointed proudly to a Gallup poll that showed that "almost twice as many people believed our charges as believed the government's defense." The number of newspapers carrying the column and the volume of lecture invitations coming in to Anderson continued the pleasant upward climb that had begun when he won the Pulitzer Prize in 1972.

The troubling aspect of their personal victory was that Anderson and Hume had turned the ITT affair, which should have been most significant as an example of the dangers of a multinational corporation's manipulation of governments to serve its own ends, into an almost petty struggle between Anderson and Hume on one side and Kliendienst, the Nixon administration, and ITT on the other. Hume went so far as to characterize Anderson and Kliendienst as "the two principal antagonists in the whole affair."

Such distortions were the inevitable consequences of Anderson's guiding philosophy that the success of his muckraking enterprise depended on "a combination of reporting and showmanship." He has been constantly engaged in promoting and defending himself and the column. Just a few days before the resignation of President Nixon, for example, Anderson produced a rather tasteless column that amounted to an ill-timed advertisement for himself. "It's no secret, of course," Anderson wrote in the column that appeared in newspapers on August 8, 1974, "that we have been in the forefront of those who have accused President Nixon of condoning lawlessness while he preached law and order." Anderson then listed several stories about Nixon wrongdoing that the column had reported first, from some details about the "hush money" paid the Watergate conspirators to more voluminous accounts of Nixon's tax troubles and the government money he spent on his San Clemente and Key Biscayne homes. It was only one of innumerable times that Anderson has used it to remind his readers, and the editors of papers buying the column, of the many scoops he has had.

Anderson also has been quick to use the column to answer critics, especially targets of uncomplimentary items in previous columns, who dared to quarrel with what was written about them. Following the ITT affair, Anderson staff member Joe Spear obtained copies of a number of secret FBI dossiers on American citizens—including author James Baldwin, singer Eartha Kitt, comedian Groucho Marx, civil rights leader Ralph Abernathy, and the widow of Dr. Martin Luther King, Jr.—who had criticized the government at one time or another. Anderson helped promote the column's revelations of the dossiers and their contents by going again to Congress, this time with Spear, to testify about them. When L. Patrick Gray then announced that the FBI kept no "secret files," Anderson wrote in an answering column that the files were all marked "secret," and he offered to give Gray the "numbers on each so he could look them up."

Following several 1974 columns criticizing the efficiency of the U.S. Postal Service and the self-serving actions of then Postmaster General Ted Klassen, the Postal Service issued point-by-point answers to Anderson's charges. Anderson and staff member Jack Cloherty, who did the research for the columns, retaliated with another that rebutted the Postal Service on even the smallest points. "We reported," the column stated, "that Klassen's favorite chauffeur (he has two) ran so many overtime errands that he doubled his regular salary. Responded the Postal Service: the chauffeur is entitled to overtime pay 'on the many occasions when Mr. Klassen is called upon to fulfill postal engagements outside of regular hours.'

"A typical occasion took place," the rebuttal column continued, "after we had written our story. A government chauffeur drove the Klassens to a department store where they purchased some curtain rods. The chauffeur waited outside in a no parking zone, the car's engine idling to power the air conditioner. When the Klassens emerged triumphantly with the curtain rods, the chauffeur popped out, deposited the curtain rods in the trunk and drove off with the Klassens in a car that had been kept cool for them."

Anderson was even more vindictive when Accuracy in Media, known as AIM, a right-wing media criticism group, began a campaign against him because of a column that had attacked the right-wing junta in Chile and the State Department's International Police Academy, which provides policemen of pro-U.S., antisocialist countries with training in counterinsurgency methods. AIM won a judgment against Anderson from the National Press Council, the nonpartisan, foundation-supported group modeled on Great Britain's press council. The council agreed with AIM that Spear and Anderson had taken out of context observations on torture made in International Police Academy student theses about interrogation methods.

Although Anderson admitted that the column in question could have been better handled, he disputed the National Press Council finding. He was then so angered by continuing, less well-founded AIM criticism of columns about Chile that he began his own investigation of the group and its chairman, a Federal Reserve Board economist named Reed J. Irvine. After an apparently hasty inquiry, Anderson produced a column that accused Irvine of using Federal Reserve Board "facilities, telephones and stationary to prepare broadsides against the press" and compared AIM's overall operation with that of "the notorious White House plumbers, whom President Nixon assigned to hound the press."

Irvine protested and both men presented their respective sides of the argument before a congressional subcommittee. The hearing ended with Anderson loudly charging that Irvine had committed perjury in denying that he did AIM work in his government office. Anderson insisted that he had proof that Irvine had made a call on behalf of AIM on his government telephone. The Federal Reserve Board then announced that its own investigation had cleared Irvine of misusing his government position, but Anderson also disputed the report. In any event, whether or not Irvine did any of AIM's work on government time, it was clear that Anderson had been pursuing a rather unseemly vendetta against a critic who, however pesky, was not even taken that seriously by the rest of the media and who had not really caused Anderson any great harm.

Anderson's reckless judgment in overreacting to AIM was all too reminiscent of his handling of what became known as "the Eagleton affair." Senator Thomas Eagleton of Missouri had won the 1972 Democratic party nomination for U.S. Vice President only to make the politically disastrous admission a short time later that he had undergone shock therapy for persistent, severe attacks of depression. This inadvertently revived rumors that Eagleton had a drinking problem, though he unequivocally denied that he had ever suffered from drunkenness, even as he admitted fully to his other psychological difficulties. A few years earlier, however, Democratic fundraiser True Davis, a Washington, D.C., businessman, had claimed to know personally that Eagleton had a serious drinking problem. When Eagleton's mental health became an issue in 1972, Anderson remembered and telephoned Davis, who told him he had been shown a photostatic copy of a long record of drunken driving arrests of Eagleton in Missouri, where he had been attorney general and lieutenant governor. Several copies of the photostat had been passed around among Democratic party leaders by Missouri highway patrol officials, Davis told Anderson.

Meanwhile, Brit Hume had begun checking independently on the rumors of Eagleton's drinking. In telephone calls to county prosecutors and other officials in Missouri, Hume found that a number of reporters were badgering them on the same subject. All that they or Hume found, however, was one 1962 speeding ticket Eagleton had gotten for driving 85 in a 65-mile-an-hour zone. Hume turned his information over to another Anderson reporter, Mike Kiernan, who was writing the script for Anderson's radio program. Kiernan decided to include in the broadcast a short item on how reporters converged on Missouri searching desperately for evidence of drunk driving by Eagleton and had found only the speeding ticket.

But by the time Anderson arrived at the downtown Washington studio where he taped his radio broadcasts, he had talked to the Missouri highway trooper and other sources indicated by Davis, who confidentially assured Anderson that the photostat Davis saw was authentic. Although no one could supply Anderson with a copy of the photostat, he was certain he would find one soon. He also was concerned that nearly every other investigative reporter in the country seemed to be on the story. So, on a hunch, Anderson told his radio audience what he had found up to that point, exaggerating somewhat. "Eagleton has steadfastly denied any alcoholism," Anderson said, as he departed from Kiernan's script, "but we now have located photostats of half a dozen arrests for drunken and reckless driving."

Anderson had not, of course, "located" anything on paper. The story went out over a national radio network and Eagleton, then in Honolulu, immediately called a press conference to denounce it as a "damnable lie." Anderson had to admit that he had no documents and had instead been told about them by reliable sources. He also persuaded True Davis to submit to an interview with the *New York Times,* but Davis told the reporter that he had not been able to authenticate the photostat he had seen, and he could not be certain the man who showed it to him was really the Missouri state trooper he claimed to be. Two other speeding tickets, issued to Eagleton in Missouri, in 1948 and 1954, were found, as was a 1967 citation in Florida for running a red light. But no photostat of drunk driving arrests turned up. When other Missouri politicians told reporters they had been approached by persons offering them such proof of habitual drunk driving by Eagleton, the whole story began to look like part of a smear campaign against Eagleton.

Hume and Opal Ginn urged Anderson to give up and apologize to Eagleton. But Anderson was persuaded by Les Whitten to admit only that he had rushed the story onto the air prematurely. He refused to concede that the substance of the story was wrong. "I have faith in my sources," Anderson said in his statement, "and stand by this story. If this faith should ever turn out to be unwarranted, I will issue a full retraction and apology."

That was not enough for the *Washington Post* and the *New York Times,* which on the same day published editorials strongly criticizing Anderson for irresponsible reporting. In addition, the *Post* ran an article by gossip columnist Maxine Cheshire detailing how she had received exactly the same tip as Anderson. Her thorough checks in both Missouri and Washington, however, had not turned up a shred of supporting evidence.

When Anderson agreed to go on the *Face the Nation* interview program with Eagleton, his entire staff strongly urged him to apologize to the senator on the air. As soon as he had the opportunity, Anderson told Eagleton on camera: "I violated my own rules. I did not authenticate whether or not these tickets were genuine. Using these sources, I went ahead with a story that I should not have gone ahead with, and that was unfair to you. And you have my apology." Eagleton commended Anderson for his courage in admitting a mistake on a nationwide television, and that seemed to take care of everything, until the moderator inadvertently referred to Anderson's apology as a retraction.

To Eagleton's great surprise, Anderson then said he could not yet "retract the story completely," although he was willing to apologize to Eagleton. He said he still had some hope of getting documentation, and he wanted to exhaust all leads. Eagleton was stunned, but he agreed to meet with Anderson in three days.

Anderson could find nothing more. None of his Missouri sources would help by supplying documentation or allowing Anderson to quote them by name. The *Washington Post,* in another scathing editorial, scolded Anderson for his performance on *Face the Nation,* and Anderson's office was deluged with more angry mail than it had ever before received. At the appointed time Anderson went to meet with Eagleton, asked him a few final questions, and then admitted he had come up empty handed. The two men then went outside to face the reporters who had massed to record Anderson's final, unequivocal apology.

"I have exhausted my investigative abilities," Anderson said. "I did not give him a full retraction before, because I had some additional questions. I am totally satisfied there is no evidence. I have come out here to retract the story in toto . . . I think the story did damage the senator. I owe him a great and humble apology."

Whether or not the incident contributed to Eagleton's eventual withdrawal from the 1972 Democratic ticket, it greatly damaged Anderson. He had not only made a monumental mistake, but it had taken days of fumbling stubbornness for him to admit it fully. His explanations that *he* had not yet been satisfied were disturbing evidence that he had attached to himself and his role in national affairs much too much importance. He had arrogantly set himself up as Thomas Eagleton's prosecutor, judge, and jury. That was Anderson's real mistake, although he never seemed to recognize it.

The problem was that long before the Eagleton affair, Anderson had been accustomed to making his own rules about what the column published and how it obtained its information. He had no supervising editors, no institutional pressures to impose on him standards of professional behavior. He was free to do whatever he could rationalize for himself and somehow justify to his reading and listening public. Only when he was clearly unable to justify his actions, as in the Eagleton case, or when he feared the column's market might be harmed, did he pull back from the frontier of investigative journalism that he had become so used to exploring.

One instance in which Anderson never did pull back occurred shortly after Nelson Rockefeller was chosen by Ford, in August 1974, to be Vice President. Anderson produced a column, reported and written by Les Whitten, that said the Special Watergate Prosecutor was investigating "hearsay evidence" that tied Rockefeller to Republican-instigated "dirty tricks" at the 1972 Democratic National Convention. The evidence against Rockefeller, Whitten reported, was supposedly contained in seven boxes of documents stored in the White House after the Watergate burglary arrests. Whitten had been told this by the operator of a Washington photocopying service, whose friend, an employee of the 1972 Nixon reelection committee, at one time had possession of the mysterious boxes. The informant also had told his story to intermediaries, who passed it along to the Special Watergate Prosecutor's office and the Senate Watergate Committee chaired by Sam Ervin.

What Whitten did not report was that both the prosecutors and the Ervin committee had investigated the story exhaustively and could not substantiate it in any way. The boxes themselves were never found. Meanwhile, Howard Hunt, in whose White House office they had been stored, told the Ervin committee and the *New York Times* that the boxes contained only a large number of copies of a book, *The News Twisters* by Edith Efron, which purports to prove that the television networks distort the news. The Nixon reelection committee had spent $8000 buying up copies of the book in a vain attempt to make it a best-seller, and several cartons containing copies wound up in Hunt's office. Neither Hunt nor any other witness called by the prosecutors and the Ervin committee could recall anything about documents that named Rockefeller in any way.

The Ford White House theorized that some right-wing Republican opposed to Rockefeller's appointment as Vice President must have first put Whitten and Anderson onto the story. Whitten never discussed his source, and the column never cleared Rockefeller's name. Perhaps only because the Rockefeller column itself was immediately considered suspect in Washington—the *Washington Post* had excised from it all mention of Rockefeller and both it and the *New York Times* immediately investigated the charge and knocked it down in subsequent stories—was it not a factor in the Senate's consideration and eventual approval of Rockefeller's appointment.

If a Rockefeller opponent had planted the story with Anderson and Whitten, it would not have been the first time that the column had been used by sources up to no good. Even the same Nixon administration officials who later fought Anderson tooth and nail, and at one point had his home placed under surveillance by the White House "plumbers," had considerable success in the days before Watergate in using the column as a conduit for leaks. For example, when in 1970 CBS broadcast a filmed account of a South Vietnamese soldier stabbing a prisoner to death, Anderson unwittingly went along with a White House plan to discredit the film by publishing a

White House memo accusing CBS of staging the incident with a soldier stabbing an already dead communist guerrilla.

Anderson acknowledged this brief special relationship with the Nixon White House in a column he wrote in June 1974. Among the other stories he said he had gained this way was one about the purported tax problems of Alabama Governor George Wallace, whom Nixon supporters feared as a political threat to the President in 1972. The leaks ended, Anderson said, when the column began publishing stories that embarrassed Nixon rather than his enemies. But Anderson did not find anything improper in the relationship so long, he said, as the stories checked out. When you have to put out eight columns (counting the one for weekly newspapers), six radio broadcasts, and several television commentaries every week, you take your tips where you find them.

Anderson also seemed willing to publish almost everything he and his staff picked up that might titillate readers across the country and gain subscribers. After the death of Aristotle Onassis, for instance, he featured several Hollywood gossip-column-type items on Onassis's stormy relationship with his wife, the former Jacqueline Kennedy, and her effort to obtain a share of the Onassis fortune. In a particularly offensive column outlining the couple's "total incompatibility" according to unnamed sources, Anderson and Whitten reported that Onassis, in discussing his wife's friends, "was even heard, not too discreetly, calling them 'faggots.'"

Occasionally, a column of this kind has raised questions about Anderson's sense of propriety, as did the 1970 column reporting that Randy Agnew, son of then Vice President Agnew, had left his wife and moved into an apartment with a male hairdresser. Brit Hume, who got the story, explained in his *Inside Story* that he had great misgivings about its being published. He thought nothing, however, of the methods he used to get Randy Agnew to confirm it, going to his apartment and telling him, "We've been told that you were living in sort of a hippie crash pad with a lot of wild parties going on and drugs being used and we thought we'd better check it out." Once inside the door Hume added, "From the looks of this place, the report doesn't seem to be true. Can I talk to you for minute?"

"The tale about the hippie crash pad was something I had thought up on the way over," Hume later wrote. "It is a common enough technique—you persuade the person you are questioning that you have been told a truly lurid story. In eagerness to disabuse you of it, the person will frequently tell the truth."

Hume had identified himself as being "with the Bell-McClure

"I leave out anything I feel would jeopardize national security. But I take a different view from the government of what that is."

newspaper syndicate." That was true enough, because they distributed the column. But Hume hid the fact that he actually worked for Jack Anderson. "We often used (the Bell-McClure Syndicate's) name instead of Jack's," Hume explained, "where identification with the column might have a chilling effect."

According to Hume's memory of the Randy Agnew story, he had argued initially at an Anderson staff meeting against reporting it at all. Hume said there was a difference between someone who had placed himself in the public spotlight, as Spiro Agnew had, and someone like Randy, who was by chance the child of a celebrity. It was Les Whitten, Hume recalled, who successfully argued that the column should run, because sons and daughters of Presidents and Vice Presidents "have always been public figures." Whitten later told me that what had happened to Randy also was relevant at the time "because Agnew had been telling people how to raise our kids. He had been so pious about other youth going astray."

When asked if there was anything he or Anderson would *not* print, Whitten cited several stories he said they had suppressed. Included among them were accounts of what he called "sex for sex's sake" that had no discernible effect on public affairs: a U.S. senator's having sexual relations with a prominent Washington hostess (the reporter got incriminating tape recordings from a private detective), an influential homosexual congressman being blackmailed by another homosexual, and a big-city mayor having sexual relations with a young woman journalist. Other suppressed stories, Whitten said, like one about a boatload of bombs on its way to Cambodia, were considered legitimate national security secrets. "There are many things we haven't printed," Anderson said: "CIA documents in which their sources were identified, battle plans, transcripts of the SALT talks. I leave out anything I feel would jeopardize national security. But I take a different view from the government of what that is."

Other journalists, Anderson charged, had lost some of their skepticism since the resignation of President Nixon and the ensuing grumbling by some that the press had hounded him from office. "Since Watergate," Anderson said, "the editors themselves are going along with the establishment. The establishment, the Cabinet, have been shaken with what happened, that the press can topple a President. The press itself is shaken by it. A lot of editors and reporters are wearing a hair shirt—sackcloth and ashes and lace— and they're overdoing it a little bit, trying to prove too hard how patriotic and responsible we are, to prove that we're not against the establishment, the government, that we're not all gadflys. The country was better served by a watchful press."

Anderson clearly saw himself as the leader of the pack of watchdogs he would like to see unleashed on the national establishment. "I've become a symbol," he told me. "I didn't seek it, but I am. Just the other day I spoke to some Latin American journalists and they all expressed their admiration for me, even the ones from Chile and Brazil, where they could get into some trouble by agreeing with what we have written about affairs in their countries. And wherever I speak in this country, reporters covering me will come up afterwards and ask how they can come to work for the column.

"I encourage the work of all other investigative reporters. I've turned aside attempts by people to get me to downgrade Seymour Hersh, for example, because the column had some of the things he wrote about before he did. But I admire his work. On the board of the Drew Pearson Awards for investigative reporting, I made certain that Neil Sheehan got the award for the Pentagon Papers, because I thought more reporters should have the guts to print classified documents. In 1972, before anyone also recognized their work and so many were criticizing them instead, I pushed for Woodward and Bernstein to get the Pearson award. Then came their Pulitzer."

Anderson also insisted that he has enforced high standards of ethics at "Muckrakers, Inc.," with fire and brimstone staff meeting sermonizing: "I tell them, 'Get me the facts. I want the facts as they are, not as you wish they are or someone else thinks they are. I won't tolerate blackjacking people by promising to go easy on them in the column in order to get information; if I ever find out you did that, you're fired.'"

Some directives are less restricting than others: "Don't steal documents, but if somebody wants to give them to you, that's okay. If you steal, you're in as much trouble with me as with the police. But the press has a right to print what comes into its possession." Anderson himself felt free to publish transcripts of the secret proceedings of the federal Watergate grand jury after being given them by a courthouse source. But both he and Whitten said they would never approach a grand juror themselves and ask him to violate the law by cooperating with them.

"We try not to lie," Anderson told me, although he admitted stringing targets of stories along until a column about them finally got into print. "I might tell a white lie," Anderson said, "but we try not to misrepresent ourselves. We will bluff some, such as by indicating we have more information than we do so far, so that a source will tell us more. But we believe we are more responsible about this than many other reporters."

Anderson acknowledged his efforts to "dramatize" columns "to make them readable. I do not want them to be dull. Too many investigative reporters feel their stories must be dull and read like legal briefs. Les might write that 'the old man walked down the street.' Well, 'shuffled down the street' might be more dramatic. And Les might come back and say, 'I don't know he did that.' And I'd say, 'Well, he's an old man, and old men shuffle.'"

There are also the temptations and perils of fame. Financial success made possible the entire floor of drawing-room-like offices in the Sixteenth Street mansion in Washington, the eight-bedroom suburban home where Anderson lives with his wife and nine children, a beach house on the Atlantic shore of Delaware, and various business investments; Anderson is given special treatment by the staff of Washington's very luxurious Madison Hotel, where he frequently lunches and is recognized regularly by other passengers on his many airplane flights. "I'll be trying to work on the plane," he told me, "when someone invariably will recognize me and come over and interrupt me to talk. I hate it. But I guess I hate it when they don't recognize me, too."

Anderson has increasingly indulged, as Drew Pearson had before him, in self-important sermonizing on all manner of national and international concerns. "The Nixon administration was too conservative domestically," he said during one of the many television talk show appearances he has made each month, "but it still deserved credit for its diplomacy in the Middle East. If you knew what I know about these negotiations, you will find amazing what Kissinger has done."

Brit Hume, in *Inside Story,* called Jack Anderson "the best and bravest reporter I had ever known." Noting that this "matter of bravery" was a "curious notion," *New York Times* reporter Steven R. Weisman, in the Sunday *Times* Book Review, observed that "both Anderson and Hume continue to see themselves as puny little Davids pitted against the Goliaths in and out of the military-industrial-complex. To a large degree, it's a true assumption, but . . . journalists can sometimes be as self-deluding about the extent and uses of their power as the politicians they write about." Such self-delusion is the muckraker's most potent enemy and the only danger inherent in the continually expanding productivity, profitability, and influence of Jack Anderson's "Muckrakers, Inc."

6: Raising Hell

When he began publishing the upstart *San Francisco Bay Guardian* in 1966, young Bruce Brugmann took as the weekly newspaper's credo this 1861 declaration by another nonconformist editor, Wilbur F. Storey of the *Chicago Times*: "It is a newspaper's duty to print the news and raise hell." Brugmann's muckraking *Bay Guardian* has done just that for the past decade. It has printed news of wrongdoing by both government and private business in the San Francisco area that went unreported by the city's monopoly-controlled daily newspapers, and it has raised hell with continuing all-out crusades against the major villains of its exposés—the powerful Pacific Gas & Electric Company, the rich media empire of the merged *Chronicle* and *Examiner* newspapers and broadcast stations, the big banks and real estate developers remaking the face of San Francisco, and the city politicians who do the bidding of these and other big campaign contributors.

"I feel we must do more than print the news," Brugmann explained, "since disclosure itself may not be enough to bring change." His efforts have extended beyond his outside political and legal actions and his signed editorials in the *Bay Guardian* to his editing of the *Bay Guardian*'s news stories. Rather than simply presenting new facts uncovered through well-documented investigative reporting, a *Bay Guardian* news story usually also contains personal interpretations of the issue by the reporter and strong language, often edited in by Brugmann himself, that shows clearly where the *Bay Guardian* stands.

"I aim my derringer at every reporter and tell him, by God, that I don't want to see an objective piece of reporting," Brugmann declared, with a touch of the hyperbole that characterizes the *Bay Guardian*'s most purple prose. "But this is not dishonest journalism," he added. "It is 'point of view' journalism. Our facts are as straight as we can make them; we don't run a story until we feel we can prove it or

". . .this is not dishonest journalism. It is 'point of view' journalism."

make it stick; we always talk with the adversary and try to print his part of the story."

Brugmann's "point of view" reporting is a combination of traditional muckraking and advocacy journalism of the kind that flourished in the "underground" press of the tumultous 1960s, when the *Bay Guardian* itself was born. Out of the social and political upheavals of that decade emerged scores of little newspapers that condemned the excesses of midtwentieth century American society and advocated radical changes of all kinds. The *Bay Guardian,* however, as Brugmann has taken pains to point out, was intended from the beginning to be as different from this radical underground press as it was from the *San Francisco Chronicle.*

"It seems to me," Brugmann has said, "that the whole point of a newspaper is to set itself independent of all groups and movements so that on the one hand it isn't part of the usually recognized team effort where the paper is working with the city hall and the chamber of commerce, or on the other hand doesn't represent only a particular movement like the New Left or a particular political action group." Like the *Village Voice* during its heyday in New York or the *Texas Observer* in Austin, Brugmann's *San Francisco Bay Guardian* is one of a handful of truly "alternative" newspapers in the country. More reformist and hell-raising than the established daily press, but far less radical or indifferent about facts than the short-lived underground newspapers, they have made muckraking and advocacy of orderly change their specialties.

Brugmann himself is a renegade newspaperman who has become obsessed with his mission to expose and break up the conspiracies of powerful interests he sees working behind the scenes to frustrate the will of the people. A large, dark-haired man of nearly forty, who alternates between serious, almost distracted contemplation and great outbursts of productive energy, Brugmann said his reformist zeal derived from "populist strains" in his family and home town in

Iowa. At the University of Nebraska, where he edited the student newspaper during the McCarthy era, Brugmann found himself defending in print several liberal professors under fire from the American Legion and the Farm Bureau as suspected communists. He barely survived several attempts to have him expelled from the university for what he wrote.

Brugmann's preparation for a career in journalism was extensive: a master's degree from the Columbia University School of Journalism in New York, service in the Army as a bureau chief for *Stars and Stripes* in Korea, and four years as a reporter for the *Milwaukee Journal.* When he decided to start an independent newspaper of his own, Brugmann selected San Francisco as the best place to try, because "the daily press here is so uniformly bad" for a metropolitan area with so many educated people.

While looking for capital for his venture, Brugmann went to work for the *Tribune* in suburban Redwood City, just south of San Francisco. In 1965 he discovered that several real estate developers were planning large housing subdivisions on previously untouched tidal marshes on the bay inside the boundaries of Redwood City and he wrote a series of muckraking *Tribune* columns crusading against this project. Brugmann chose "Points of No Return," as a standing title for these columns, which reflected a philosophy that would later guide him as editor of his own newspaper: Actions by powerful interests that are likely to be detrimental to the public good must be exposed and stopped before they become final and irreversible. In particular, Brugmann campaigned vigorously to prevent the Redwood City government approval of a 43-acre development called Redwood Shores, which he warned would cause irreparable damage to bay marine life. Even after the *Tribune* itself gave editorial support to the Redwood Shores project, Brugmann continued crusading against it until pressure from city officials and the newspaper's own hierarchy forced him to leave the *Tribune* in October 1966.

By that time he had already raised $35,000 capital—much of it from his own family and a wealthy San Francisco heir to a shipping fortune. Brugmann quickly found a printer and a small office in San Francisco and began the *Bay Guardian.* In his first issue, on October 27, 1966, Brugmann picked right up with his crusade against Redwood Shores. Later he took out after the other bay shore projects (one issue's front-page banner headline read: "Can Bay Be Saved?"), as well as proposed development threatening the environment of other important natural areas around San Francisco. In an editorial that first year Brugmann vowed: "It will be a purpose of the *Bay*

Guardian, in its news columns and its editorials, to show that these environmental problems exist, that something can be done about them . . . This is neither a scientific nor a technological problem, but a political problem. The first priority is to bring the pressure of conservation, planning and good sense to bear on the political process. This the *Guardian* will seek to do."

Brugmann had little difficulty finding additional targets for his muckraking. The *Bay Guardian* campaigned against supermarket pull-date codes for fresh foods that could not be deciphered by customers and eventually published an article showing shoppers how to break the codes; other publications from the *Los Angeles Times* to *New York* magazine followed the *Bay Guardian's* lead, and supermarkets eventually converted to open dating of foods.

In 1969 the *Bay Guardian* charged that the city of San Francisco was losing millions of dollars each year by generating hydroelectric power in the Sierras and bringing it only to within thirty miles of San Francisco. There the electricity passed to the control of Pacific Gas & Electric, which distributed it at a profit. If the city marketed the electricity itself, the *Bay Guardian* argued, it and the customers would come out ahead. The newspaper then revealed in 1971 that the city lost still more money by putting most of its $250 million investment portfolio into three big banks at low interest rates and allowing big, idle surpluses to build; the city treasurer subsequently resigned and new investment policies were instituted that gained San Francisco about $1 million in additional interest income each year. Brugmann also displayed his independence from other activist liberals by becoming the first journalist to report and criticize the profligate expense-account spending of editor Warren Hinckle of the radical *Ramparts* magazine.

But mostly Brugmann has gone after those who hold power in government and private business in San Francisco—not, he explained, to put anybody in jail, but to make changes in the system. "We try to expose the power structure of the city and what makes things wrong," Brugmann said. "The power structure is ruining the greatest city in the world by building skyscrapers, doubling the size of the airport, building a new convention center, and uprooting the living conditions of the city. We try to carry out strategic campaigns to stop things like Manhattanization of the city or to accomplish things like municipalizing Pacific Gas & Electric."

Doing the investigative reporting for all this is "enormously difficult, tedious work," Brugmann said. Much of it is now done by young volunteer reporting interns Brugmann has found in local colleges or who simply walked into the newspaper's office. For little pay they work in teams under a full-time *Bay Guardian* reporter or editor. The muckraking stories based on their research are meticulously documented with the data found in the records, but then the conclusions and interpretations are hyped by Brugmann or one of his editors to make clear what they think is wrong and what should be done about it.

"There are good guys and bad guys in everything for them," said one former *Bay Guardian* reporter now working for a large East Coast metropolitan daily. "Brugmann was simply obsessed about some of his villains, like Pacific Gas & Electric. He thought anyone on their board was bad and would print lists of all their directors in the *Guardian.* Once I wrote a story about some propaganda PG & E had put out in its fight against attempts by the city of Berkeley to municipalize it there. My editor added at the beginning of it: 'Here's more of the smelly fish being peddled out of PG&E's pushcart.' When I complained, I got an angry call from Brugmann who went on for two hours about how he was absolutely against objectivity and about what the *Guardian*'s purpose was."

Explaining how he operated, Brugmann himself said in late summer 1975, "We've got this election coming up, and we've had a team of interns working all summer on special-interest profiles of the politicians. We're going through campaign contributions with fifteen people, and we will show how much money from Pacific Gas & Electric, the various corporations responsible for Manhattanization, and the others flows to the mayor, city attorney, and council. They're almost like bribes, except that you call them campaign contributions. We'll show it all in boxes and charts in the newspaper and show how they've voted in the past on issues affecting these special interests. We'll put pressure on them to show that we're wrong and that there is no relationship between the money and their votes. We're telling each one of them that we're going to watch their votes on things like the feasibility study for the city to buy out Pacific Gas & Electric. We're telling them, 'the burden's on you.'"

Through similar research in 1971, a *Bay Guardian* investigative reporting team found from election contribution records that the campaigns of "14 winning supervisors, mayors, and assessors in recent elections . . . were largely funded by land development interests, and that the top 244 contributors to winning campaigns were mostly connected to real estate development." Another *Bay Guardian* study, made at the same time, of the "Manhattanization" of San Francisco showed that the city's "downtown high-rise district contributed $5 million less in taxes than it cost in municipal services in fiscal 1970" and that "property tax payments from the downtown actually declined by 16 percent." All this and more muckraking reporting about the power and plans of real estate developers in San Francisco, plus instructions on how to fight them, was put together in a special four-page *Bay Guardian* "investigative reporting supplement" in September 1971, and later expanded into a *Bay Guardian* book entitled *The Ultimate Highrise*, which Brugmann hoped would become "the text for high-rise battles across the country."

In the book Brugmann accused much of the rest of the media in the San Francisco area of a conspiracy of silence about the threat he believed developers posed to the traditional city scale and lifestyle of San Francisco. He blamed this on the involvement of several media firms in real estate in the San Francisco area: "ABC/KGO owns Marine World, a marshland fill project in (the) Redwood Shores development off Belmont. KRON/*Chronicle-Examiner* have extensive real estate holdings. Kaiser (which was building subdivisions outside San Francisco) owns KBHK and KFOG . . . ."

San Francisco's newspapers and broadcast stations have long been a favorite target of Brugmann's crusades. In 1968 he revealed secret details of the 1965 corporate marriage between the previously independent *Chronicle* and the Hearst-owned *Examiner*. "The *Chronicle*," Brugmann wrote, "was willing to give up its dominant position, its traditional independence and all that was meant by its long-time slogan, 'the city's only home-owned newspaper,' in exchange for higher profits promised by a joint operation that would destroy the need for expensive competition." (The *Examiner* and *Chronicle* had been competing morning papers until 1965, when Hearst folded its afternoon *News-Call-Bulletin,* moved the *Examiner* to the afternoon, and entered a joint operation arrangement with the *Chronicle*.)

When congressional hearings were held in 1969 on the proposed Newspaper Preservation Act, Brugmann went to Washington to argue that the legislation—ostensibly intended to keep failing newspapers from folding by allowing them into joint business, advertising, and production arrangements with stronger newspapers—was actually designed to protect already existing joint operations, like the one in San Francisco, from antitrust action. It created news-suppressing media monopolies in place of once competing newspapers, he said. Brugmann cited several controversial issues that, he pointed out, each San Francisco newspaper had refused to cover, including several instances of local wrongdoing uncovered by the *Bay Guardian*. In 1970, just two days after final passage of the Newspaper Preservation Act and its signing by President Nixon, Brugmann filed a suit in federal court in San Francisco asking the judge to declare the new law unconstitutional and break up the *Chronicle-Examiner* joint operation.

While his suit moved slowly through court, Brugmann also encouraged a challenge before the Federal Communications Commission of the license of the Chronicle Broadcasting Company's KRON-TV and KRON-FM stations. At one point Brugmann revealed in the *Bay Guardian* that Chronicle Broadcasting had hired private detectives to investigate two of its former employees who had charged in FCC filings that KRON-TV distorted the news and presented programs promoting the *Chronicle's* cable television interests. After the *Chronicle* printed a short article acknowledging this, Brugmann followed with this characteristic reaction in the next issue of the *Bay Guardian*:

When General Motors was caught red-handed trying to harass and intimidate Ralph Nader with private dicks, the president of GM . . . publicly apologized to the young auto critic. His apology got nationwide publicity. Three years later when the *Guardian* caught Superchron using private dicks in the Ralph Nader case of communications, the *Chronicle* publisher, Charles de Young Thieriot, admitted retaining the private dicks and said it was "entirely reasonable and proper to do so." This admission got four inches in his paper. This, ladies and gentlemen, is in microcosm the state of monopoly journalism in the summer of 1969.

Brugmann suffered a setback in his suit against "Superchron" and the Newspaper Preservation Act when a federal judge decided in 1972 that the law was constitutional and that Congress had a right to pass it, even though "it may be," the judge wrote, "that Congress could have adopted a less heavy-handed piece of legislation to accomplish the objective of maintaining the solvency of large metropolitan daily newspapers." Brugmann was encouraged, however, to press his case against the *Chronicle-Examiner* joint operation in particular. The attention of the nation's journalists began to focus on the expected trial in the summer of 1975, in which Brugmann's lawyers promised revealing evidence about the financial manipulations between the closing down of the *News-Call-Bulletin* and the creation of the *Chronicle-Examiner* monopoly.

But Brugmann surprised everyone, and disappointed some of his more idealistic supporters, by suddenly settling out of court. For $500,000 that theoretically compensated Brugmann and his little newspaper for the disadvantages they face in trying to compete for advertising with the *Chronicle-Examiner*, Brugmann agreed to abandon his effort to break up "Superchron." Brugmann did it, he explained later, because he was able to use the money to provide his newspaper with larger offices and, more important, to make the *Bay Guardian* a weekly again. It had begun as a weekly back in 1966, but financial problems had forced Brugmann to publish as infrequently as every month until an influx of some new capital in 1972 enabled him to put out the newspaper biweekly for the next three years. By returning to weekly publishing and being able to afford vigorous promotional mailings, Brugmann said he hoped to be able to steadily increase the *Bay Guardian*'s circulation well beyond its present 27,000 paid subscribers and attract more advertising as well.

"This is our big opportunity," Brugmann said. "Circulation of the *Examiner* is down; the *Oakland Tribune* is down. This is our chance to show that a weekly newspaper like ours, with a strong point of view, can work and prosper in the bay area. I want to show that it can and should be done in any metropolitan area in the country."

The hell-raising advocacy journalism of Bruce Brugmann's *Bay Guardian* has deep roots in the American experience, going back to antiestablishment colonial editors like John Peter Zenger of the *Weekly Journal* in New York and Revolutionary-era agitators like Thomas Paine, who crusaded for emancipation of slaves, equality for women, easy divorce laws, prohibition of dueling, and acceptance of atheism in his *Pennsylvania Gazette*. The tradition was carried on during the nineteenth century by abolitionist pamphleteers, crusading frontier-town newspaper editors, and, in the teeming cities back east, reform journalists like E. L. Godkin, who edited both the *Nation* magazine and the *New York Evening Post* in the late 1800s. Advocacy journalism then reached an apogee in the brief era of the original muckrakers at the beginning of the twentieth century.

After World War I, when muckraking disappeared from the popular press, crusading was left to a few small magazines like the *Nation* and the *Progressive* and radical newspapers and newsletters supported by left-wing trade unions, various prosocialist factions, and the American Communist party. With the notable exception of *In Fact*, a newsletter in which former foreign correspondent and emigré George Seldes exposed shocking conditions in the auto, drug, tobacco, and other industries during the 1930s and 1940s, most of these radical papers were devoted to political commentary and propaganda, rather than nonpartisan muckraking. In 1939 several veteran New York newsmen started a liberal, muckraking daily newspaper called *PM*. But in an era of increasing economic prosperity and rising national opposition to leftist dissent, the paper never won sufficient readers or financial support and survived only until 1946. It was succeeded for a time by the *New York Star* and then the *New York Daily Compass,* which finally expired in 1952.

Out of the ashes of *PM* and its successors, however, arose an unlikely phoenix—I.F. ("Izzy") Stone, a gnomelike, squeaky-voiced, nearsighted, cheerfully angry man who breathed new life into American advocacy journalism. Left unemployed after thirty years in journalism when the *Daily Compass* folded, Stone began a mail-subscription newsletter in Washington, *I.F. Stone's Weekly,* in which for nearly two decades he railed against political duplicity, military adventurism, bureaucratic waste, and other ills of American government. Stone's carefully crafted, strongly opinionated, bitingly witty, and impressively documented writing attracted an influential audience in journalism, academia, and government that grew steadily from 5300 subscribers for the first issue in January 1953 to more than 70,000 for the last in December 1971.

Born in 1907 of Russian immigrant parents in Philadelphia and raised in nearby Haddonfield, New Jersey, Stone briefly published his first radical newspaper when he was just fourteen years old. Called *The Progress,* the monthly paper attacked William Randolph Hearst's "Yellow Peril" campaign, praised Mahatma Gandhi, and called for cancellation of World War I debts in return for a twenty-five-year moratorium on arms build-ups in Europe. After three issues Stone's father made him stop publishing the paper because it interfered with his studies, so the determined teenager began working after school as a reporter for the *Haddonfield Press* and the *Camden Courier-Post.*

Stone read voraciously and largely educated himself, devouring the works of Whitman, Keats, Shelley, Wordsworth, Spencer, Heraclitus, Cervantes, Gibbon, Charles Beard, Stephen Crane, and Jack London while still an adolescent. But because he never did well in the structured atmosphere of school, he finished near the bottom of his high school graduating class and quit college after three years at the University of Pennsylvania, where he had worked nights at the *Philadelphia Inquirer.* He was then a full-time reporter for the *Camden Courier-Post* and, later, both Philadelphia newspapers. He worked as a reporter and editorial writer for the *New York Post* in the late 1930s, when its editorial staff was still considered one of the best and most liberal in the country. Yet Stone, an unusually intense and

" . . . I couldn't get a job doing and saying what I wanted to say, so I started my own little flea-bite publication."

uncompromising journalist who grew gruffly impatient with those who did not always show similar dedication, "would always chew out the other editorial writers" for not putting enough into their work, according to free-lance writer Robert Sherrill, also a *Post* editorial writer at the time.

Stone had grown up an idealist who searched through the philosophy he read for answers about evil and suffering in the world and what could be done about it. He had rejected religion, including the Judaism he was born to, because, as he told a Harvard Divinity School student who interviewed him for *The Christian Century* in 1970, "I've always felt there's no way to reconcile the existence of evil with the existence of the kind of God that is envisaged in Western religions." He ultimately also rejected doctrinaire socialism and Marxism because of the injustices and restrictions on freedom of expression that persisted in communist and socialist states. He came to believe, he told the *Christian Century* interviewer, that "the basic problems are moral, in the sense that if you could change people's moral attitudes, then you could solve economic and political problems much more easily . . . If by some magic you could raise the level of altruism in ordinary human beings by 30 per cent, it would change the whole picture. If you could change the level of concern for others, we could all be saved."

"Like so many other radical journalists of his time, Stone began writing for the *Nation* magazine and was an associate editor there from 1938 to 1940, when he moved to Washington to follow more closely the national issues he was drawn to. He still contributed regularly to the *Nation* as its Washington editor from 1940 to 1946 and also worked from the capital as a reporter, columnist, and editorial writer for the *Post.* Then came *PM* and its successors, which

were run by and for journalists like Stone, who believed in the
morally enlightening power of printing unpopular truths. Commer-
cially, however, "it just wasn't a viable idea" at the time, according to
Stone. "There were lots of people talking about wanting a liberal
daily paper, but they didn't support it. So it got smaller and smaller,
with diminishing returns."

When the *Daily Compass* folded in November 1952, on the day
before the presidential election was lost by the liberals' great hope,
Adlai Stevenson, Stone was out of a job at age forty-four. He wanted
to go back to the *Nation* but, there was no longer enough money to
pay him. Other publications turned him down because of his strong
liberal views. "It was a bad time then, of course, and I couldn't get a
job doing and saying what I wanted to say," Stone recalled, "so I
started my own little flea-bite publication."

"I had to support my family in some way," Stone later told radical
journalist Andrew Kopkind, who contributed to the *Weekly* for a
time. "Also, I hoped I could comfort some of the people under attack
and all alone those days. And there was something else; I remember
walking across the Capitol grounds one day back then and thinking
about the McCarthy crowd: 'Well, I may be just a Red Jew son-of-a-
bitch to them, but I'm keeping Thomas Jefferson alive.'"

Stone began his weekly with $3500 in severance pay, a $3000 loan,
and old *PM* and *Compass* mailing lists, which produced the first 3500
subscribers. He wrote most of each four-or-more-page issue himself
and supervised the jobbed-out printing and make-up that gave it an
austere but readable appearance. "My idea," Stone said, "was to
make the *Weekly* radical in viewpoint but conservative in format."
Working out of his home, he shared with his wife Esther the business,
subscription, and back-issue chores. He covered every major issue in
Washington, often digging up shocking facts that the capital's press
corps had overlooked and illustrating his analyses with juxtaposed
items and officials' quotations that revealed dramatic inconsistencies
and apparent lies.

"I made no claim to inside stuff," Stone said. "Obviously, a radical
reporter in those days had few pipelines into the government. I tried
to give information which could be documented so the reader could
check it for himself. I tried to dig the truth out of hearings, official
transcripts, and government documents, and to be as accurate as
possible. I also sought to give the *Weekly* a personal flavor, to add
humor, wit, and good writing to the *Weekly* report. I sought in
political reporting what Galsworthy in another context called the
'significant trifle'—the bit of dialogue, the overlooked fact, the buried

observation which illuminated the realities of the situation. Those I often used in 'boxes' to lighten up the otherwise solid pages of typography unrelieved either by picture or advertising. I tried in every issue to provide fact and opinion not available elsewhere in the press."

Stone had difficulty with his hearing from the late 1930s until corrective surgery in 1964 and 1965, so he developed the habit of thoroughly combing printed transcripts of meetings and hearings, usually finding and linking together significant tidbits of information other reporters missed. He went through the *Congressional Record* each day, as well as dozens of American and foreign newspapers and periodicals he picked up during daily tours of magazine stands and bookshops. He skimmed everything rapidly, yet carefully, thumbing through the pages one by one as he leaned close to his work table to see through his thick glasses, ripping out numerous items he saved in scattered piles of files, where somehow he could always find exactly what he wanted.

Stone's methods of reporting were quite different than those of most Washington correspondents, who depended heavily on the spoken word from selected government contacts. "Establishment reporters know a lot I don't know," Stone said, "but a lot of what they know isn't true, or they can't print it." He despised the "pseudo-objectivity" of the daily press, which, he said, "just parrots government sources." Instead, Stone operated on two basic assumptions: "Every government is run by liars; that is a *prima facie* assumption until proven wrong. And the second is that a government always reveals a good deal, if you take the trouble to find what it says."

Stone often was able to use information freely made available by one part of the government to prove that another part of the government was peddling a big lie. In an admiring documentary film about Stone by young director Jerry Bruck, Jr., entitled simply *I.F. Stone's Weekly*, Stone tells how he was able to prove that the government was lying about detection of underground atomic explosions, which was a crucial issue in Soviet-American test-ban negotiations in the late 1950s. Edward Teller, a nuclear scientist opposed to any agreement with the Soviet Union, had predicted that underground tests could not be detected more than 200 miles away, and the *New York Times* published a story saying that U.S. monitoring of its own underground tests had confirmed this theory. Tucked inside later editions of the *Times*, however, Stone noticed several additional little stories reporting that scientists in Toronto, Rome, and Tokyo had detected the U.S. tests. "I thought, gee, I wish I had enough money to cable those places and find out what's going on," Stone said in the film. Instead, he contented himself with clipping the articles and putting them in a file on one of the stacks in the basement office of his northwest Washington home.

Stone waited and watched as the Soviet Union offered to allow atomic monitoring stations 580 miles apart. "Two days later," Stone said, "the Atomic Energy Commission, which is in my opinion the most mendacious agency in Washington," made public a report reiterating its conclusion that underground tests could not be detected more than 200 miles away. Stone remembered the *Times* clips and decided to look into the matter, even though, he said, "I've never been on a seismology story before." He called around Washington until he discovered the seismology branch of the U.S. Coast and Geodetic Survey in the Commerce Department. Stone did what no other reporter writing about the test-ban negotiations thought to do. He got into his car and went to see the government's own seismology experts about the monitoring of underground explosions.

"And they were so glad to see a reporter," Stone said. "I don't think they'd seen a reporter since Noah—since there was a tremble from Mount Ararat when Noah's Ark landed and there was a wide squiggle on the seismometer." Stone was told that the seismologists in Washington had easily monitored the AEC's underground nuclear tests conducted in Nevada. He copied down the seismology figures and published them, emphasizing how the AEC had lied, presumably to sabotage the test-ban treaty negotiations. After that the AEC admitted publicly that the reports it had released were untrue.

In 1970 Stone also took the trouble to find out whether the limited treaty banning above-ground tests that had emerged from the U.S.-Soviet negotiations had really discouraged nuclear testing. He found out it that it had not. "The Atomic Energy Commission press officer told me," Stone wrote, "there had been ninety-eight U.S. tests from 1945 until the treaty went into force on August 5, 1963. Since then there have been 210 U.S. tests, or more than twice as many in the seven years since the treaty as in the eighteen years before it." Stone added that Sweden, "which monitors everybody's testing, has evidence to show that the 210 tests we're admitting to is a low figure." Furthermore, Stone said, while the AEC claimed the Soviet Union made thirty-eight tests since the treaty went into effect, Sweden contended that the Soviet tests totaled twice that much. "All this is part of a phony charade in which the AEC has been engaged ever since talk of a nuclear test ban began in the fifties," Stone wrote. "It is designed to support the AEC's view that we would never be absolutely sure an underground test had taken place without on-site inspections."

"His appeal is not only informational," Andrew Kopkind wrote of Stone. "What was most enjoyable was the way he demolished windbags with a clean stroke or direct hit. He pored through otherwise unread government documents and always came up with the perfect example of villainy, mendacity or double-dealing to make his point." Kopkind cited as an example an item in May 1965 issue of the *Weekly,* which read, in part:

The Department of Commerce publishes a daily bulletin in which the government advertises various wants for bidding. There in the issue of 29 April, as our Marines were landing in Santo Domingo, appeared an ad which deserves to be preserved for the historian . . .
Service and materials to perform a RESEARCH STUDY ENTITLED "PAX AMERICANA" consisting of a phased study of the following: (a) elements of National Power; (b) ability of selected nations to apply the elements of National Power; (c) a variety of world power configurations to be used as a basis for the U.S. to maintain world hegemony in the future . . .

Thereafter, Stone repeatedly referred to heavy-handed American foreign policy or military actions with which he disagreed as more "Pax Americana." Kopkind wrote that such "delicious polemical bonbons exemplified Izzy's style: somewhere between cantankerous and whimsical, angry right up to the point of self-righteous—but only up to that point."

If he was not self-righteous in his writing, he could be in his work style, always daring other journalists to be as determined, skeptical, high-minded, and hard-working as he. In the process he wore out countless young journalists who foolishly agreed to work as his apprentices. "He was one of the most difficult people ever to work for on the face of the earth," remembered Peter Osnos, a *Washington Post* reporter who worked for Stone longer than any of his other young assistants—ten months in 1965 and 1966.

Each day started, Osnos said in an interview in the Bruck film, "about 7:30 in the morning when Izzy's on the phone, and he's saying, 'Pete!' and you're beginning to shake already and he's already been through the *New York Times,* the *Washington Post,* the *Baltimore Sun,* at that point it was also the *New York Herald Tribune,* and the *Wall Street Journal.* And you're still struggling through the A-section of the *Washington Post*. And the first thing he wants to know is if you saw the item, on page Z-12, in which J. Edgar Hoover was proven to be the fool we all knew he is. And, of course, if you've seen it, you're just in heaven for the rest of the day, but if God forbid you missed it, you just don't recover all day.

"From then on in, it's just run, run, run, until generally I would fall asleep usually about one or two o'clock in the morning, with three or four *Congressional Records* stacked on my chest or under my chin, gaga with the day's debate on some particularly boring subject that Izzy wanted indexed. And, of course, you could never index it adequately because he could always index it infinitely faster. I mean he could take an enormous volume of congressional hearings and in the course of maybe what would seem to me ten seconds, but was probably about two hours, he would leaf through these things and come up with some jewel that other people would devote a lifetime to. People read, but they miss most of what they see. Izzy misses nothing."

Stone forgot nothing. More than any other journalist in Washington during all the years of the Vietnam war, Stone kept referring back to the 1964 Gulf of Tonkin resolution and the evidence he had presented almost immediately afterward that the alleged attack by North Vietnamese gunboats against the U.S. fleet was an American fraud. He also never forgot during the years Senator J. William Fulbright was celebrated by other liberals as an opponent of the war that he had also been one of the important proponents of the Tonkin Gulf resolution. During all the years when others blindly supported the war or took no stand on it, Stone argued against it week after week, pointing out lie after lie in the Johnson and Nixon administrations' justifications for their military policies.

"I think the most important fact about Izzie's career," Peter Osnos told me, "is his permanent sense of outrage. He has never become cynical or blasé about Washington or the world, and that is what keeps his edge sharp. He sees blacks and whites where others are willing to see grays. A scandal or an injustice is not to be excused. Compromise when it is a sell-out is not to be excused."

Stone could be rather exasperating to talk with, despite his engaging, puckish sense of humor. He surprised and angered other Jews with his criticism of Israeli militarism and his insistence that the Palestinians, as well as the Israelis, were entitled to their own home in the Middle East. While other liberals expansively eulogized assassinated President Kennedy, Stone judged him shortly after his death to have been "a conventional leader, no more than an enlightened conservative, cautious as an old man for all his youth, with a basic distrust of the people and an astringent view of the evangelical as a tool of leadership. It is as well not to lose sight of these realities in the excitement of a funeral; funerals are always occasions for pious lying." Stone also disappointed the young New Left radicals of the 1960s by decrying bomb-throwing, iconoclastic revolution as a self-defeating means for achieving necessary change. "I think the oppressed can't afford to be *reasonable*," he said, "but they can't afford to be *irrational* either."

Stone steadfastly insisted that he was not a muckraker or an investigative reporter, arguing that "all journalism is investigative." He expected all good reporters to be like himself, but he never found one acceptable as his successor. He discussed with Robert Sherrill and Andrew Kopkind, among others, the possibility of taking over the *Weekly* when he retired, but he inevitably found the free-lance work he solicited from them not to be entirely suitable. "Izzy just wasn't in his heart of hearts willing to take on a real collaborator," concluded another would-be successor. "He is, as nearly as I can judge, a completely fulfilled man. He has, as he often said he might, survived his time as a pariah and a tolerated eccentric to become something of a national institution. And that, for a wild-eyed socialist, a confirmed radical, is something to be proud of."

Stone finally closed down the *Weekly* at the end of 1971. (It had actually been a biweekly since 1968 when Stone suffered a heart attack.) He devoted more time to articles for the *New York Review of Books,* to which he had become a contributor, accepted a few more speaking engagements and collected the awards and honorary degrees belatedly bestowed on him, and set out to add to the ten books he had already published. He decided to tackle first the history of human freedom and turned to Plato to discover the truth about the silencing and execution of Socrates. "Everybody else is on Watergate," Stone said in 1974, "and I'm trying to expose the trial of Socrates."

The Vietnam war and Nixon created a new skepticism in a fresh crop of young journalists," Stone said, and he was pleased that they had picked up where he had left off with the *Weekly*. Some were directly inspired by Stone: Carl Bernstein had regularly read his father's copy of the *Weekly* when it came in the mail, and Seymour Hersh had begun following it closely after coming across Stone at the Associated Press Washington bureau. But Stone worried about the faddishness of muckraking and feared that both muckrakers and their readers might become so caught up in the excitement of each new exposé that they would miss the point. Using himself as an example, Stone mused in Jerry Bruck's film that "I really have so much fun, I ought to be arrested. Sometimes I think it's wrong of me because . . . to be able to spit in their eye, and do what you think is right, and report the news, and have enough readers to make some impact is such a pleasure that you forget what you're writing about. It becomes like—you're like a journalistic Nero fiddling while Rome burns, or like a small boy covering a hell of a big fire. It's just wonderful and exciting, and you're a cub reporter, and God has given you a big fire to cover. And you forget—*that it's really burning.*"

Molly Ivins, an admirer of Stone and co-editor of the *Texas Observer*, now the oldest surviving local alternative newspaper in the country, knew just what Stone was talking about. "I've got a vindictive streak," Ivins admitted during a speaking appearance at a workshop for midwestern newspaper reporters in Minneapolis in 1974. "I really like to nail those bastards' hides to the wall. I enjoy that," she said, referring to targets of the *Observer*'s muckraking in Texas. "I have fun."

It had not always been fun for Ivins, a tall, big-boned, strawberry blond woman who enjoys telling everyone just what is on her mind. She had too many disagreements with her editors at the *Minneapolis Tribune* over how much of her personal interpretation belonged in the articles she wrote as a reporter. So she quit and went back home to Texas to help run the biweekly *Observer* in Austin, the state capital. Despite its small circulation, which for years has hovered just above 10,000, the *Texas Observer* has for more than two decades been one of the state's most influential publications. Responsible for this are its deadly accurate investigative reporting and irreverently critical political commentary—two lamentably rare commodities in the rest of Texas journalism.

Since Ivins joined editor Kaye Northcott at the *Observer* (its full-time editorial staff is rounded out by an associate editor), the newspaper's muckraking has nailed the hides of several state officials to the wall. It spurred investigation of the Sharpstown Bank scandal, which eventually involved a former governor, lieutenant governor, and attorney general of the state, as well as the speaker of the Texas house of representatives and several prominent financiers, in improper collusion between bankers and state officials. Continuing years of *Observer* revelations of financial boondoggles inside the giant University of Texas, the newspaper reported that university regents had appropriated $1 million for a new chancellor's mansion and more money to enlarge the football field while they raised students' tuition and cut teachers' salaries and research funds. Ivins also wrote two muckraking articles about private child-care facilities in the state, which have involved the *Observer* in a protracted libel suit against the newspaper, four other publications, and NBC, which picked up the story.

The *Observer* was begun in 1954 by Ronnie Dugger, a University of Texas graduate who ran it as editor until 1967. A group of liberal Texas Democrats had decided that the state needed a journalistic alternative to the conservative editorial policies and passive reporting of the daily newspapers of Austin, Dallas, Forth Worth, and Houston. When they approached young Dugger, who had just returned to Texas from a year's studies in Oxford, England, he said he would edit such a newspaper if it would not be a party organ. The original publisher and principal financial backer, Mrs. Frankie Randolph, called the "Eleanor Roosevelt of Texas" by author and *Observer* alumnus Willie Morris, agreed to give Dugger exclusive control over the new independent weekly he characterized on its front page as a "journal of free voices."

The *Observer* soon became invaluable for its detailed, authoritative coverage of state government and Texas politics, devoting at least half of each issue to the workings of, and bills before, the state legislature when it was in session. Dugger and regular contributors over the years like Morris, Robert Sherrill, and Larry King added incisive, sometimes stinging, sometimes whimsical commentary on politics and the issues of the day. The *Observer* also contained book reviews and regional cultural notes.

But Dugger was best at muckraking. He and an ever-changing sparse staff, operating out of a small, cluttered office near the University of Texas campus and the state capitol in Austin, exposed corruption among legislators and lobbyists, gift-taking by state officials, tax-dodging and environmental pollution by Texas oil companies, the financial manipulations of Billy Sol Estes, noncompetitive rate-setting by insurance companies, horrible conditions in state reform schools and mental hospitals, and abuses of budget and power at the University of Texas. Playing no favorites, the *Observer* frequently criticized President Lyndon Johnson for his conduct of the Vietnam war and liberal Texas Senator Ralph Yarborough for such things as putting his son on his government payroll at a higher salary than any other congressional relative was getting from the taxpayers.

The *Observer*, which had never made money, slid into a sharp

"You can find out more in one night of drinking with the capital press corps than you do in six months of reading the daily papers."

journalistic and financial decline in the mid-1960s, after Morris, Sherrill, and King had all left and Dugger, too, decided to trade the responsibility for producing a 40,000-word newspaper each week for comparatively leisurely magazine and book writing. The *Observer* had to be reduced in size and published biweekly to be saved by Dugger's successors, first Greg Olds, and then Kay Northcott, who has worked at the newspaper since 1968. Olds was editor when the *Observer* made national news by revealing that President Johnson's appointee to the second highest position in the U.S. Department of Health, Education, and Welfare, who was then the president of Southwest Texas State College, Johnson's alma mater, had won his doctoral degree with a dissertation strongly resembling both his wife's master's thesis and a U.S. Marine Corps report on the Marines' 1915-1934 occupation of Haiti. Circulation of the *Observer* was up to 12,000 by the end of 1974, when the newspaper made a profit of $158 and published a 64-page slick twentieth-anniversary edition.

Molly Ivins, who had earned degrees from Smith College and Columbia University, studied for a year in Paris, and worked as a reporter for the *Houston Chronicle* as well as in Minneapolis, joined Northcott at the *Observer* in 1970. She almost immediately made her presence known with bold muckraking reporting and a strident writing style. She had left behind a nasty critique of her former employer, published under the title "The *Minneapolis Tribune* is a Stone Wall Drag" in the *Twin Citian* magazine, and one of her constant targets since moving to the *Observer* has been the lackluster Texas press. Like I.F. Stone and Bruce Brugmann, she does not believe in the "objective" journalism of what she calls the "straight" press.

"I've seen truth murdered too many times in the name of

objectivity," Ivins wrote in the *Twin Citian* article. She complained that the *Tribune* prevented reporters from writing much of what they knew or could interpret for the reader. Later, after four years back in Texas, she said, "You can find out more in one night of drinking with the capital press corps than you do in six months of reading the daily papers. Straight journalists know but don't tell. The establishment structure keeps them from it."

On the other hand Ivins believes that the alternative press must not be reckless. "I don't think advocacy journalism can cop out," she said. "There has to be an internal attempt to abide by the standards of professional journalism—accuracy and fairness." She told the midwestern reporters meeting in Minneapolis that the *Texas Observer* is carefully professional in this way and therefore "unique among its several imitators" in the "underground" press that grew up during the 1960s. The *Observer,* Ivins pointed out, "is pre-underground, so it's not confused with the underground press. It's considered terribly radical in Texas, but actually it's mildly liberal, I'm afraid."

Much the same thing could be said about the country's other notable "pre-underground" newspaper, the weekly *Village Voice,* founded in 1951 by two residents of New York's Greenwich Village, psychologist Edwin Fancher and writer Dan Wolf. The *Voice* became a forum for the new liberal, bohemian, intellectual, and professional Greenwich Village residents who were alienated from the big New York dailies and the snobbish, ultraconservative *Villager,* which had been supported by the neighborhood's business interests since 1933. While campaigning to keep the Village polyglot, culturally exciting, and safe from urban renewal and excessive crime, the *Voice* naturally became involved in muckraking. Led by Jack Newfield, the *Voice*'s resident investigative reporter, its writers revealed local government corruption, social problems, real estate exploitation, and courthouse injustices. *Voice* exposés frequently became tips for the city's dailies to follow up.

Newfield, a chunky man with glasses and curly hair, has sought both to uncover and correct injustices in the intensely personal campaigns he has conducted against everything from lead paint poisoning to nursing-home fraud to nepotism and corruption in the giant New York City municipal bureaucracy. In a relentless crusade against bad judges, he gathered from countless interviews and courtroom observations—plus internal studies, reports, memoranda, and court transcripts—enough information to publish impassioned articles like "The Ten Worst Judges in New York," which resulted in the removal of some judges and the prosecution of others. The Association of the Bar of the City of New York gave Newfield's court exposés a mixed review typical of his work: grudging confirmation of most of his charges and condemnation of a few others as "irresponsible journalism." Similarly, because Wolf, editor of the *Voice* for twenty-three years, seldom edited or cut contributions to his "writer's paper," bright, experimental writing, new ideas, and bold muckraking were often offset by preachy advocacy, overwriting, parochial griping, unconfirmed gossip, and seriously slanted or even wholly untrue reporting.

Yet the *Voice*'s readership grew rapidly as it increasingly identified itself with the social and cultural changes of the 1960s, typified by sexual freedom, protest politics, off-Broadway theater, Pop art, and "new journalism." After its circulation had increased from 17,000 in 1962 to 140,000 by the beginning of the 1970s, the *Voice* was bought by Clay Felker, the ambitious publisher of *New York* magazine. Felker had hoped to make the *Voice* a national weekly able to compete successfully with *Rolling Stone,* the tabloid combination of rock magazine and radical political newspaper. But the *Voice*'s circulation suddenly leveled off, and its huge profits dwindled.

What had happened was that the *Voice* stood still journalistically during the late 1960s and the early 1970s when the true underground press rose and collapsed. The scores of radical alternative newspapers started throughout the country between 1964 and 1969 were freer in form and much more strident and outrageous in content than the *Voice.* John Wilcock, a British-born journalist who wrote for the weekly before becoming a traveling guru of what he christened the "underground" press, said the *Voice* was left "in the position of a teacher outsmarted by its students. It was the *Voice,* with its pseudo-liberalism and willingness to print what at one time seemed far-out, that paved the way for all the underground papers that followed."

The most successful of these were patterned rather obviously on the *Village Voice,* but with the addition of more polemical writing, frequent obscenities, approving references to drugs, and a growing emphasis on sex. The *Los Angeles Free Press,* for example, the first and largest of these papers, was launched with a little money and several volunteers by Art Kunkin, a former student of New York's New School for Social Research who had been working in Los Angeles as a tool- and die-maker. The paper eventually had a circulation of 90,000. In Berkeley, California, the cradle of student protest, Max Scherr, a resident off-campus radical then in his fifties, sold a local bar he owned to start the *Berkeley Barb* in 1965. Soon it was almost as big a success as the *Free Press*. In New York that same year John Wilcock and some bohemian friends founded the *East Village Other* as a more radical competitor to the *Voice;* its circulation grew to nearly 50,000.

Smaller and sometimes even more radical papers were begun by college students, campus community hangers-on, members of the "New Left," and militants in such cities as Boston (*Avatar* and the *Old Mole*), Philadelphia (the *Distant Drummer* and the *Free Press*), Washington, D.C. (the *Free Press* and *Quicksilver Times*), Atlanta (the *Great Speckled Bird*), Detroit (the *Fifth Estate*), Chicago (the *Seed*), Milwaukee and Madison, Wisconsin *(Kaleidoscope),* San Francisco (the *Oracle*), and many others. Some of these papers lasted only months or a couple of years. While a few had salaried staffs, many functioned with shifting groups of volunteers. Most of them took advantage of a technological advance that in large part helped make the underground press of the 1960s possible: offset printing, a low-cost photographic method that could directly reproduce typewriter copy and eliminate costly print-shop typesetting.

The vast majority of these radical newspapers spoke the rhetoric of youthful left-wing revolution and reported on the protests and confrontations of the 1960s exclusively from the side of the students and radicals. They baited the police (invariably called "pigs") and narcotics agents, opposed U.S. capitalism and the Vietnam war and promoted the counterculture lifestyle of long hair, scruffy dress, drug experimentation, casual sex, and psychedelic music and art. In many cases they felt no responsibility to report both sides of a controversy or even to present accurate details of an event. Instead, as propaganda organs for the movement, they felt free to distort facts to fit their line of argument.

"We were not sticklers for accuracy," acknowledged Ray Mungo, who helped start the short-lived "Liberation News Service," which began by supplying radical newspapers with articles and photographs from the October 1967 March on the Pentagon. "But our factual errors were not the product of any conspiracy to mislead the young," Mungo wrote in his memoir of that period, *Famous Long Ago.* Instead, he explained, they were the consequence "of our lack of organization, shorthandedness and impatience with grueling research efforts. *Facts* are less important than *truth* and the two are far from equivalent, you see; for cold facts are nearly always boring and may even distort the truth, but *Truth* is the highest achievement of human expression" (emphasis his).

To illustrate what he meant, Mungo referred to a 1967 article in Boston's *Avatar*, headed, "Report from Vietnam, by Alexander Sorensen," which appeared to be, in Mungo's words, "a painfully graphic account of Sorensen's encounter with medieval torture in a Vietnamese village." According to Mungo, however, the article was fiction. "Because we know Brian Keating, who wrote the piece," Mungo explained, "we discover that Alexander Sorensen doesn't exist and the incident described in *Avatar*, which moved thousands, never in fact happened. But because it has happened in man's history, and because we know we are responsible for its happening today, and because the story is unvarnished and plain and human, we know it's true, truer than any facts you may have picked up in the *New Republic*."

Mungo's Liberation News Service was later absorbed into the older "Underground Press Syndicate," which had been started in June 1966 by the ubiquitous John Wilcock and other radical editors as a national advertising agent and clearinghouse for articles and artwork of member alternative newspapers.

Not all underground editors wanted to be thought of as far out of the mainstream or as doctrinaire left-wing radicals, however. "We don't see ourselves as an instrument of revolution, because we don't see any revolution," said editor John Kois of *Kaleidoscope*, "At this paper," Kois said in 1969, "We are almost traditional reformists—we pose alternatives and try to make them happen. We're gadflies."

A few underground papers attempted to engage in traditional muckraking, although they seldom had the staff or financial resources for extensive research. In conservative San Diego, the *Street Journal* published a lengthy exposé of the financial manipulations of local banker and civic leader C. Arnholdt Smith. Much of the material came from an earlier story on Smith in the *Wall Street Journal*, but the San Diego paper also linked several other prominent local businessmen with Smith's questionable business practices. Later, other underground papers pursued stories and rumors connected to Watergate and the 1972 election campaign financing scandals, occasionally providing tips for establishment investigative reporters.

By the time of Watergate, however, most of the underground press movement had splintered and started to die. Many radical papers lost their audiences and folded, while at some of the biggest and most profitable papers, including the *Los Angeles Free Press* and the *Berkeley Barb*, the most left-wing staff members left to start more militant but far less successful offshoots like the *Berkeley Tribe*.

Radical women journalists, unable to change the sometimes offensive editorial content and sex advertising of many male-dominated underground papers, staged coups, like that at New York City's *Rat,* or started militant feminist publications like *Off Our Backs* and *Underground Woman* that struggled to stay alive. Dissident servicemen published alternative GI newspapers opposing the Vietnam war, fighting for expanded rights, and exposing injustices on local bases. These servicemen's publications, which tended to be less strident and more accurate than the rest of the underground press, helped bring about significant changes inside the military until the winding down of the Vietnam war and the end of the draft took away their two most important targets.

By the mid-1970s the underground press had been largely displaced by more traditional muckraking newspapers like the *San Francisco Bay Guardian.* Typical of newcomers of this kind was the *Oklahoma Observer,* an Oklahoma City biweekly that had been published by the local Catholic diocese before it was bought in 1970 by veteran newspaperman Forrest "Frosty" Troy. He soon shocked the Oklahoma capital with his exposés of corruption, conflicts of interest in state and local government, and heavy-handed lobbying for favoritism by the state's giant oil, gas, and insurance industries. Perhaps because no newspaper there had done anything like this before, the little *Observer* gained the attention of state officials and achieved some Troy-supported reforms: An inhumane form of solitary confinement was ended at the state penitentiary at the governor's order; the governor and legislature acted to require Oklahoma-based corporations for the first time to pay tax on their dividends; and the legislature voted more money for books, teachers, and special education. At the bill-signing ceremony for the tax-reform law, the governor told the forty-year-old crusading editor, "This is your program."

The approach to muckraking taken by Troy, a college dropout who twice was the *Tulsa Tribune*'s Washington correspondent before he bought the *Observer,* has often been quite heavy-handed. Targets of his crusades are labeled "featherbrain" and "moron," and in an article on illegal conflicts of interest in the awarding of state construction contracts, he wrote: "Spending a weekend reading the transcript from the Oklahoma County grand jury is like being trapped in a sewer for two days. Pustules of corruption sear your senses and you search in vain for some escape from the smothering putrefaction."

Such stridency has offended potential advertisers (two local utility companies pulled their ads after Troy campaigned for a state law limiting the amount of money utilities could spend on advertising), offended other Oklahoma editors, and kept the paid circulation of the *Observer* down around 4000 (although most members of the Oklahoma legislature are subscribers). But none of this has dismayed Troy or persuaded him to modify his newspaper. As he himself has said in responding to his critics, "I'm a zealot."

Some similar papers, however, have tried to attract additional readers and keep solvent by adding to their muckraking the kinds of service features that made "city" magazines like *New York* so successful: calendars of community events, cultural news and reviews, and consumer guides. Even Bruce Brugmann has filled much of the *Bay Guardian* with lists of college extension courses in the San Francisco area, directories of women's services, tips for finding lower-priced food, guides to San Francisco's Chinatown and waterfront and California's wineries, and a directory of banking services, including tips on where and how to obtain checking accounts without service charges. "We're trying to provide features that will make people read the paper who disagree with our point of view," said Brugmann. "They may resent our positions, but they have to buy the paper. Then eventually we might convert them with the rest of the newspaper."

In New Orleans, Philip Carter, a former *Washington Post* reporter and son of the crusading southern editor, Hodding Carter, has created a successful balance of muckraking and entertainment and service features in the weekly *Courier.* Carter bought the alternative paper in 1972 and overhauled and expanded what had been a cantankerous neighborhood journal of the French Quarter. In addition to expanded features on the arts, books, and New Orleans night life, Carter has published investigative reports on local political corruption, Mafia activities, corporate price-fixing, police brutality, hospital and prison conditions, and massive tourist-attraction development projects that threaten to radically alter the appearance and atmosphere of the old city. The formula increased the *Courier's* circulation, advertising, and influence.

In Boston, the *Phoenix* was created in 1972 by the merger of a highly political "underground" paper, the *Phoenix,* and a weekly cultural and entertainment newspaper, *Boston After Dark.* The new *Phoenix* has combined entertainment and service features with aggressive muckraking to build a circulation of 65,000 (one of the largest in the country for a "hell-raiser") and attract ample advertising. The *Phoenix* also has drawn several young investigative reporters with its "commitment" to muckraking, according to reporter Peter Lucas, who left the daily *Boston Globe* to work for the weekly. "It keeps the big guys on their toes," Lucas said of the *Phoenix*. "It embarrasses them, and it is small enough to stay honest. The *Globe* will rip off stories from us, but that is all right with me."

One of the best investigative reporters working for the *Phoenix*, twenty-five-year-old Howard Husock, insisted, however, that he did not feel driven by any special sense of mission. "People feel they read the truth in the *Phoenix*," he said, "but we don't have a monopoly on truth. We just put things in the broader context of political and economic interpretation. This actually would be allowed now at many daily papers, but something about the atmosphere inside them still discourages it."

Husock has detailed in articles how wealthy Boston slum landlords profit from tax shelters and government rehabilitation programs without improving living conditions in their rundown housing properties, how Boston's banks were ruining a still livable inner-city neighborhood by refusing to put more mortgage money into it, how the mayor steered lucrative urban-renewal construction contracts to developers linked to Boston politicians, and how a federally funded public job program for the chronically unemployed was being exploited for political patronage by city hall. Husock pointed out that most of these stories were later picked up and pursued by the city's daily newspapers, and the exposé of the public job program led to a federal investigation. This is not radical or advocacy journalism, Husock insisted, but merely "aggressive reporting" that had come of age in the 1970s and could be done with a little more freedom at a newspaper like the *Phoenix*.

"What happened during the 1960s has influenced young people now in journalism not to emulate the undergrounds, but to become a lot more aggressive reporters," Husock said. "We have a certain role to play at the *Phoenix*, but it's not really the 'let's change the system' idealism role. We talk here about breaking good stories, just as reporters at traditional newspapers do. That's why people in their forties read the *Phoenix*. We're doing the stories that appear in the dailies and on TV."

Although a handful like the *Phoenix* (and a competitor, *The Real Paper*) in Boston, the *Courier* (and its competitor, *Figaro*) in New Orleans and the *Bay Guardian* in San Francisco have survived and prospered, the number of alternative big-city newspapers remains small, and their future uncertain. But Bruce Brugmann believes that any "good metropolitan weekly, starting small, but speaking with integrity, can soon have influence in inverse proportion to its size. There is nothing stronger in journalism," Brugmann said, "than the force of a good example. The *Bay Guardian* can succeed, despite the galloping contraction of the press in San Francisco, because there are many of us who still believe that the newspaper business is a trade worth fighting for. That is what this newspaper is all about."

7: ■ Free-lance Muckraking ■ and the "New Journalism"

The ride up the slow, rattling, unsteady elevator to the Greenwich Village offices of the *Nation* magazine was almost a journey backward in time. The dusty old building and the *Nation*'s dimly lit corridors, worn functional furniture, and wood-encased manual switchboard could have formed the set for a vintage 1930s movie. Editors and other staff members—most of them plainly dressed, cigarette-smoking, older men and women—moved almost noiselessly from one cluttered, dark little cubicle to the next, casting long shadows on the bare walls. The scene was altogether appropriate for the century-old magazine, which has never tried to keep up with the times in its appearance. Yet under Carey McWilliams and his predecessors as editor, the little magazine had been consistently ahead of its time in exposing corruption, abuse of power, and other evils of government and big business, especially during the many years when little of this was being done by the rest of the media.

On one wall of McWilliams's modest office hung framed awards won by the magazine and its contributors during his quarter-century as editor. On the other side of his office were a row of well-worn unmatched filing cabinets, stretching from a solid wooden one bought long ago to a tinny new model. Besides bearing witness to the passage of McWilliams's years at the *Nation,* they contained evidence of how he sustained the magazine's long tradition of unorthodox social criticism and untimely muckraking during the 1950s and 1960s when other editors ignored or even discouraged it. McWilliams, a short, stocky man with glasses, thinned dark hair, and the careful speech, controlled demeanor, and neat habits of a veteran lawyer has always methodically sorted and saved clippings. Whenever he found something significant or troubling in the mail, newspapers, journals, popular magazines, *Congressional Records,* books, and other material that regularly came across his desk, he tucked them away in a particular file folder in one of the cabinets, until they began forming what McWilliams recognized as an alarming pattern still unnoticed by the rest of the media. He then wrote or telephoned one of the devoted newspapermen and free-lance writers who have periodically done articles for him for relatively little money.

"He would collect pamphlets and articles from a huge range of sources, bundle them together, and ask if you'd like to do a piece," recalled Bernard C. Nossiter, London correspondent for the *Washington Post,* who frequently moonlighted for the *Nation* while working at the old *New York World Telegram and Sun.* "He'd suggest questions," Nossiter said, "but carefully avoided steering you in any direction."

McWilliams published Ralph Nader's first muckraking essays, including "The Safe Car You Can't Buy" in the *Nation* of April 11, 1959, six years before Nader finished *Unsafe at Any Speed.* It was at McWilliams's suggestion that Hunter Thompson, then an unknown free-lance writer, went off to observe the Hell's Angels and wrote a 1965 *Nation* article that grew into the popular book on the motorcycle gang that launched Thompson's gaudy career. McWilliams also encouraged and published the early work of Fred J. Cook, Robert Sherrill, and Joseph Goulden, who all later became best-selling muckraking authors.

In this way McWilliams helped create a new post-World War II magazine and book market for free-lance muckrakers, whose numbers had dwindled to a very few since their turn-of-the-century popularity. Not until the late 1960s did this market suddenly expand to include large-circulation, slick magazines like *Harper*'s and the *Atlantic,* the newer "city magazines" like *New York, Philadelphia,* and *Washingtonian,* and even several magazines like *Ramparts, New Times,* and the *Washington Monthly,* which were started especially to publish free-lance muckraking. By the early 1970s book publishers, who in the 1950s and 1960s were somewhat reluctant to put Fred Cook's early FBI and CIA exposés between hard covers, were ardently courting muckraking authors.

Even then, until his retirement at the end of 1975 at the age of seventy, McWilliams remained an important pacesetter, publishing articles from young free-lancers on previously untouched subjects. He recalled the effect of a former FBI agent's first-person account in the *Nation* of how the bureau monitored civil rights and political activists by infiltrating their groups, tapping their phones, and keeping dossiers on them. "You could almost hear the rest of the press listening," McWilliams said. "Then you could see the delayed reaction here and there with the press saying, 'There might be some merit to the argument.'" Soon, interviews with other FBI agents and informers, plus Army intelligence officers and CIA operatives who also were engaged in spying on civilians, began appearing everywhere.

"Other editors try to find out what the trend of the moment is and then get with it," observed another former McWilliams contributor, *Washington Post* columnist Nicholas von Hoffman. "McWilliams doesn't cash in on trends, he makes them."

McWilliams was only the latest of several strong editors of the *Nation* who consistently saw its primary purpose as that of serving, in the words of one early contributor to its pages, as "an external conscience of other publications." The magazine was founded in 1867 with the money of a philanthropic Philadelphia abolitionist and run as a reform journal of social criticism by several wealthy young writers who were shocked by conditions during the postslavery, early industrial sweatshop era. From the beginning the magazine was partially filled, as it still is, with avant garde book and art criticism. But it soon became especially noted for its vivid descriptions of wretched social conditions, as well as its ardent advocacy of full civil rights and educational and economic opportunities for freed blacks. In time came biting, revealing essays railing against militarism, robber-baron economic monopolies, and the plight of the impoverished in cities and rural areas.

One longtime staff member, A.G. Sedgwick, later wrote that the policy of the *Nation* under its first great editor, E.L. Godkin, was one of "attack . . . a policy that preserved it from the popularity for which, of course, it never made the smallest bid." The *Nation* seldom had more than 25,000 subscribers and never carried much advertising. Because of its continually shaky financial condition its austere appearance has changed little over the decades. It has remained a relatively thin, rather scholarly-looking weekly printed on dull, cheap paper. It has never had a glossy cover and has rarely published photographs.

The *Nation's* plain appearance and lack of wide popularity left it considerably overshadowed during the decade between 1902 and 1912, when vivid exposés of corruption in the cities and the tyranny of big industrial monopolies written by the original "muckrakers" became wildly popular. But the national craze for muckraking subsided just as suddenly as it had grown up; only the *Nation* kept up its attack. And even with its relatively tiny circulation, the magazine grew steadily more influential as it came to stand more and more alone.

Under editor Oswald Garrison Villard, the liberal pacifist son of the railway magnate, the *Nation* offered a journalistic home to reporter Paul Y. Anderson when he left the *St. Louis Post-Dispatch* in 1923 to pursue a U.S. Senate investigation of the transfers of the Teapot Dome and Elk Hills oil reserves during the Harding administration. Anderson's free-lance dispatches to the *Nation* from Washington made coherent and compelling the voluminous documentary evidence being gathered by the committee and Anderson himself, and they helped reveal Teapot Dome as a national scandal. *The Post-Dispatch's* managing editor was so impressed that he rehired Anderson, who then worked for the next dozen years as the Washington correspondent for both that newspaper and the *Nation,* investigating the favoritism of the oil-depletion allowance, the questionable selection of the jury that acquitted Fall and Doheny of the Teapot Dome scandal, and the disappearance of $250,000 in Liberty Bonds, for which he received the Pulitzer Prize in 1929. "If the *Nation* had done nothing more than publish Paul Y. Anderson in these years," Carey McWilliams later wrote about the Villard-Anderson era, "it would have made a significant contribution to the continuance of the muckraking tradition."

Following Anderson's lead, other newspapermen sent to the *Nation* articles based on investigative reporting that their own papers would not print; they were joined by academicians and free-lance writers for whom it did not seem to matter much that the magazine could not afford large fees. The *Nation* "never paid well," Lewis Gannett, who worked there for a time as an editor, once wrote, "but people wrote avidly from universities and from mining camps, eager to tell a story that the newspapers were missing."

More threatening to the venerable but frail magazine than its chronic shortage of money were occasionally deep staff policy rifts on such issues as how to react to political repression in the Soviet Union. Following World War II such disagreements undermined the magazine's editorial direction, discouraging free-lancers and causing circulation to fall. It was during this particularly gloomy period that Carey McWilliams was lured to New York.

McWilliams's parents had moved their family to California from Colorado, where Carey was born in 1905 and later watched his father, a cattle rancher, slide into bankruptcy during the recession of 1920. McWilliams worked his way through the University of Southern California, receiving a bachelor of law degree in 1927, and went into private legal practice in Los Angeles. Among his clients were a group

"This radical tradition is the only tradition I've ever been able to identify myself with."

of mostly Mexican-born migrant workers striking against citrus orchard farmers to obtain better wages and working conditions. By 1933 these workers were joined in their struggle against big California farmers by "Dust Bowl" refugees from Oklahoma, Nebraska, Texas, and Arkansas.

"Not only did he have the family experience to tell him that all stories don't necessarily end well," Nicholas von Hoffman later wrote of McWilliams, "but he also grew up in a time when native American radicalism was still a force, particularly in the western states where people were fighting the railroads, the mining companies, and the eastern banking interests." McWilliams himself said that "this radical tradition is the only tradition I've ever been able to identify myself with. It's discontinuous, it disappears, it breaks off, but it always comes back."

McWilliams's radicalism is not anarchistic, cynical, shrill, or violent. It is instead soft-spoken and constructive, optimistic and profoundly patriotic in the Jeffersonian tradition. As he has gone about trying to help change American institutions without destroying them, McWilliams has always been a plodding toiler—never hasty nor doctrinaire. "He was absorbed and amused by the way those in power abused it," Bernard Nossiter told me. "But he communicated his own belief that exposure and sunlight would somehow cure."

In this way McWilliams helped irreversibly alter the struggle for social justice in the United States, beginning with his exposure of the suffering of migratory farm laborers at the hands of agricultural land barons in California in the 1930s. Shocked by the hard labor, poverty wages, and violent repression endured by California fruit and vegetable workers, "I became interested in what I found to be a fascinating problem," McWilliams recalled wryly. "I wondered why nice Christian citizens of California would allow this to happen. Then I discovered the Associated Farmers."

The Associated Farmers was the fearfully powerful organization of large growers who each owned tens of thousands of the state's best agricultural land. Through painstaking research McWilliams discovered that these landowners had gained much of their holdings and their power by seizing control of vital water sources and irrigation networks for arid Southern California. Small landowners either paid high prices and political homage to the big growers for the irrigation of their farms or sold out to them. After a depresing tour of migrant labor camps in the San Joaquin Valley in 1935 McWilliams decided to write about the miserable conditions he had seen set against the background of the facts about land and water rights ownership that he had found in state and local records. He successfully offered his first article to the *Nation* and then wrote a series of six more detailed and localized articles for a weekly Pacific Coast magazine under the title "Factories in the Fields." These articles and McWilliams's work with others in the successful campaign of reform gubernatorial candidate Culbert Olson helped finally to bring the abuse of migrants and other working men in the state to the attention of depression-weary California voters in 1938.

McWilliams went to work in Olson's administration as state commissioner of imigration and housing, using the once-dormant little agency to investigate with hearings throughout the state living conditions of the migrants and to establish and enforce state standards for their treatment. The Associated Farmers, aided by a conservative state legislature and editorials, opinion columns, and planted news stories in the *Los Angeles Times* and *San Francisco Examiner*, aggressively fought McWilliams's crusade and called him "Agricultural Pest Number One in California, outranking pear blight and boll weevil."

At the same time McWilliams gained a national reputation with publication in 1939 of his first book, *Factories in the Field*. The book, which had grown out of his earlier magazine articles, became a bestseller, in part because its appearance was closely followed by John Steinbeck's *The Grapes of Wrath*, a fictional account of agricultural oppression in California. The national attention they had focused on the problem brought Populist Senator La Follette to California with a congressional committee.

But by the time La Follette's sensational hearings and a companion investigation by a U.S. House of Representatives committee had ended and reform legislation was drawn up, the pre-World War II economic recovery and resurgence of nationalism had already begun. The legislation to protect agricultural workers from exploitation died in Congress. And Culbert Olson was ousted from the California statehouse in 1942 by voters converted by the propaganda of the Associated Farmers and their allies.

On taking office, the new governor, Earl Warren, "issued a statement saying that his first official act would be to remove me from the state government," McWilliams recalled. "It wasn't necessary though. I would have resigned anyway because of differences with him, when he was state attorney general, over the La Follette hearings (which Warren opposed) and the setting up of the Japanese refugee camps. For most of the next decade, McWilliams continued to practice law and write. Another book on California agricultural exploitation, *Ill Fares the Land*, was followed by *Southern California: An Island in the Sun*, in which McWilliams retraced the turn-of-the-century conspiracy by several large San Fernando Valley landowners, including owners of the *Los Angeles Times* and local politicians, to divert water from elsewhere in the state to the San Fernando Valley, thereby greatly increasing the value of their holdings there. McWilliams's account was resurrected for the screenplay for the 1974 film *Chinatown,* which superimposed a 1930s-style detective mystery on the story, and he was properly credited in the production notes for the film. McWilliams also wrote book-length essays about race, class, and religious prejudice in the United States and lectured frequently on college campuses, though occasionally invitations provoked controversy after he was twice publicly labeled as a communist sympathizer. In June 1949 the un-American activities committee of the California state senate included McWilliams on a list of persons it said "followed or appeased some of the Communist Party line program over a period of years." And in 1952, Louis Budenz, a university professor who had renounced his Communist party membership in 1949, named McWilliams in congressional testimony as one of the thirty persons he knew to be communists. Despite repeated denials by McWilliams, the accusations stuck for a time during the early 1950s.

In 1951 McWilliams, who had continued writing for the *Nation*, itself the victim of frequent red-baiting, was asked by publisher Freda Kirchway to come to New York to work on a special issue McWilliams had proposed on endangered American civil liberties. "It was a come-on," McWilliams said in 1974. "She told me about all the problems of the magazine, and I thought I could help. I thought I was going to stay just two weeks, but like the man who came to dinner I've been here ever since." He was first named associate editor, then editorial director in 1952, when he effectively took control of the

"In the fifties, there were damn few places to write openly . . . on the injustices of the loyalty-security madness."

magazine. He held the title of editor from 1955 until his retirement two decades later. McWilliams set the magazine back on its feet editorially with his determination to publish facts on important national issues ignored elsewhere, without taking any kind of "party line." This did not bring the *Nation* immediate popularity or financial success in the Cold War era, however. When McWilliams finally put together his special issue ("How Free Is Free?"—June 28, 1952), it was attacked by Richard Rovere (now *The New Yorker's* man in Washington) in the *New Leader* "on the ground," McWilliams recalled, "that by describing what was happening to civil liberties at that time we were in effect giving aid and comfort to the men in the Kremlin." Nevertheless, respect for the *Nation* as well as its circulation began to grow again among journalists, academics, and others looking for unvarnished truth in a troubled time.

"In the fifties," according to Bernard Nossiter, "there were damn few places to write openly and without apologetics, on the injustices of the loyalty-security madness. The *Nation* stood almost alone, apart from the socialist and Marxist organs. For a nondoctrinaire eclectic, a reporter with an ethical bias but no other, it was *the* magazine in which to write."

Nossiter was then with the Scripps-Howard *World Telegram and Sun*, which he said "was filled with professional red-baiting." So when he decided to write something he knew his paper would not print, "an article on William Perl, a classmate of Julius Rosenberg, who was railroaded to jail on a phony perjury rap," Nossiter sent it to McWilliams, who published it. "I was troubled about how Scripps-Howard would react to the *Nation*, so I dropped my by-line," Nossiter said. "But after that one, I decided this was silly nonsense," and he wrote many articles for McWilliams under his own name.

"Carey's apartment on the upper West Side was a wonderful oasis in those days," Nossiter recalled. "The intelligent and decent civil liberty types all drifted in, and as discouraging as the country seemed, the possibilities of an open and sane society seemed alive there."

Working with Nossiter was an older, brilliant writer, Fred J. Cook, who in the mid-1950s was already a veteran of nearly twenty-five years in newspapers. Born in Point Pleasant, New Jersey, in 1911, Cook had graduated Phi Beta Kappa with a bachelor of literature degree from Rutgers and worked as a reporter and editor for small New Jersey newspapers for fourteen years before moving to New York and the *World Telegram and Sun* in 1944. Cook had the unusual ability to analyze and organize vast amounts of incoming information and transform it quickly into smooth, exciting prose. He soon became a star rewrite man turning out front-page stories in minutes on deadline with information phoned or brought in by "leg-men" reporting on the street. Nossiter thought Cook was "the best and smartest rewrite man at the *World Telegram and Sun*" and the kind of person Carey McWilliams might want writing for him.

"Like Carey, Fred seethed over injustice and treated it with devastating wit and irony," Nossiter said. "He was also the fastest writer I ever saw in a newsroom. So when Carey began looking for someone to do a long civil liberties piece, I suggested Fred, and a happy marriage was born."

McWilliams asked Cook to analyze the suspicious contradictions McWilliams thought he saw in the evidence presented against Alger Hiss. Cook had detected just those kinds of flaws in a Brooklyn murder case and had written newspaper stories that helped lead to a reversal of a conviction. Cook was wary, however, of writing anything for the *Nation*. "In those days, Roy Howard ran the *World Telegram and Sun*," Cook said, "and to him the *Nation* was akin to communism." Besides, Cook had always figured that Hiss "was probably guilty. I guess my own paper's headlines had gotten to me.

"Then I talked about it with some people from the paper at lunch," Cook recalled, "and they all said I shouldn't do it. Well, I guess I'm an obstinate cuss, so all someone has to do is tell me not to do something, and I'll be sure to do it. Besides, McWilliams was persistent. He kept asking me to just look through the material he had on the Hiss case. 'You can't refuse to look,' he said. So I did and I found doubts about what had happened to Hiss."

The result was a special issue of the *Nation* in 1957, which prompted others to wonder whether Hiss had been railroaded to disgrace and brought Cook some book offers. It was the first of several reexaminations of the Hiss case that McWilliams printed through the years, as he turned up new questions and contradictions, especially in what has since been written and said by Hiss's chief accuser, Richard M. Nixon. Looking back in 1974, McWilliams kept steering the conversation back to the Hiss case and the unrelenting efforts he and Cook made to show that Nixon had framed Hiss in a headline-grabbing effort to boost himself out of obscurity. McWilliams regretted that Nixon's fall from the Presidency did not prompt more journalists to inquire once again into the Hiss affair—especially in light of what was learned about Nixon from the Watergate tapes—and find a way to prove Hiss's complete, unarguable innocence.

Cook followed the special issue on Hiss with several more over the next few years. In 1958 came "The FBI," a 60-page, 10-chapter report examining and largely confirming the sensational charge made by Cyrus Eaton, the maverick Cleveland, Ohio, industrial millionaire, that the FBI had been "snooping. . . creeping up on people . . . (and) violating the rights of free men" with informers, electronic surveillance, and sometimes illegal detentions. Cook documented abuses from the thousands of arrests during the "Palmer Red Raids" of 1919-1920 to the use during the 1950s of double agents, wiretaps, leaks of FBI files to politicians, and J. Edgar Hoover's alarmist estimates of the size and strength of the thoroughly infiltrated American Communist party. Behind the FBI's carefully projected public image of All-American virtue and infallibility, Cook argued, was a reality of disregard for civil liberties, unchecked aggrandizement of power, and frequent "Keystone cops" bungling. Even more than the Hiss issue, "The FBI" attracted wide attention to Cook and the *Nation*, winning for them a Page One Award of the New York Newspaper Guild, which usually was presented only for newspaper reporting.

Cook also wrote for the *Nation* on City Hall corruption in New York (winner of another Page One award in 1960), the U.S. arms industry's peacetime profiteering and manipulation of national defense policy (1961), the CIA's secret interference in foreign governments (1961), and the resurgent power of the radical Right (also 1962). These were Cook's most important years, when he stood out to those who followed his work as a modern Lincoln Steffens, breaking new ground and making it possible for the muckraker to once again be an important force in American journalism.

Unlike Steffens, who had enjoyed great financial success, however, Cook never had the time nor the money to make first-hand investigations of the many varied subjects he explored. Instead, just as he had done with the Hiss case, the consummate rewrite man produced densely detailed, strongly argued narratives from files given him by McWilliams, plus information Cook found himself in newspaper and magazine clippings, congressional hearing testimony, court files, and other records. "He had a way of putting it all together so that it showed things in an entirely new light," McWilliams said. "He made it interesting and wrote fast and accurately."

"I always liked to look through records and transcripts. I was always happiest with a pile of good records in some vault-like repository somewhere," recalled Cook, whose ability to glean dark, important secrets from searches of the public record would not be widely emulated by other newspapermen until reporters like Jerry Landauer and Stanley Penn of the *Wall Street Journal* and Donald Barlett and James Steele of the *Philadelphia Inquirer* came along years later. "All the stuff I found had been there all the time in records lying around all over the landscape," Cook said. "But nobody else was picking it up. Nobody else was looking at it with a critical eye during the 1950s. There was really a dearth of investigative reporting then.

"At the *World Telegram and Sun*, there were definite limits on investigative reporting. If you went beyond the story the editor expected, you soon stepped on someone's toes. I worked on a Yonkers raceway scandal following a killing there in 1953, and the blame was beginning to wind up in Governor Dewey's lap. He was a good friend of publisher Roy Howard's, so I was told this thing is going kind of far and I better go on to another story. After two or three times of that, you get discouraged."

The *Nation* was "so suspect in many quarters" when Cook began writing for it, that he fully expected to be fired by the *World Telegram and Sun*. "But they held their hands for a time," Cook said, "while they were looking for a good excuse to dump a guy writing things like that for the *Nation*." The excuse came after Cook and other reporters followed an investigation too close to a local institution considered untouchable by the New York press: Robert Moses.

Cook and his best legman, a blustery, hulking, nonwriting reporter named Gene Gleason, started it all with a series of articles in the late 1950s on how federal urban renewal money had been used to tear down healthy neighborhoods along with slums in New York, and how little had been rebuilt on most of the sites after landlords had been paid handsomely for buildings taken over by the city. Cook's editors remained cool to the possibility of misuse of power by Moses, who at age seventy ran with an iron hand the city's urban-renewal agency, along with several other independent public authorities that built and controlled much of New York's highways, bridges, parks, and public housing. The city's press had been alternatively awed, charmed, and cowed by Moses for the four decades in which he had wielded unchecked power.

But Cook and Gleason and a suddenly growing group of much younger reporters from the *Times, Post,* and *Herald-Tribune* kept expanding the urban renewal scandal, until they were able to show how political cronies of Moses were allowed by him to pocket urban renewal money in return for their support of his increasingly unpopular bulldozer methods. Moses fought back tenaciously, publicly attacking Cook and Gleason as "irresponsible guttersnipes" and meeting with New York newspaper publishers and editors to ask for their help in stopping what he characterized as a smear campaign. Some of the best stories produced by Cook and Gleason were relegated to inside pages under modest headlines, while Moses' lengthy replies to articles were published verbatim under their own, sometimes larger headlines. Although the reporters persisted in their digging and even shared information on occasion to prevent the editors of any one newspaper from killing the urban renewal scandal stories outright, no government agency offered to make a full investigation of the program.

So Cook turned to the *Nation* to explain, with the help of Gleason's reporting, how Moses' abuse of power in his handling of urban renewal and other city programs was characteristic of the generally undemocratic control of New York by unresponsive officials, Tammany Hall grafters. city employees' unions, and big gambling syndicates. The resulting October 31, 1959, special issue of the *Nation,* entitled "The Shame of New York," caused a sensation in that city. Cook and Gleason were invited onto a television interview program where Cook repeated accusations Gleason had made to him about city officials and others trying to influence the reporting of the story. Although the *World Telegram and Sun*'s city editor later acknowledged being told by both reporters that Gleason had been offered city jobs and other favors, Gleason himself inexplicably denied it all under questioning at the district attorney's office. Moses, Mayor Wagner, and District Attorney Frank Hogan made a fuss about Gleason's retraction, which conveniently deflected public attention from the original scandals and finally gave the *World Telegram and Sun* the excuse it was looking for to fire both men.

Cook, then forty-eight years old, decided to try to make his way as a free-lance writer, beginning with the several special issues he produced for the *Nation*. McWilliams later pointed out that he was not able to pay Cook much and that "not a penny of foundation money was used to finance any of these projects, although it would have been most welcome." Instead, they depended on McWilliams's files and Cook's resourcefulness and writing talent. "We improvised, we made do," McWilliams recalled. "But we got the issues out, they sold remarkably," and became collectors' items years ago when McWilliams's supply of reprints ran out.

Like many of the free-lance muckrakers who have since contributed regularly to the *Nation*, Cook helped support himself by writing for better-paying magazines, including the *Saturday Review* and the Sunday *New York Times* magazine. Cook has also produced nearly forty books, including paperbacks and histories and stories about the American Revolution, as well as several muckraking classics: *The Warfare State, The FBI Nobody Knows, The Corrupted Land,* and *The Plot Against the Patient.*

Books had been important vehicles for American muckrakers since the turn of the century, when there appeared, among others, David Graham Phillips's *The Great God Success* (1901), Lincoln Steffens's *The Shame of the Cities* (1904), Upton Sinclair's *The Jungle* (1906), and Theodore Dreiser's *Sister Carrie* (1900) and *The Financier* (1912). Even when muckraking was much less in vogue, there occasionally appeared books like Jacob Riis's *How the Other Half Lives* (1888), Matthew Josephson's *The Robber Barons* (1934) and *The Politicos* (1938), Michael Harrington's *The Other America* (1962), and Ralph Nader's *Unsafe at Any Speed* (1965). The 1950s had been a particularly bleak period for muckraking of any kind, however, and Cook's first attempts at putting some of his work between hard covers were somewhat frustrating, even after Morrow published his book on Alger Hiss.

"Two major houses came to me after the special *Nation* issue on the FBI (in 1958), but then they mysteriously backed off," Cook told me. "Later, I signed a two-book contract with Macmillan, with the first book being *The Warfare State* (on the military-industrial complex). The second book, about the police state, was *The FBI Nobody Knows*, but there was a long period there when nobody knew if it would ever come out. Two directors of the publishing house were close friends of J. Edgar Hoover. So advance proofs were sent to the FBI, where they stayed for three months. Finally, Clyde Tolson called the publisher and said, 'This is a terrible thing, unpatriotic, a terrible slur on the bureau,' and things like that, but they could find no facts wrong, except for one thing I agreed to put a footnote on. Once we had agreed to that, which was the only specific point they could cite, they had no alternative but to let it be published. It was a great victory back then, although the book only sold about 15,000 copies, because it was still before its time."

In all his muckraking books and articles Cook has been idealogically and politically partisan, a fact he has never tried to hide. Together with McWilliams he always believed that passionate advocacy was a necessary part of muckraking, and both men have tried to use the facts in a particular situation to influence their readers to fight against what they believed to be wrong and support what they believed to be right. Such advocacy set free-lance muckraking apart from much less impassioned investigative reporting in newspapers, where the reporter was expected to let the facts speak for themselves.

"*The Nation* is not a news magazine," McWilliams once explained. "It is a journal of critical opinion. As a publication we are not well adapted to the needs of muckraking journalism. We have a small staff and meager resources. We have no full-time staff writers to assign to various subjects. We are unable to finance extensive research or investigation."

But McWilliams also told me before his retirement that "not a week passes that does not bring to the office clippings, documents, and miscellaneous intelligence from all parts of the country, in many cases from individuals who, so far as our records indicate, have never at any time been subscribers. So in that way I have a bigger staff than *Time* or *Newsweek*. It just happens to be an unpaid staff. The magazine has been around so long that people are attached to it. Frequently, and particularly back during the McCarthy period, information has come without a name or address of the sender in envelopes addressed simply to '*The Nation*, New York.' "

In 1964 "a friend in California" sent McWilliams a curious report by the state's attorney general, condemning the Hell's Angels motorcycle gang and "other disreputables," as growing menaces to the welfare of the state. Wondering what this was all about, McWilliams sent the report to a foot-loose free-lance writer then living in San Francisco, Hunter S. Thompson. McWilliams had never met Thompson, an unsuccessful novelist and former newspaperman who had been separated from jobs at several papers and *Time* magazine following monumental displays of temper in disputes with his editors. But McWilliams said he admired an essay Thompson had written for the *Realist*, "so I sent him the stuff on the

Hell's Angels and said, 'You might be interested in this.' I keep sending out queries like that to young writers, and I once found that out of 100 letters I sent, I got five or six pieces."

By Thompson's account "at that point I was stone-broke, writing fiction, living in a really fine little apartment in San Francisco— looking down on Golden Gate Park, just above Haight Street. The rent was only $100 a month—this was 1965, about a year before the Haight-Ashbury madness started—and I got a letter from Carey McWilliams, and it said, "Can you do an article on the Hell's Angels for us for $100?' That was the rent, and I was about ready to get back into journalism, so I said, 'Of course, I'll do anything for $100.'"

Thompson pushed himself into the gang's inner circle in their hangouts in San Francisco's industrial slums and began riding with them throughout California. He discovered a fascinating American subculture of "rejects, losers—but losers who turned mean and vengeful instead of just giving up." Their drinking and brawling was wild, although Thompson's research, including the searching out of original police records, disproved many of the reports of gang rapes and terrorizing of entire towns that had been reported as fact in the California attorney general's report and other articles. Thompson demolished the myth created in *Time, Newsweek,* and newspapers like the *New York Times* of "outlaw motorcyclists . . . the Menace . . . the hundred-carat headline" and substituted for it the equally fascinating and disturbing reality of the Hell's Angels' brutal alienation in a five-page article in the *Nation* on May 17, 1965, that immediately caught the attention of New York publishers.

"My mailbox piled up with book offers," according to Thompson. He took one and eventually wrote *Hell's Angels: A Strange and Terrible Saga,* which sold well and attracted considerable attention with its blend of old-fashioned investigating, contemporary history, popular sociology, and flashy narrative style. It led directly to Thompson's considerable success as a maverick author and star contributor to *Rolling Stone,* although as his writing and drug-taking lifestyle grew increasingly bizarre, Thompson moved light years away from Carey McWilliams's serious little magazine.

McWilliams also received unsolicited contributions from other writers who could find no respectable forum for what McWilliams has called "a piece with something to say that is not yet part of the general dialogue." Robert Sherrill said he always regarded the *Nation* "as a place of last resort, in the good sense of what that means." When it came time to decide where to sell a particular article idea, Sherrill said, "you didn't think of the *Nation* first, because of its small circulation and low pay. You turned to the *Nation* when you knew you had something out of the main channel. It is an unhappy circumstances generally, but the great virtue of the *Nation* is that it still is one of the few places you can go with those kind of pieces.

"It is very important, however, that McWilliams doesn't think of the *Nation* as a muckraking journal in the seamy, titillating manner of a Hearst Sunday supplement. What McWilliams really is doing is always taking a fresh look. He is seldom in the corner of an extreme. He's been accused of being a communist sympathizer by the far Right, but he is really not extreme.

"In fact, Carey himself is a dull subject in a way," Sherrill said. "I've never heard anything negative about him from anyone who knows him or has worked with him. And if he had a negative side, I'd tell you."

Sherrill probably would. The lanky, white-haired southerner whose acid wit is well known and feared by politicians and other journalists in Washington has made his reputation by saying in print what most other correspondents in the capital only dare gossip about at cocktail parties. In writing about the Alaska oil pipeline, for instance, Sherrill showed how both the project's supporters and opponents had lied in presenting exaggerated self-serving cases to a confused public. Sherrill's books include an irreverent biography of Lyndon Johnson, *The Accidental President*, published long before most Washington reporters ventured to criticize Johnson in print; an equally acerbic study of Hubert Humphrey, *The Drugstore Liberal*; and the controversial *The Saturday Night Special*, which savaged both the gun lobby *and* gun-control advocates who, Sherrill argued, were wrong to believe legislation could solve a problem so symptomatic of an underlying pathology of American society.

Sherrill caused his most mischief, however, with an article in the July 24, 1974, issue of the *New York Times* magazine, arguing that existing evidence of the 1969 Chappaquiddick Island drowning of Mary Jo Kopechne contradicted much of Senator Edward M. Kennedy's account of the accident. Working from records and accounts of the incident that had previously been made public, Sherrill, like Fred Cook at his best, simply analyzed the evidence more perceptively than had been done before. He asked questions about Kennedy's veracity, sobriety, and conduct during the investigation of the accident that other journalists (with the notable exception of Jack Anderson) had been chary to ask so directly in print. Washington newsmen became obsessed by Sherrill's article and its unspoken implication that five years earlier they had not subjected

"What McWilliams really is doing is always taking a fresh look."

Kennedy to the same scrutiny that Richard Nixon had to endure for Watergate. Editors were debating whether they should assign Watergate-wise investigative reporters to new inquiries into Chappaquiddick when Kennedy announced in September 1974, two months after the appearance of Sherrill's article, that he was withdrawing from consideration as a presidential candidate for 1976.

Sherrill told me he was surprised the *Times* magazine had printed the article. He had expected it be rejected and was ready to send it to the *Nation* instead. But Sunday editor Max Frankel said later he had specially commissioned just that kind of muckraking analysis from Sherrill, because "it became apparent to me that by the standards of Watergate we hadn't done right by Chappaquiddick."

It had also become apparent that the *Times* magazine and other mass-circulation, general-interest magazines were now ready to publish free-lance muckraking articles they certainly would have turned down a few years before. In January 1972 McWilliams had published a long article, "Kangaroo Grand Juries," by civil liberties lawyers Frank J. Donner and Eurgene Cerruti, who revealed how the internal-security division of the Nixon Justice Department had directed a nationwide witch hunt of young political activists, using federal grand juries to force them to testify about themselves and their friends or go to jail for contempt of court. The exposé won the *Nation* another Page One award. Thirteen months later the *New York Times* magazine printed a similar article, "The New Grand Jury: A Kind of Immunity That Leads to Jail," by Paul Cowan, who covered the same ground and gave credit to the *Nation*. Free-lance muckraking had made it into the mainstream.

By the mid-1970s the market for free-lance muckrakers had become vast and lucrative. Magazines like *Harper's* and the *Atlantic*, which had specialized in political, literary, and social commentary, were now publishing exposés of everything from drug experimentation on penitentiary prisoners to congressional lobbying of giant oil companies, from profiteering inside major universities to the rigging of Soap Box Derby races. Even a girlie magazine like *Penthouse* featured articles exposing domestic skullduggery of the CIA and the questionable issuing of less-than-honorable discharges to half a million Vietnam war veterans. The *New Yorker*, which had over the years published excerpts from muckraking books like Rachel Carson's *Silent Spring*, greatly increased the number of those excerpts and added original investigative reporting by both its own staff writers and free-lancers, until a majority of its weekly issues each year featured muckraking articles on such subjects as the My Lai massacre cover-up, defoliation in Vietnam, problems of the American legal system, the unaccountability of multinational corporations, the dangers of oil supertankers, nuclear energy safety and security problems, occupational diseases, and such endangered species as whales.

There were also new magazines devoted primarily to muckraking. *Ramparts*, which had been founded in 1962 as a forum to encourage reforms of the Catholic Church, was taken over by a former public relations expert and *San Francisco Chronicle* reporter, Warren Hinckle, III, who increased its circulation from 3000 to 300,000 with muckraking articles, slick packaging, and imaginative promotion. Discussions about trends in Catholicism were replaced by revelations of American atrocities in Vietnam and the CIA's secret financing of supposedly independent student and labor organizations like the National Student Association. The CIA story, *Ramparts'* most important exposé (although some of the information had first appeared in the *Nation* months earlier), made front-page news across the country and won the magazine the George Polk Memorial Award. Hinckle, an immense man with long black hair, a black eye patch, and a flamboyant manner, announced such *Ramparts* revelations at frequent press conferences in advance of their publication and ordered up outrageous magazine covers, such as one that depicted Christ on a cross in the middle of a Vietnam battlefield.

Hinckle ran *Ramparts* in a perpetual state of frenzy, brainstorming ideas for its articles, appearance, and promotion on the run as he traveled the country from the magazine's San Francisco offices to New York's Algonquin Hotel, wining and dining wealthy liberal patrons lured to underwrite the enormous debt Hinckle himself helped create with his chaotic direction of the magazine and his extravagant expense-account lifestyle. When the magazine's debt grew unmanageable, contributors went unpaid, and accuracy and credibility became lost under Hinckle's heavy hype, he was ousted during one of *Ramparts* frequent staff insurrections. Other editors came and went as the magazine reorganized financially and just managed to survive into the 1970s, publishing free-lance muckraking articles on such subjects as philanthropic foundations, environmental destruction, the ills of American capitalism, and even the shortcomings of the New Left.

In 1969 a quite different man than Hinckle—quiet, cautious, frugal Charles Peters, a West Virginia lawyer who had come to Washington as an official of the Peace Corps—left government to start the *Washington Monthly*, a new magazine "with a new purpose—to help you understand our system of politics and government, where it breaks down, why it breaks down, and what can be done to make it work." Working with a small staff and depending on the growing number of free-lancers in Washington, Peters examined in the *Washington Monthly* how the system has been exploited by defense contractors, other big businesses and big unions, and the highway, oil, dairy, and other lobbies in Washington. He also exposed how the system has failed to care for the needy, cope with crime, or work toward international peace. Peters encouraged critics inside the government, whom he called "whistle-blowers," to write articles for him exposing federal waste, mismanagement, and corruption, and periodically focused on shortcomings of the press, which Peters believed, even after Watergate, to be much too timid in its role as watchdog. Although run tightly, the small magazine has not been a big financial success, and Peters has kept it going by marketing articles reprinted from the magazine and soliciting help from foundations and wealthy patrons.

Ironically, both *Ramparts* and the *Washington Monthly* have ultimately suffered from the competition of the new muckraking efforts of newspapers, many mass-circulation magazines, and the highly successful, much more commercial "city magazines" like the *Washingtonian* in Peters's own backyard. *Philadelphia*, for example, had been a business community journal before it was taken over during the 1960s by a group of young editors and writers who used it as a vehicle for the kind of local investigative reporting that Philadelphia's newspapers had seldom before attempted. To almost everyone's surprise, *Philadelphia*'s business readers were captivated by the focus on local political scandals, organized crime, consumer fraud, and conflicts of interest. Local gossip items and film, theater, restaurant, and other recreational activity listings and reviews broadened *Philadelphia*'s circulation and made it by the late 1960s a fat monthly filled with lucrative national as well as local advertising. Although its great commerical success led to some diluting of the magazine's content with trendy, customer-pleasing light features, *Philadelphia* continued its muckraking, won four national Sigma Delta Chi Distinguished Service Awards for public service in magazine journalism, and doubtlessly was one reason why the *Philadelphia Inquirer*, after its purchase by the Knight newspaper chain, and the afternoon *Bulletin* greatly increased their local investigative reporting in the early 1970s.

New York, the most successful and influential of the city magazines, rose from the ashes of a dead newspaper, the *New York World Journal Tribune*, doomed successor to the *World Telegram and Sun, Journal American,* and the *Herald Tribune*, in which it had been a Sunday supplement. Clay Felker, a non-newspaperman who had worked for Viking Press, *Life,* and *Esquire*, became editor of *New York* in 1963 and remade it, while still part of the *Tribune*, into a brashly written magazine featuring the experimental impressionistic journalism of *Herald Tribune* writers like Tom Wolfe, Dick Schaap, and Jimmy Breslin. Wolfe, who had become bored with conventional newspaper reporting, followed his breakthrough *Esquire* magazine article on stock-car racing, "The Kandy-Kolored Tangerine-Flake Streamline Baby"—which began: "There Goes (Varoom! Varoom!) That Kandy-Kolored (Thphhhhhh!) Tangerine-Flake Streamline Baby (Rahghhh!) Around the Bend (Brummmmmmmmmm mmmmmmmmmmmm)"—with *New York* articles filled with loud sounds, vivid scenes and bizarre punctuation. There were pieces on the audience at a Rolling Stones concert, for example, and the habit of prisoners in the Women's House of Detention in Greenwich Village of yelling down to young men on the street outside.

Felker added to this cacophony his own first attempts at what he later characterized as "consumer journalism," beginning with an article he commissioned to match a catchy title suggested by a *Fortune* magazine article, "Con Edison—the Company You Love to Hate." Felker later wrote in a memoir of his early days at *New York* that "I had the advantage of having a reporter I had inherited from the *Journal American* who knew something about Con Edison . . . Thinking himself freed from the kind of restrictions that had been built into the *Journal American*, he went all out and did an absolute first-rate job, coming up with an appalling account of a company that was politically pernicious, backward in its services and arrogant to its customers." Con Edison put great pressure on the *World Journal Tribune*'s editors to kill or alter the series the reporter wrote, and they succeeded, according to Felker, in forcing "some severe editing in favor of Con Edison" in some but not all of the articles. Otherwise, the series ran intact, heralded by promotional ads on radio, and won prizes and attracted readers. "I discovered then that an article that put itself on the side of the readers could elicit enormous response," Felker later wrote.

Felker's opportunity to strike out on his own came rather suddenly, when the *World Journal Tribune* died in 1967 and Felker was left without his Sunday magazine. He used $6575 of his severance pay to buy the rights to the *New York* name and spent more than a year looking for money with which to revive the magazine. With the help of Armand G. Erpf, a Wall Street investment banker, Felker found enough investors, successfully conducted a public stock sale, and produced the first issue of an independent weekly, *New York*, on April 8, 1968. Several of Felker's favorite writers from *New York's Herald Tribune* days, including Wolfe, Breslin, and Peter Maas, were among the new magazine's first contributing editors and received stock in the venture.

Their impressionistic essays on New York personalities, sights, and sounds were combined with "consumer journalism" muckraking of local business, government, and the courts, and a myriad of popular reader services that featured reviews of movies, plays, books, and both *haute cuisine* and "good meals for $2.50 or less." There were also weekly listings of local events and entertainment, guides to bargain shopping, "taste tests" of everything from wines and beers to pizza and cheesecake, periodic evaluations of institutions like private schools and hospitals, and advice on such matters as renovating a house, buying a co-op apartment, or protecting against burglars, muggers, and car thieves. All this was unusually and attractively packaged inside catchy covers. The formula was an instant success, generating large circulation, advertising revenue, and profits for Felker and his investors. It also produced a proliferation of *New York* look-alikes across the country: *Boston,* the *Washingtonian, Cleveland,* the *Chicagoan,* the *Texas Monthly* (out of Austin), and others.

The best of what has been offered as muckraking in the city magazines has been daring and good, including Gail Sheehy's unmasking of the owners of Times Square massage parlors, peep shows, and hotels of prostitution in *New York*; exposés of white-collar criminals, incompetent judges, and unethical lawyers and doctors in the *Washingtonian*; and investigations of Texas legislators, professional criminals, and the state's newspapers in the *Texas*

Monthly. The worst has amounted to trendy gossip and self-indulgent "new journalism" versions of reality, such as the *Washingtonian*'s "wide-eyed investigation of strippers and B-girls" that turned out to be little more than a voyeur's prowl of tawdry Washington night life, or Gail Sheehy's notorious *New York* exposé of a prostitute and her pimp, "Redpants and Sugarman," who turned out to be fictional composite characters drawn from some observations and interviews and much imagination. The popularity of such writing has sometimes led to confusion of muckraking and "new journalism."

Felker is credited with coining the phrase "new journalism" to explain what Wolfe, Breslin, and others were writing in *New York*, and Wolfe expounded on it in essays there and in *Esquire*. Essentially, Wolfe described it as detailed reporting presented with the techniques of fiction: colorful style, extensive description, experimental use of language and punctuation, changing points of view, personal commentary from the writer, juxtaposed facts creating a desired dramatic effect, and even views from inside the minds of the characters in the narrative. Wolfe and other "new journalists" argued that such writing came nearer to presenting the reader the truth about a person or event than conventional, often dull who-what-where-when reporting and exposition. Too often, however, the "new journalist's" reality has been inaccurate in specific detail and shaped too much by his own ego. Even at their best, "new journalists" record only the surface realities of our times, without really digging for important and revealing facts.

"New journalism" and muckraking nevertheless have had one characteristic in common: whether with sexy writing or scandalous revelations, they both attract and titillate readers. One magazine, *New Times*, was expressly started in 1973 to become a national vehicle for both "new journalism" and muckraking. Founder George A. Hirsch, the money manager of *New York* before he lost a power struggle with Felker, raised $1.7 million in capital from several large banks and attracted such luminaries as Jimmy Breslin (who left *New York* himself following an ego struggle with Felker), Dick Schaap, Larry L. King, Nora Sayre, and Nicholas von Hoffman to be contributing editors. Although the content of *New Times* has been decidedly uneven, it has published muckraking articles on such varied subjects as the corruption of doctors by drug salesmen, radiation damage suffered by Navajo uranium miners, and damage done by overpopulation to the Southern California environment. Although it did not immediately attract as much advertising as

"I'm having more impact than at a newspaper . . . "

expected, its circulation grew steadily and the magazine remained strongly alive at this writing.

As the market for muckraking has grown, so have the ranks of free-lance muckrakers, some of whom have achieved recognition and financial success that has rivaled many "new journalists." One of those was Tad Szulc, for many years a star foreign correspondent for the *New York Times*, who covered the coup that exiled Juan Peron from Argentina, the overthrow of another dictator in Venezuela, and the crushing of the "Prague Spring" in Czechoslovakia by Soviet tanks. Szulc also engaged in investigative reporting uncharacteristic of many foreign correspondents, uncovering plans for the Bay of Pigs invasion in advance (the *Times* suppressed the story, although President Kennedy said afterwards that he and the country probably would have been better off if it had been printed) and disclosing that the United States was sending arms to Pakistan despite a State Department ban. Szulc's sources inside the government's top foreign policy circles were so good that the Nixon administration had his telephone tapped by the FBI. But his unorthodox diplomatic reporting techniques, unpopularity with officials like Henry Kissinger, and arguments with his editors over potentially explosive stories ultimately made him uneasy at the *Times*, despite his two decades on its staff.

Szulc began offering some of his more controversial information to magazine editors and book publishers and received encouraging responses. After landing several lucrative free-lance assignments and two book contracts, and receiving an unexpected inheritance, Szulc waited until his twentieth year at the *Times* ended—which earned him the equivalent of a year's wages in a lump sum from the newspaper's profit-sharing plan—and quit in late 1972. The four books and more than forty magazine articles he produced during his next two years of free-lance muckraking earned him an annual income of $50,000, more than enough to continue providing himself, his wife, and their two children with a comfortable life in their twelve-room Washington home. Even more important, Szulc said, was that he could "write what I want" about Kissinger, U.S. intervention into the internal affairs of Chile, other adventures of the CIA, and similar matters in publications ranging from *Foreign Policy*, the *New Republic* (of which he is now a contributing editor), and the *Columbia Journalism Review* to *Rolling Stone* and *Penthouse*. "I'm having more impact than at a newspaper," he said. "I like this life."

Free-lance muckrakers who fail to achieve Szulc's financial independence have had to continue to work for newspapers while moonlighting as free-lancers, or seek retainers and regular assignments as contributing editors to magazines, or gamble on writing a best-selling book, like Joseph Goulden's *Superlawyers*, that could provide a nest egg for several years of free-lancing. Beginning in the mid-1960s with the first of Ralph Nader's and Fred J. Cook's books, as well as the best-selling exposé of the CIA, *The Invisible Government* by David Wise and Thomas B. Ross, the number and sales success of muckraking books has steadily increased until a bumper crop appeared in 1974. That year the nation's bookstores were filled with muckraking books on the Watergate scandal (led by the million-dollar best-seller, *All the President's Men* by Bob Woodward and Carl Bernstein), the corruption investigation and resignation of Vice President Spiro T. Agnew (*A Heartbeat Away* by *Washington Post* reporters Richard M. Cohen and Jules Witcover), occupational diseases in industrial plants (*Expendable Americans* by *New Yorker* staff writer Paul Brodeur and *Muscle and Blood* by a twenty-seven-year-old free-lancer Rachel Scott), fraud and scandalous conditions in American nursing homes (*Tender Loving Greed* by a Cleveland, Ohio, community planning consultant, Mary Adelaide Mendelson), academic finances and politics (*Our Invaded Universities* by Texas free-lancer Ronnie Dugger), rampant fraud, theft, and mismanagement in the stock market (*The Great Wall Street Scandal* by a former securities analyst, Raymond Dirks, and writer Leonard Gross), the environmental dangers created by huge oil-carrying supertankers (*Supership* by free-lance shipping writer Noel Mostert), incompetence among the federal judiciary (*The Benchwarmers* by Joseph Goulden), and the aggrandizement of the power of independent public agencies by New York City public works czar Robert Moses (*The Power Broker* by former *Newsday* reporter Robert A. Caro), among many others.

Most of these books sold much better than the average for non-fiction and several were best-sellers. Several also opened up new subjects for muckraking by the mass media. *Tender Loving Greed* began as a modest investigation pursued by Mendelson with a small legacy from her mother's estate. Her first manuscript was contracted for and then rejected by a major publisher frightened off by the prospect of libel suits from nursing-home owners. Knopf later accepted a revised version, braved both threats of legal action from the nursing-home industry and denunciations from supposed public watchdogs—including the staff of the U.S. Senate Subcommittee on Long-Term Care—and published it. The book eventually caught the attention of newspaper investigative reporters who confirmed Mendelson's findings with front-page exposés in papers across the country, and new government investigations of nursing-home operators were begun in Congress and several states, including New York, where a major scandal with serious political ramifications was uncovered.

Occupational diseases, which kill an estimated 100,000 Americans each year, have received significant attention following publication of *Expendable Americans* and *Muscle and Blood*. Brodeur, on assignment from the *New Yorker*, examined in meticulous detail the asbestos industry, where factory workers inhale tiny fibers of the insulating and fire-resistant material and eventually suffer cancers of the lung, colon, or stomach. Brodeur showed how, despite years of warnings from independent medical researchers, asbestos companies have resisted expensive retooling to protect its workers from inhalation of the fibers. Scott, formerly a reporter for the *Baltimore Sun* specializing in industrial safety and environmental problems, quit her newspaper job to roam the country investigating occupational disease problems in the mining, auto manufacturing, foam rubber, printing, and other industries, pointing out the reluctance of most corporate executives to take the problem seriously. Both books were discussed in great detail in news magazines, book reviews, and on television, and led to a spate of investigative articles on occupational diseases.

The Power Broker, one of the most controversial and influential books of the 1970s, has called into question the history and journalism of New York City for the past half-century. Robert Caro, a native of Manhattan who won awards for his investigative reporting of suburban real estate frauds, became interested in the immense power exerted throughout the New York area by Robert Moses, who had never been elected to public office. Caro discovered in greater detail and on a much wider scale what Fred Cook had begun to write about years before. In collusion with mayors, governors, legislators, and business leaders, Moses used independent public works authorities, with their powers of condemnation and endless flow of money from tolls, legislative appropriations, and federal grants, to build highways, bridges, and housing projects throughout the New York area, including Long Island, which Moses criss-crossed with auto freeways and deprived of most public transportation. As a reporter for *Newsday*, Caro kept coming across evidence of Moses' power.

"I started getting interested in public works because I saw that they shaped things," Caro said in an interview with *Planning* magazine after *The Power Broker* was published. "When you build a road or a bridge, you have changed the city forever. Whenever I started investigating public works, the thread would start leading back to Robert Moses. You could never get to Robert Moses, because he was never directly connected, and his records, unlike the records of public officials, were closed, because he did it all through the public authorities.

"I was supposed to be a good investigative reporter," Caro said. "But, as I started to get more and more interested in why decisions crucial to Long Island were made, I could see this tremendous frustration . . . How could I make people understand that there's a fourth branch of government, public authorities, which is insulated from public opinion, which the public can't touch, which nobody can touch, and which has this immense power that's absolutely outside the democratic process? Wherever I went, whatever I started to look at, the trails started to lead back to Moses, and they always stopped before I could investigate them."

Caro needed time—much more time than a newspaper reporter could envision spending on a single project—to discover just how Moses inevitably worked his will. "You could never learn much about the decision-making process, since Moses' empire operated so secretly—just that Moses seemed to be the power behind every issue I looked into," Caro said. "It seemed impossible to really show the influence he had unless I wrote something on the scale of a book."

Caro won a Nieman Fellowship to study for a year with other journalists at Harvard, where he took urban planning courses that only increased his desire to investigate Moses' empire. "I sat in lecture halls and listened to planners explaining how highways or housing was built," he said, "and I realized how ridiculous it was. Rational planning considerations have nothing to do with it. Decisions were made for reasons far outside the planning process, like the hidden movements of banks, civic authorities, and politicians."

In 1967, while on a Carnegie Fellowship at the Columbia School of Journalism in New York, Caro began his arduous research. The project, which Caro first guessed might take two years, eventually consumed seven. He and his wife Ina conducted 522 interviews and studied countless city, state, and public authority records, including those of the Triborough Bridge and Tunnel Authority, which Moses had successfully kept secret for years. Caro doggedly pursued one confidential source after another to gain access to those records, which showed how Moses used the Triborough tolls to help finance his other public works projects rather than to pay off the bridge and tunnel, as well as other secrets of Moses' manipulation of public bodies. Meanwhile, Ina Caro found farmers and homeowners Moses had cavalierly dispossessed to build his highways and other projects during the 1920s and 1930s. Caro also conducted seven lengthy interviews with Moses himself in 1967 and 1968, but the older man abruptly broke off the dialogue after Caro began bringing up unflattering evidence he and his wife had gathered independently.

When Caro finished his 1296-page book its partial serialization by the *New Yorker* and subsequent publication by Knopf in 1974 made news in New York with its copious evidence of just how Moses had ruthlessly shaped the city. The book suffered only from excessive documentation in many places, which made it laborious to read, and from Caro's occasionally strident tone—flaws that seem to be endemic to muckraking books. Caro, a determined but modest and soft-spoken man, won both the Pulitzer Prize for biography and the Francis Parkman Award of the Society of American Historians for *The Power Broker*—ironic honors for an investigative biography and revisionist history, and new incentives for muckraking free-lance authors.

Muckraking books had become so popular with publishers and book buyers that one young man who saw the trend developing early has gotten rich in a very few years of working as an agent for muckraking authors. David Obst, the bearded, frenetic entrepreneur who marketed Seymour Hersh's Dispatch News Service stories on My Lai, sought out newspapermen and free-lance writers who had never had big-time book publishing contacts before and talked his way into New York publishers' offices with muckraking manuscripts like Woodward and Bernstein's *All the President's Men*, Daniel

Ellsberg's *Papers on the War*, and Colonel Anthony Herbert's *Soldier*. Obst sold a hundred books and took his 10 percent from millions of dollars in royalties during his first few years as an agent, operating out of a cubbyhole office in Washington while commuting to New York and a farm outside Wilmington, Delaware. He has often angered clients and dismayed publishers by disappearing on journeys across the country or around the world, but his ability to spot a highly salable subject before anyone else has enabled him to exploit handsomely what Seymour Hersh called the "muckraking mythology" of the 1970s.

One of Obst's typical Washington clients has been John D. Marks, co-author with ex-CIA agent Victor Marchetti of best-seller *The CIA and the Cult of Intelligence*. Marks was once a U.S. foreign service officer and an assistant to the State Department's director of intelligence before he resigned in 1970 to protest American policy in Southeast Asia. While working in the State Department, and later on Capitol Hill, Marks began leaking to Washington investigative reporters information about U.S. policies with which he strongly disagreed. He even described, in an article under the pseudonym Terry Pollack in the January 1973 issue of *Ramparts*, what it was like to be a "leaker."

Marks helped Marchetti write the CIA book because he believed the spy agency badly needed reforming. With the book's success, inadvertently aided by the CIA's attempts to censor parts of it, came lucrative free-lance writing opportunities. Marks began turning out muckraking articles about the CIA and American foreign policy-making for *Rolling Stone, Playboy,* and the *Washington Monthly*. His opinions on U.S. intelligence activities were sought out by television talk-show producers and presented in the pages of the *New York Times* and the *Washington Star*. Marks has also taken a bread-and-butter job with a Nader-like Capitol Hill group that is trying to establish itself as a watchdog of the intelligence establishment, and he has continued acting as a sought-after tipster for Washington investigative reporters.

For free-lance muckrakers unable to find such a job or write a best-selling book one financial resource is the Fund for Investigative Journalism. Founded by philanthropist-journalist Philip Stern (himself the author of *Rape of the Taxpayer, The Great Treasury Raid*, and other muckraking books) with money from the Stern Family Fund and several other foundations, the fund's board of Washington journalists has approved grants of a few hundred to many thousands of dollars for fresh investigative inquiries "into how the institutions of our society are performing," according to executive director Howard Bray.

Typical of the fund's beneficiaries was Harvey Katz, a former Justice Department lawyer who turned to free-lance muckraking in 1970. Katz received a grant to support several months of research into white-collar crime and Washington's criminal justice system, from which he produced a series of four articles for the *Washingtonian*. One of them, "Some Call It Justice," examined the competence of judges serving in courts in the Washington metropolitan area, and won for the magazine a Sigma Delta Chi Distinguished Service Award. In 1972 Katz received another Fund for Investigative Journalism grant that enabled him to investigate corruption in the Texas legislature and write both an article about it for the *Washingtonian* and a book, *Shadow Over the Alamo*.

However, publication of that book, for which David Obst was Katz's agent, suddenly imperiled Katz's career. A relatively minor figure mentioned in the book sued for libel, charging that Katz had confused him with someone else. Promotion and sales of the book were stopped immediately by the publisher, Doubleday. And Katz's expected royalties and a subsequent exposé of charities he did for Doubleday, entitled *Give*, have been tied up in the legal defense of the libel suit, which has cost both Katz and Doubleday many thousands of dollars in lawyers' fees and court costs. For Katz, years of work on two books produced nothing in collectable royalty income and made very little impact on the reading public.

Similar libel actions, including clearly unjustified nuisance suits, have been a crippling problem for many financially vulnerable free-lance muckrakers. Without the money and lawyers that, for example, major newspapers have to back up their investigative reporters, free-lancers can be wiped out by the expense of fighting a libel suit, even if they win in court. Under a standard clause in most book contracts, publishers can shift to the author most or all of the expenses of defending against libel suits and paying judgments in losing cases. Typically, Seymour Hersh had to pay his publisher, Random House, $7000 and his own lawyer another $3000 to fight a nuisance suit he eventually won in court against a soldier named in his book, *My Lai 4*, though Hersh was fortunate in that his book earned well over that amount.

Authors are justifiably vulnerable to libel suits if they carelessly defame someone with serious errors in published books, but many of the increasing numbers of suits that have been filed against muckraking authors are little more than attempts by controversial figures to stop unfavorable publicity resulting from entirely accurate accounts of their activities. Even if they are destined eventually to lose in court, they can in the meantime financially immobilize an author, put a good scare into his publisher, and possibly discourage anyone else from writing about them. Sol Stein, president of Stein and Day publishers, has said he also believes that a number of lawyers who have had their auto negligence business decrease because of no-fault insurance have now turned to libel law to become "ambulance chasers of the literary trade." Large newspapers and magazines can afford to fight back vigorously in court. But smaller publications and free-lance writers may be successfully intimidated into abandoning certain kinds of muckraking projects.

Finally, there is the instability and trendiness of the book business itself. Not all muckraking books become welcome best-sellers for their publishers; many more sell only a few thousand copies and are considered publishing failures, even though they may have a much greater, financially unmeasureable impact by drawing the attention of the readers that count, including other journalists, to the subject being examined. As the publishing business continues to be increasingly owned and dominated by conglomerates like RCA (Random House, Knopf, and Pantheon) and ITT (Bobbs-Merrill), who are determined to make these subsidiaries more profitable, there will undoubtedly be less and less of a market for this kind of marginal book.

Thus, the future of free-lance muckraking remains uncertain. To a great extent it will be determined by book and mass-circulation magazine editors and publishers, who are, in turn, heavily influenced by what they perceive to be the trend of the times. The outcome likely will be quite important, because the future of all investigative reporting may well depend on the fate of the free-lancers. From Fred Cook's first tackling the FBI and CIA to Seymour Hersh's uncovering the truth about My Lai, they have been the pathfinders for the new muckrakers.

8. The Future of Muckraking

Judging from the contents of its inside pages—folksy reports of family doings and farm life from part-time correspondents in Blair Branch, Linefork, and other mountain crossroads and hollows—the Whitesburg, Kentucky, *Mountain Eagle* would appear to be just another country weekly. But on its front page there have been muckraking stories that have justified the paper's motto, "It Screams." Editor Tom Gish, a fifty-year-old former United Press International reporter who bought the newspaper "on impulse" for $40,000 during a weekend home in Whitesburg in 1957, has crusaded against environmental damage caused by strip mining in the county, exploitation of miners by both the coal companies and the union, unchecked power of the giant Tennessee Valley Authority, and the casual brutality of local deputy sheriffs.

While the *Mountain Eagle* earned the loyalty of 5800 subscribers, including scattered admirers throughout the eastern United States, its muckraking angered most of those who hold power in Whitesburg and surrounding Letcher County. The newspaper was boycotted by many potential advertisers among local businessmen, and editor Gish, a gentle, round-faced man with glasses and a neatly trimmed beard, was barred from mine company offices, TVA record rooms, and county agency meetings. This hostility reached a climax in August 1974, when the *Mountain Eagle* office was burned by arsonists. Only after first refusing to investigate and then insinuating that Gish himself might be to blame did law enforcement officials finally issue warrants for four suspects, including a local deputy sheriff. With the continuing help of his wife Pat, several other relatives, and young volunteers from colleges and jobs elsewhere, Gish continued publishing the *Mountain Eagle* under a new motto, "It Still Screams!" But the newspaper remained in a precarious financial position.

Of course, Tom Gish has not been the nation's only unpopular muckraker. Other crusading country editors have been run out of

232

their towns by advertiser boycotts and print-shop vandalism. In cities like Washington, St. Louis, and Los Angeles investigative reporters who angered law enforcement officials with police, court, and prison exposés have been subpoenaed to court and ordered to reveal confidential sources for their stories or go to jail. In Indianapolis and Philadelphia reporters who made local officeholders their muckraking targets have subsequently become victims of police harrassment, false arrests, and even criminal indictments on trumped-up charges. Numerous muckrakers have been served or threatened with financially crippling libel suits by wealthy subjects trying to keep their names and misdeeds out of print. Investigative reporters who challenged the Nixon administration too often were subjected to telephone wiretaps, audits of their income tax returns, and public attacks on their credibility. Nixon White House consultant and Watergate burglar E. Howard Hunt has even told of aborted plans to drug or poison muckraking columnist Jack Anderson.

Although the American public made Woodward and Bernstein celebrities in the wake of Watergate, it has not entirely supported the mission of the new muckrakers. Even after the release of the Nixon White House tape transcripts, which irrefutably confirmed almost everything that investigative reporters had written about the Watergate cover-up and Richard Nixon's role in it, half the people interviewed in national opinion polls believed the media's coverage of the affair had been excessive and biased, and that the press generally had been less fair to Nixon than had the courts or Congress. From 1972 through the summer of 1974 it had been left to the press to make public most of the ugly details of Watergate, while the courts and Congress moved slowly against the cover-up conspirators, and Nixon defended himself by attacking the press. So the press became, in the public mind, Nixon's inquisitor.

"If the press sometimes seemed obsessed with Watergate," wrote editor Henry Grunwald in a *Time* magazine essay before public impeachment proceedings began during the traumatic summer of 1974, "the reason is partly to be found in the default of other American institutions, including Congress. No thunderous voices have lately been heard on Capitol Hill. Congress seems to be floundering, anxiously listening for public opinion . . . It almost seems as if new outrages were required each week to keep the whole case real. This has created a moral and psychological vacuum that the press has filled. Congress, long subdued by the presidency and unaccustomed to lead, has been quite content to sit back and let the press perform as the cutting edge against Watergate."

Although investigative reporters and their editors saw the final resolution of the Watergate affair as clear justification of their mission, others expressed considerable concern that the new trend might go too far. Veteran journalist John Osborne, the *New Republic*'s thoughtful Nixon watcher, concluded that the press played a "necessary and proper" role in the Watergate investigation but added, "I have to say at the same time that they're like dogs who have scented blood and are running the fox right down to the death." A suburban Washington man writing to the *Washington Post* asked: "Now that the *Post* has dispatched Richard Nixon with one-sided journalism, what new crusade will the *Post* undertake? There are many of us out here who are honestly fearful since we know that the newspapers and broadcast stations have become both completely invincible and wholly unaccountable for their actions. Will it be nuclear power? Or will the *Post* somehow decide that the farmers are responsible for our high food prices?"

The next targets, ironically, turned out to be Henry Kissinger, Nelson Rockefeller, and the men who run the Central Intelligence Agency, all of whom had important friends in the media. Stories about Henry Kissinger's role in the telephone-tapping of government aides and newspaper reporters, for example, prompted Kissinger allies in the press, including columnists Marquis Childs, James Kilpatrick, and Joseph Alsop, to decry such investigative reporting, which Alsop said was the result of the "enormous, Watergate-induced self-importance of the American press."

When investigative reporters began digging into the past of Vice President-designate Nelson Rockefeller and uncovered his habit of slipping expensive gifts to public officials and others in positions to further Rockefeller family interests, there were more howls. "At the moment, this town is manic with suspicion," complained Washington columnist Tom Braden, himself a recipient of Rockefeller largesse. "Rumors see print under no greater legitimacy of source and fact than 'It has been reported . . .' Newspapermen scramble over each other to call upon those who ever knew Nelson Rockefeller and to ask whether he gave Christmas presents—'What? How much do you think it cost?' Nobody is above suspicion; the higher the office or the more seemingly unimpeachable the character, the greater the suspicion." CBS television commentator Eric Sevareid declared that the Rockefeller confirmation hearings had been helped to "drag on" by the stories of "journalists who, if they can't be Solzhenitsyn, want to be prize-winning, gimlet-eyed investigative reporters."

Even *Washington Post* publisher Katharine Graham, in a

December 1974 speech to the Magazine Publishers Association, expressed serious misgivings about the treatment of Rockefeller. Graham, a staunch supporter of investigative reporting generally, observed that "there is a new sensitivity to wrongdoing abroad in the land, and that is obviously to the good." But she questioned the wisdom of "a new and rather indiscriminate emphasis on disclosure as the index of fitness for public office." She said that "an emphasis on candor and an absence of wrongdoing, although primary and vital, can distort the process of assessment if it is carried to extremes and distracts the public and press from other, equally significant questions." Graham also wondered aloud whether, in the new muckraking atmosphere, there had been a "tendency to jump on Rockefeller . . . to compensate for (press) failures in the past or to avoid the possible sin of underplaying what might be tomorrow's scandal."

The efforts of investigative reporters in 1975 to reveal clandestine activities of the nation's intelligence agencies caused national public television reporter Carolyn Lewis to complain that such reporters seem "unable to function without a government scapegoat to publicly humiliate and denounce." She wrote in a column contributed to the *Washington Post* that

we have become addicted to incessant scandal and shock . . . We need a "fix," but Watergate is gone. So now, each day, we seek new "highs," new media excitements. We dig and probe and prod and cast a jaundiced eye on everyone and everything . . . .
The headlines imply it all: the FBI is wicked, the CIA is evil, and NSA is so secret, it is positively satanic . . . Clutching our tumultuous breasts, we thunder our journalistic hymn: "We of the media shall give you the truth and the truth shall make you free." . . . But do we really have to clothe our findings in religious fury and the ecstasy of self-sainthood? Do we have to besmirch and besmudge even the honest, innocent bureaucrat who did the right thing as he saw it, even though you and I in hindsight think he was wrong? Do we have to sanctify the paranoia of the fearful and stoke up the slumbering fires of the subterranean haters?

Was this a foreboding echo of the words of Theodore Roosevelt, which helped end the brief era of the original muckrakers seventy years ago? "The man who never does anything else, who never thinks or speaks or writes save of his feats with the muckrake," Roosevelt had warned, "speedily becomes, not a help to society, not an incitement to good, but one of the potent forces of evil."

There is legitimate concern that excessive muckraking zeal can lead to serious mistakes and abuses. While pursuing Watergate Bob Woodward and Carl Bernstein wrongly named three innocent men as recipients of wiretap transcripts. The Santa Ana, California, *Register* published a widely reprinted but completely unsubstantiated report that Senate investigators were looking into the possibility that surplus campaign funds had been used by President Nixon to purchase his San Clemente estate. During the last days of a recent West Virginia gubernatorial primary, the *Charleston Daily Mail* published a grossly inaccurate account of an allegedly improper, supposedly $500,000 land deal made by one candidate for governor, who lost the election by 10,000 votes before it became clear that he had done no wrong and had earned only $14,000 from the land investment.

Even when an investigative reporter has drawn a deadly accurate bead on his target, as Seymour Hersh had in his exposé of illegal domestic spying by the CIA, he might be tempted to push flimsy follow-up stories onto the front page in an advocate's effort to keep his charges alive until they can be proven. Hersh followed his original December 1974 CIA domestic spying revelations with twenty-one front-page and eight inside-section stories, most of which contained little new information. Several of these stories were no more than overblown reports of reactions to Hersh's original story, while others misleadingly presented as new revelations information that had been published in other newspapers, books, and even the *Times* itself as much as two years earlier.

There is also the question of whether there can be too much of even the most meticulously responsible muckraking. Might the nation become so inundated with stories of scandal that citizens will despair or become jaded or lose confidence in their society? Such worries presuppose the existence of considerably more investigative reporting than now actually goes on. Despite the many examples of an obvious resurgence of muckraking in the United States in recent years, the fraction of the nation's newsmen involved in investigative reporting is still quite small, and many of the most influential institutions and powerful forces in our society have so far escaped muckraking scrutiny.

While concerns about the volume, effects, and propriety of muckraking "are legitimate for both the (journalism) profession and the public," concluded Michael Levett, author of a recent study of U.S. investigative reporting, "they may in fact be an instance of locking the barn door before the purchase of the horse." Levett, who helped make the study for the Urban Policy Research Institute in Los

Might the nation becom so inundated with stories of scandal that citizens will despair . . . ?

Angeles, said this was "another way of saying that neither the quality nor the quantity of investigative reporting on local, state or regional levels has reached a stage justifying the general caveats aimed at investigative journalism." Levett contended that "most media . . . still barely—if at all—support serious investigative activities."

Even in Washington, there are not many muckraking reporters— no more than a few dozen in a press corps of hundreds—and only a very few of them, Woodward and Bernstein at first and perhaps five to ten others later, were involved in the investigative reporting of Watergate. Both the White House and the Congress are covered by large crowds of reporters, but the truth of presidential statements, the way decisions are arrived at in the White House, the dangerous senility and venality of some powerful congressional leaders, and the way legislation is really enacted on Capitol Hill are seldom investigated by journalists on those beats. The federal regulatory agencies, which wield immense influence over both citizens and private business, are barely covered at all, much less subjected to the scrutiny of investigative reporters—with the notable exceptions of Morton Mintz of the *Washington Post*, Steve Aug of the *Washington Star*, and a few *Wall Street Journal* writers.

Away from government the picture dims more. Aside from aggressive, probing coverage of the *Wall Street Journal* and scattered consumer reporting by a few newspapers, private business is almost never examined. When the Watergate Special Prosecutor's office moved against several large corporations later convicted of making illegal campaign contributions, there was scant attention from the media. It was left to the Securities and Exchange Commission to reveal that American corporations had spent millions on illegal campaign contributions in U.S. elections and huge bribes to foreign officials to do business overseas.

height of interest in the public officials caught in the
net, free-lance writer Andrew Kopkind pointed out in
journalism review, that "at least a score of business
have run through the Watergate mill so far. But despite
crucial role in the system of scandal, they remain unknown and
actually ignored by a press that is attracted only by political stars.
While the minutest detail of the hierarchy of the Committee to
Reelect the President was investigated and exposed (by investigative
reporters), the inner sancta of Ashland Oil . . . Phillips Petroleum
. . . Gulf Oil . . . and the Carnation Company were unentered.

"What happens in Business is nobody's business," Kopkind wrote.
"The impenetrability of the 'private sector' is a canon of the American
Creed as it is custom of reportage. Any comparison of the press
treatment of executives and politicians in Watergate and attendant
operations shows just how little attention is paid to the mechanisms
of corporate life . . . Decisions made in the great corporate offices of
the country are certainly as significant for public policy as those made
in many governmental agencies or legislative councils." Citing
another example, Kopkind added, "what went on in David
Rockefeller's bank had as much to do with the quality of life for the
people of New York as what went on in Nelson Rockefeller's capitol
office. And yet the bank chairmanship is given only a fraction of the
scrutiny afforded the state governorship."

The *Columbia Journalism Review* pointed out in 1974 that "at
perhaps hundreds of papers and (broadcast) stations where editors
relish exposing crooked politicians caught with their hands in the till,
there's not a moment's thought about exposing supermarket
operators who put their thumbs on the scale. There's hardly a paper
or a station in the nation that fails to report fluctuations in the prime
interest rate (set by the U.S. Federal Reserve system for banks
borrowing from it), yet one would be hard-pressed to find more than
half a dozen that report, by name, changes in the rates (charged by
banks) for mortgages or other consumer loans." In sum, investigative
reporters have revealed little about what goes on inside banks,
corporations, factories, or supermarkets, which can exert at least as
much control over our daily fortunes as government.

Why in this new era of muckraking is there not even more
investigative reporting? Many newspaper publishers and broadcast
station owners still discourage it, because they do not want to anger
friends in business or local government or because they fear losing
advertising revenue. According to the Urban Policy Research

Institute study, some publishers may allow exposés of "petty payoffs and welfare abuse but draw the line at stories dealing with the institutional foundations of a city or state, the relationships of banks, corporations, elected officials and—perhaps—newspapers." Even when it does not antagonize advertisers, investigative reporting can prove costly to a publisher by tying up a newspaper's highest salaried reporters for weeks on end, possibly forcing the paper to hire more reporters for routine news coverage. Editors and publishers surveyed by the institute also feared losing money defending libel suits that could arise from investigative stories. Most of them doubted that muckraking would increase circulation at all, much less enough to offset the various financial risks they enumerated.

Many reporters and editors have shied away from investigative reporting because it seems too tedious, difficult, lonely, and unpredictable in payoff. Editors, who seldom are former investigative reporters, often have trouble conceiving worthwhile investigative assignments, directing the research productively, giving the reporter psychological support, or shaping the resulting story into the strongest and yet safest form. The investigative reporter himself runs the risk of alienating valuable news sources, withstanding threats or worse from targets of his stories, or becoming ostracized by colleagues who are jealous of his freedom from daily deadlines or the covering of mundane events.

Perhaps for these reasons, good investigative reporters are a breed apart—for example, Jack Nelson of the *Los Angeles Times* Washington bureau, who first worked for the Biloxi, Mississippi, *Daily Herald* at age eighteen and was soon uncovering gambling payoffs and slot machine concession corruption. He has been threatened with death by racketeers in Mississippi, assaulted by a burly deputy sheriff in Georgia, and besmirched in Washington by the late FBI Director J. Edgar Hoover, who tried repeatedly to persuade the *Los Angeles Times* to fire him. Nelson, a cocky little man who stands five feet, nine inches tall and weighs 135 pounds, braved these adversities and others to write about vice and corruption, the Ku Klux Klan, violations of civil liberties by the FBI, and Nixon administration lawbreaking during the Watergate scandal. Stories Nelson wrote at age twenty-four for the *Atlanta Constitution* about corruption in Liberty County, Georgia, produced twenty-two indictments of local officials and organized criminals. A later series of articles revealing horrible conditions in the huge Milledgeville State Hospital in Georgia won Nelson a Pulitzer Prize in 1960.

Nelson, a classic loner, was one of the few newspaper reporters doing investigative work in the 1950s and early 1960s and one of the first to go beyond exposés of vice and Justice Department leaks of information about organized crime. In 1970, for example, Nelson turned aside warnings and pleas for secrecy from his sources in Justice, the FBI, and the Anti-Defamation League to reveal in detail how criminal informants were paid $36,000 by the FBI to trap two Ku Klux Klan hit men in the process of planting a bomb at the home of a Jewish businessman in Meridian, Mississippi. The Ku Klux Klan agents, a man and a woman, were killed in a bloody shootout when the trap was sprung, which is why the FBI and the Anti-Defamation League tried to keep secret the fact that paid informants had set them up.

Nelson also is something of a generalist who covers a variety of issues in Washington, in addition to continuing his investigative reporting. Instead of disappearing from the *Los Angeles Times* for months while pursuing a single investigation, he balances several inquiries at once and covers occasional breaking news stories, which prevents him from sinking into the typical investigative reporter's rut. Saul Friedman is a similar kind of Washington bureau reporter for the Knight newspaper chain who broke several important investigative stories during the federal investigation of former Vice President Spiro T. Agnew. He too believes that full-time investigative reporters can become too isolated from their colleagues, their readers, and reality. Too often, they end up writing "long, exhaustive pieces that are not read by anyone but contest judges," he said. Morton Mintz of the *Washington Post* is still another reporter who mixes muckraking with daily coverage of Washington—in his case the regulatory agencies and congressional committees that deal with multinational corporations, antitrust investigations, product safety, and consumer protection. He keeps up with the news on his beat while also pursuing his own beneath-the-surface investigations of wrongdoing. Mintz believes there is too much for him to report to remove himself entirely from daily coverage.

At the other extreme, of course, are investigative reporters who concentrate on a single subject for months or even years, like Woodward and Bernstein on Watergate, Seymour Hersh on the defense and intelligence establishments, or Denny Walsh, among others, on organized crime and its connections to business, unions, and politics. There have also been teams of reporters formed to carry out a specific investigation, like the group of six reporters and editors of the weekly *Sun* papers in Omaha that penetrated the financial secrecy of Boys Town. After months of research the *Sun* team found that that well-known institution for disadvantaged youths, which sends out pathetic-sounding fund-raising letters around Christmas each year, had an annual income of $26 million, a net worth of more than $200 million, and untold millions of dollars lying around earning interest. The *Sun* stories prompted the Boys Town board to invest $70 million in new philanthropic projects for children and won the *Sun* papers a Pulitzer Prize. A similar *Indianapolis Star ad hoc* team—which included a police reporter, a science writer, a local government reporter, a feature writer, and a photographer—won the Drew Pearson investigative reporting award in 1974 and a Pulitzer Prize in 1975 for a year-long investigation of corruption and mismanagement in the Indianapolis police department and the county prosecutor's office.

The growing trend among newspapers and news magazines, however, has been to form more lasting, independent investigative reporting teams that, like the pair of Donald Barlett and James Steele, tackle whatever subject seems important or topical at the moment. These elite teams may operate quite independently of the rest of their newspaper's staffs and more or less direct themselves. The larger teams, like those of *Newsday* or the *Boston Globe*, even have their own editors, researchers, and secretaries.

The forerunner of these special teams was the flying squad of muckrakers assembled by *Life* magazine in its dying days during the late 1960s. The stars of that team were William Lambert, a middle-aged, former government investigator with good contacts in the Nixon administration; Sandy Smith, a burly Chicago newspaper veteran who specialized in investigative stories about the Mafia during two decades with the *Tribune* and *Sun-Times*; and Denny Walsh, a tough-talking, cigar-smoker who shared a Pulitzer Prize for helping uncover labor union corruption for the *St. Louis Globe-Democrat*. Lambert, Smith, and Walsh had all made many good friends in the Justice Department and FBI during their years of reporting on organized crime activities, so the *Life* team, under the direction of Russell Sackett, focused mostly on Mafia and big-name criminal figures and their connections to prominent politicians— including mayors, governors, congressmen, senators, and a judge. Smith produced a major *Life* series on organized crime, entitled "The Mob." Walsh explored St. Louis Mayor Alfonso Cervantes's dealings with organized crime figures and Ohio Governor James Rhodes's questionable use of campaign money. Lambert won a national prize for exposing the relationship between convicted stock manipulator Louis Wolfson and then U.S. Supreme Court Justice Abe Fortas, including the fact that Fortas, while sitting on the court, was paid $20,000 from the Wolfson Family Fund, a tax-free foundation set up by Wolfson and his brothers. After Lambert's *Life* story appeared, Fortas, who was the choice of his close friend, President Lyndon Johnson, to become Chief Justice, was forced to resign from the Court instead.

Life's investigative reporting team consumed hundreds of thousands of dollars each year in salaries and cross-country travel expenses and drew $80 million in libel suits. However, *Life*'s editors and publisher, the Luce communications conglomerate, hoped to use what they called the "Blue Team" to boost the magazine's prestige and attract badly needed new advertising. "*Life* was convinced that investigative reporting was profit-making," Denny Walsh said years later. "They put the Blue Team on the rubber chicken circuit to show us to the advertisers."

But ultimately muckraking, too, proved unprofitable for *Life*. It failed to attract sufficient advertising to keep the magazine from folding, and the "Blue Team" scattered. Sandy Smith rebounded the most successfully, taking his Justice Department contacts to *Life*'s sister news magazine, *Time*. Walsh on the other hand, floundered at the *New York Times*. He produced only a handful of stories that contained more suspicions than facts before being fired over a story about San Francisco Mayor Joseph Alioto that the *Times* refused to publish. Walsh later went to work for the *Sacramento Bee*.

The oldest and most effective newspaper investigative reporting team has been maintained since February 1967 by the tabloid-sized Long Island paper, *Newsday*. Begun just a few months after former White House aide Bill Moyers took over direction of *Newsday*, which is owned by the wealthy Guggenheim family, the team was given three reporters, a file clerk-researcher-secretary, and its own office. There, under the direction of its own editor, Robert W. Greene, a rotund veteran investigator from the Senate Rackets committee in Washington, the *Newsday* team concentrated first on zoning practices in fast-growing Long Island townships. It quickly became clear that developers were bribing local officials to obtain rezonings for new construction, and after two years of stories, seven persons were convicted in Long Island courts, thirty public officials resigned from office, and about twenty new local laws were enacted to better curb conflicts of interest. For their work the *Newsday* team won the 1970 Pulitzer Prize.

After a 1971 investigation that resulted in a six-part series on the questionable financial dealings of Richard Nixon's friend, Bebe Rebozo, and Senator George A. Smathers of Florida, the "Greene team," as it was called at *Newsday*, was selected to be the nucleus for an extraordinarily ambitious project conceived by Moyers's successor, publisher William Attwood: It was to follow the trail of illegal heroin from the poppy fields of Turkey to the streets of Long Island and discover why the drug traffic can't be stopped.

In all, fourteen *Newsday* staff members and $100,000 in expenses, in addition to the salaries of the participants, were committed to the project. Greene headed a three-man team that went to Turkey, after a three-week, five-day-a-week, six-hour-a-day, Berlitz course in Turkish. For three months the group lived in a rented house on the outskirts of Istanbul and traversed Turkey, risking their lives interviewing poppy farmers, opium dealers, and clandestine heroin chemists about who the illegal traffickers were and how they operated. The reporters then repeated the process in investigating the "French Connection" route to the United States, during three more months on the south coast of France near Marseilles. Another part of the *Newsday* team ranged from Long Island to Washington, D.C., Miami, and Mexico to discover how the heroin entered the United States and reached New York's streets. The two groups then met back in the paper's Garden City offices to write their story on how social conditions and official corruption and malfeasance in several countries made it all but impossible to block what they called "The Heroin Trail." The resulting series of articles, which ran in *Newsday* in 1973, won a 1974 Pulitzer Prize and was published the same year by Signet as a paperback book.

Newsday's executives believe that such muckraking *has* increased their newspaper's prestige and readers. Greene, who has become an investigative reporting guru, giving frequent interviews and lectures on the subject, has said: "It is not only a matter of increasing circulation but of not losing out to electronics. TV can and will cover immediate beat stories of interest with greater and greater speed. Newspapers must establish themselves as delivering something else, investigative and interpretative stories, in order to stay alive."

Greene also believes that this is not a difficult or mysterious task for any self-respecting newspaper to undertake. "While a few good stories are generated by tips," he told prospective investigative reporters and their editors at an American Press Institute seminar, "most preplanned investigations originate with the paper itself. When a newspaper employs reporters, there is a reasonable presumption that these reporters are trained observers. These reporters should be able to detect or at least smell unusual happenings, patterns of events on their routine beats. And they should be able to learn what things are bothering people and what people suspect is going on, even though they cannot always prove it. It is largely from this net of information that investigative stories are born. And once a paper commits itself to this type of story, not only will one story lead to another, but also an encouraged public will begin to generate tips leading to more."

In the late 1960s the *Boston Globe* started a "Spotlight Team" that closely resembles the Greene team: three reporters supervised by one of their number, a research secretary, and their own office. The *Globe* team won a 1972 Pulitzer Prize for a series of articles on municipal corruption in Somerville, Massachusetts, and it has claimed, overall, responsibility for the indictment of twenty-nine people, the censure of three judges, and the defeat of one prominent politician at the polls. For several years the *Chicago Tribune* also has operated various investigative "task forces" that have produced exposés of everything from police brutality to voter fraud in that scandal-ridden city.

In 1967 the Associated Press began a national investigative reporting team based in Washington. Although it once included ten reporters, it has shrunk considerably since Seymour Hersh resigned, James Polk became a free-lancer, and Jean Heller moved to the Cox newspaper chain and then *Newsday*. With the Associated Press unwilling to spend any more money on what had once been a pet project of AP general manager, Wes Gallagher, Brooks Jackson remained the only outstanding member of a four-reporter team.

Generally, however, the trend toward muckraking teams has continued, with the *Cleveland Plain Dealer* and the *Providence Journal* and *Evening Bulletin* among the papers starting new ones during 1974. It was unclear, however, how much these would increase the quality or even the quantity of investigative reporting. The formation of supposedly new teams at some newspapers amounted to little more than a reshuffling of reporters already doing occasional investigative work or the awarding of new titles without committing sufficient time, resources, or mandate to produce real muckraking. Judging from stories they produced, other teams became so isolated in their quarantined offices that they generated only rather stale exposés of long-recognized problems rather than breaking new ground. Investigative teams also ran the risk of overplanning and overcoordinating, which could result in less investigating and stories of relatively little consequence.

A similar fate can, of course, befall lone reporters working without close supervision or the temporary relief of noninvestigative work. Such journalists often wind up running in circles, another reason why in this new era of muckraking they have not expanded significantly beyond organized crime, traditional corruption in government, or obvious wastes of the taxpayers' money. There has been a natural tendency, even among investigative reporters, to take the path of less resistence where others have already blazed a trail.

One way to combat these problems and help investigative reporters remain as productive and flexible as possible is to integrate them with other writers in the newsroom, so that they keep in touch with daily developments in the community and the rest of the world. The *Washington Post*, with about 100 reporters on its metropolitan and national news staffs, has only two truly full-time investigative reporters—Bob Woodward and Ronald Kessler. Both work with everyone else in the *Post*'s large main newsroom, exchanging ideas with reporters covering daily events. Both Woodward and Kessler also work with a variety of editors, which avoids special relationships that can isolate an investigative reporter or remove the necessary distance between him and a vigilant editor.

Meanwhile, at any one time several other *Post* reporters are working on investigative assignments, frequently as an outgrowth of their regular coverage of a specific beat or subject area. Fred Barbash and Edward Walsh, the senior metropolitan reporters covering Maryland's government and politics, have done the investigative reporting that revealed, consistently ahead of the rest of the media, important details of a federal investigation of Governor Marvin Mandel. Barbash uncovered evidence of conflicts of interest involving Mandel and some of his close friends in business that federal prosecutors had not yet discovered. The prosecutors subsequently incorporated this information into their investigation and November 1975 criminal indictment of Mandel. Walsh and Richard Cohen, another metropolitan reporter then covering Maryland government, did the *Post*'s investigative reporting of the earlier federal prosecution of Spiro T. Agnew. They disclosed much of the evidence against Agnew, as well as his plea-bargaining with the government. Walsh and Barbash have periodically produced other investigative stories: on Maryland election campaign financing, nursing homes in the state, mismanagement of the state health department, and lobbying pressures, conflicts of interest, and scuttling of reforms in the Maryland legislature. At the same time they have kept up their daily coverage of state government and

Assigning investigative tasks to regular reporters assures they will have plenty to keep them busy during less productive stages of an investigation.

politics, maintaining the contacts and understanding of Maryland affairs that has given them a strong edge over everyone else.

Similarly, the *Post* reporter covering Washington, D.C.'s City Hall revealed in investigative stories that a nominee for deputy mayor had not paid his city income taxes for years; and the reporter covering local courts has done extensive investigative reporting of judicial misconduct. The reporter covering housing news has revealed fraud in the sale of condominiums in the Washington area, mismanagement of the federal government's "new town" development program, and "reverse blockbusting" by white real estate dealers driving low-income blacks out of "renewed" Washington neighborhoods. Even the reporter on the special Bicentennial beat has mixed stories of celebrations, historical observances, and human interest with revelations of costly mismanagement in government Bicentennial commissions and the crass, sometimes fraudulent exploitation of the event by some businesses and promoters.

Assigning investigative tasks to regular reporters assures they will have plenty to keep them busy during less productive stages of an investigation. This is essential for smaller newspapers that could never afford to assign any of their reporters to investigative reporting full-time. At larger newspapers increasing the number of reporters able to do investigative reporting improves newsroom morale and increases the number of productive exposés the paper can undertake.

Implementing such a policy, however, requires close, expert supervision by editors able to train reporters in investigative techniques and make certain they are not away too long from their normal assignments on wild goose chases. To help editors and reporters acquire these skills, the American Press Institute, supported by newspaper publishers, has periodically conducted intensive seminars. In addition, about a dozen editors and reporters with experience in these areas recently formed a national Investigative Reporters and Editors group, which intends to set up a clearinghouse for information on muckraking techniques and projects and conduct national meetings and seminars. Among its founders are Jack Anderson and Les Whitten, David Burnham of the *New York Times* and Harley Bierce and Myrta Pulliam of the Pulitzer Prize-winning *Indianapolis Star* investigative reporting team, who first thought of the idea and are running the new venture.

Investigative reporting has also been encouraged by a variety of journalism reviews that have sprung up in recent years—ranging from the mass-market *Columbia Journalism Review*, a slick magazine published out of Columbia University's graduate School of Journalism in New York, and [MORE], a privately owned tabloid published in New York, to struggling local reviews started by groups of reporters in Philadelphia, Chicago, St. Louis, Minneapolis-St. Paul, Denver, Dallas, Houston, Los Angeles, San Francisco, and Honolulu, among others. Unfortunately, many of these local reviews have already failed financially. Assisted in part by grants from the Fund for Investigative Journalism in Washington while they were alive they exposed unprofessional behavior, conflicts of interest, and self-censorship of journalists, broadcasters, and media owners; in some cases reporters writing voluntarily for these local reviews endangered their jobs by sharply criticizing the performances of their own newspapers. Occasionally, some of these publications even did the kind of local investigative reporting that newspapers in the same cities were not yet willing to undertake. For example, in 1969, the *Chicago Journalism Review* (the nation's oldest local review, founded by reporters there in 1968, and one of the most recent to go under, in 1975) revealed that a special Chicago police squad had infiltrated, wiretapped, and pilfered records from antiwar groups in Chicago in the mid-1960s. The *Chicago Daily News* became the first daily newspaper in the city to "break" that same investigative story six years later, in the spring of 1975.

Outside the mainstream of mass media are other publications engaged in notably competent investigative reporting that could provide valuable tips and even competition for newspaper reporters and editors. Several examples can be found in the professional and trade press, which has been wrongly assumed by many to consist only of uncritical house organs. *Modern Medicine*, an international

journal for physicians published in Minneapolis, has produced a
series of award-winning investigative reports on the poor treatment
of Vietnam veterans by military and Veterans' Administration
hospitals as well as related problems of Vietnam veterans. *Overdrive*,
a national 60,000-circulation magazine for independent truckers
published out of Los Angeles, has printed numerous articles by
investigative reporter Jim Drinkhall revealing fraudulent loans and
financial assistance to organized crime figures by the giant Teamsters
Union pension fund. Some of these reports, which have appeared
incongruously amid technical articles, truck ads, and cheesecake
photos, have led to federal investigations and indictments. No other
publication has burrowed so deeply into the Teamsters' finances and
apparent ties to organized crime.

Some of the most vigorous investigative reporting of federal
regulatory agencies has been done by a number of independent
newsletters sold to subscribers in businesses and trade associations
who want to keep up on developments in Washington. Dissident
employees inside some federal agencies also have produced their own
muckraking newsletters, including one put out by Department of
Housing and Urban Development employees that alerted the
Washington press to mismanagement and financial difficulties in
HUD's "new town" program.

Lobbyist Ralph Nader also has been an influential, if not especially
thorough, muckraker who has gotten maximum publicity for his
work with dramatic congressional testimony, well-timed leaks to
intimates in the Washington press corps, his own contributions to
magazines and newspapers, and the many lengthy reports his legions
of volunteer students, lawyers, and journalists have turned out—
nearly twenty of which have been published as books by Grossman
Publishers. Nader's raiders have studied air and water pollution, auto
safety, federal regulatory agencies, food additives, land use, banks,
nursing homes, and antitrust enforcement. While these reports have
seldom been as exhaustive or accurate as advertised, they have
provided good leads for investigative reporters willing to dig more
deeply into the same subjects. Nader himself has vigorously
encouraged this process with flattering, chatty phone calls to his
favorite journalists.

In 1973 Nader spent $40,000 from his Public Citizen fund-raising
organization to help start a new Washington news bureau, the
Capitol Hill News Service, to cover the activities of congressmen
seldom scrutinized by the rest of the media. Its five reporters have
produced a number of investigative stories on campaign finances,

congressmen's expensive Capitol Hill prerogatives, and the financial favors they receive from big lobbyists. At times the fledgling news service has been sloppy in its reporting and made much ado of relatively petty congressional foibles. It has nevertheless created some needed investigative competition for Capitol Hill correspondents, who have traditionally been among the most complacent reporters in Washington.

Unfortunately, television, the medium on which more Americans depend for news than any other, has provided relatively little investigative reporting. Since the late 1960s the national television networks have produced a few attention-getting documentaries, including "The Selling of the Pentagon," the controversial CBS examination of Defense Department public relations efforts; "What Price Health?" NBC's investigation of the costs and shortcomings of American medical services; "Hunger in America," the CBS inquiry into U.S. poverty and malnutrition; and "Pensions: The Broken Promise," NBC's exposé of the systematic shortchanging of American pensioners. A few local stations have also put together such programs as "The Slow Guillotine," a dramatic report on air pollution, and "Powers That Be," a frightening inquiry into the safety of nuclear power, both done by KNBC-TV in Los Angeles. But altogether there have been no more than a few dozen muckraking television documentaries during the past decade, while investigative reporting elsewhere has increased dramatically. Otherwise, television has occasionally followed up on investigative stories already done by newspaper reporters or free-lance writers.

Very little muckraking has shown up on the networks' early evening national news shows, which more than 50 million Americans watch each night. The coverage given by these shows to Watergate during the presidential election of 1972, for example, was minuscule in quantity and limited in substance to "a fairly straight serving of headlines from the *Washington Post*," according to media critic Edwin Diamond. Diamond, co-director of the Massachusetts Institute of Technology's Network News Study Group, which surveyed nightly news shows on that subject, reported, "There was little original reporting by any network and almost nothing that could be called investigative reporting." Even after the Watergate inquiry gained momentum with the Senate investigation in 1973, the Special Watergate Prosecutor's activities, and the looming impeachment and resignation of President Nixon in 1974, the television networks continued to do little more than report, albeit in greater quantity, what had been publicly revealed elsewhere.

To some extent the networks may have been intimidated by the immense political and regulatory pressure put on them by the Nixon administration, which ironically felt persecuted by isolated instances of skeptical television coverage of Nixon, the rest of his administration, and the Vietnam war. No matter how unwarranted they may have been, these pressures troubled the networks, over which a vengeful federal government could hold considerable sway. The Nixon administration mounted a rather successful public relations campaign against "The Selling of the Pentagon," by capitalizing on undeniable flaws in its production to cast doubts on its overall credibility. Later the Federal Communications Commission, which regulates television, ruled that the award-winning "Pensions: The Broken Promise," was "one-sided" because it "created the impression that injustice and inequity were widespread in the administration of private pension plans." Actually, there was ample evidence to indicate that this "impression" was an accurate reflection of the truth and that the documentary was far less hard-hitting than investigative reports on the same subjects in newspapers and magazines had been. Nevertheless, the FCC invoked its fairness doctrine and required the network to give an opportunity for reply.

Despite the medium's immense income, money is another factor limiting TV investigative reporting. Network news documentaries cost several hundred thousand dollars each to make and usually produce a revenue deficit, because they attract few advertisers. Local television muckraking that in any way impugns local businesses has frequently cost station owners large advertising accounts and lost station news directors their jobs. Local television station news staffs are small compared to those of newspapers in the same cities, and usually lack the manpower and expertise to undertake extended investigations of complicated subjects. Moreover, television news executives believe that it would be difficult to illustrate this kind of program or to make it sufficiently entertaining.

There have been increased attempts at investigative reporting by local television stations in recent years, but they seldom have involved digging in fields not already well plowed by newspapers, magazines, or books. Instead, many of these efforts have amounted only to shallow explorations of problems already well known to the viewing public—slum housing, rising prices, consumer fraud, prison and hospital conditions, and crime—because they can be more easily illustrated and dramatically presented. Thus, consumer reporters who follow up viewer complaints about food prices, auto repair bills, or dirty restaurants have become staples of many local news formats. And at least one local television muckraker, Geraldo Rivera of WABC-TV in New York, has capitalized on aggressive, dramatically staged exposés of New York's welfare hotels, overpriced prescription drugs, narcotics abuse, and an antiquated state home for the retarded to become a local media superstar and talk show host.

Marilyn Baker, then with public station KQED-TV in San Francisco, won national attention and a lucrative book contract with her television scoops on the investigation of the Patricia Hearst-Symbionese Liberation Army case. Baker actually did little more than beat other reporters to police and counterculture sources for such information as the names of members of the Symbionese Liberation Army, and all too frequently she reported rumors that turned out to be baseless. It is sadly indicative of the depressed state of television muckraking that, for this, she gained a high-paying new job with the CBS television affiliate in San Francisco, extraordinary publicity, and serious critical consideration for her hastily thrown-together book, *Exclusive! The Inside Story of Patricia Hearst and the SLA*, as well as a public reputation as an accomplished investigative reporter.

Daniel Schorr of CBS, a former newspaperman and free-lance writer, who recently earned notoriety by obtaining and selling to the *Village Voice* a secret congressional report on the CIA, comes closer to being an investigative reporter. Schorr, a gray-haired bespectacled man of nearly sixty, has burrowed beneath the surface of events and institutions in Washington with a skepticism and a disdain for conventional detached television demeanor that are clearly foreign and often irritating to his colleagues. During the early years of the Nixon administration, while reporting on federal social programs, Schorr angered the White House by refusing to parrot on the air pronouncements made by the President. When, for example, Nixon told a Catholic group in New York City that "you can count on my support to rescue the parochial school," Schorr searched the federal bureaucracy and reported there was no evidence of any program to aid parochial schools. At one point, the Nixon White House ordered an FBI investigation of Schorr in an attempt to intimidate him. But the effort backfired when this harassment became public knowledge.

During Watergate Schorr was one of the few television reporters to take the *Washington Post*'s revelations seriously and report them as fully as possible, although Schorr did little original digging himself. Following Seymour Hersh's exposé of the CIA's illegal domestic activities, Schorr became one of the most aggressive investigative reporters on that story. After picking up a rumor from an off-the-record private luncheon that top editors and reporters of the *Times* had with President Ford at the White House, and then confirming its accuracy with CIA sources, Schorr scooped the sworn-to-secrecy *Times*men by reporting Ford's concern that congressional investigations of the CIA might reveal "possible CIA involvement in assassinations" of foreign leaders. Schorr later reported solid information from retired Air Force Colonel Fletcher Prouty that the CIA attempted several times to assassinate Cuban Premier Fidel Castro. Richard Helms, who was director of the CIA at the time of the assassination planning, publicly denounced Schorr, shouting at him in a congressional office building corridor: "Killer Schorr, Killer Schorr."

The difference between Schorr and the best newspaper investigative reporters, however, has been his relative lack of thoroughness. In 1974 Schorr broadcast a rumor that forty people would be indicted by a federal grand jury for the Watergate cover-up; only seven were. Later, during the furor over the CIA's domestic activities, Schorr rushed Colonel Prouty on the air with an exclusive which, this time, turned out to be unsupported by facts. Prouty asserted that former Nixon aide Alexander Butterfield was a spy inside the White House. Everyone involved categorically denied the story, and Schorr later admitted that he had not taken the time to try to reach Butterfield himself or the two Air Force officers from whom Prouty said he had gotten his information. At most newspapers editors would insist that a reporter in Schorr's position do better than that and would likely maximize with close supervision his effectiveness and credibility. But no one in television really knows how to handle a reporter like Daniel Schorr because there are so few, if any others, like him.

Since Watergate there has been something of a revival of documentary-style muckraking by the networks. CBS's highly professional and exceptionally well-financed *60 Minutes* follows up smartly on investigative stories its large production staff discovers in newspapers and magazines. Since late 1973 ABC has countered with periodic ABC New Closeups on single subjects: abuses by the Internal Revenue Service of its tax-law-enforcing powers, the Federal Aviation Administration's laxity in protecting air passengers' safety, the dangerously low fire safety standards in the United States, the federal government's lackadaisical enforcement of mine-safety laws, and the suspicious circumstances surrounding

President Nixon's freeing of former Teamsters' boss Jimmy Hoffa from prison, under the condition that he refrain from further union activity. Through 1975 the two networks' dedication to *60 Minutes* and *Closeup* remained ambiguous. Both have received unusually generous financial support and plenty of promotion from the networks, expenditures that have been somewhat repaid to CBS and ABC in prestige, if not corporate profits. But CBS continued until late 1975 to allow its schedule-makers to push *60 Minutes* all over the Sunday night spectrum, and the show has disappeared from the air completely during the autumn months when professional football telecasts dominate. *60 Minutes* was finally given, in the middle of the 1975-1976 season, its own prime-time slot, something *ABC News Closeup* has never had. Its godfather, ABC Vice President Avram Westin, has spent much of his time wrestling with network lawyers over contents of the program, especially when it steps on the toes of big corporations. Acknowledging to a news magazine reporter that ABC's commitment to *Closeup*, a big money-loser for the network, may well be transitory, Westin said, "The business has a cyclical nature. It takes a conscious decision by management to support an aggressive news organization. For the moment, this corporation has put its money where its mouth is."

There also has been some effort to entice investigative journalists into television on the assumption that their expertise is what broadcast attempts at muckraking have primarily lacked. Brit Hume went to work for *ABC News Closeup* after leaving the employ of Jack Anderson. The *Closeup* producers also enlisted reporters like Karl Meyer, the author of a book on the international smuggling of art objects, to write scripts for individual shws, including one based on his book. Hume was encouraged by his *Closeup* experiences, but Meyer came away disillusioned with efforts to attract the largest possible viewing audience by overdramatizing and distorting his material.

The fledgling, low-budget public television network, PBS, has been unable to undertake its own investigative projects, although reporters for some local public stations have. One who was unusually successful was Selwyn Raab, who actually worked most of his career for newspapers before joining the staff of public station WNET-TV in New York in 1971. Born of Polish and Austrian immigrants in New York in the 1930s and raised in a tough lower East Side neighborhood, Raab is a nonconforming, intensely curious man who repeatedly left jobs on newspapers in Connecticut, New Jersey, and New York to travel aimlessly around South America. In 1964, while working for the old *New York World-Telegram and Sun*, he came across clippings about George Whitmore, Jr., who had confessed to killing two young women in New York in 1963 and was then in Bellevue Hospital for "observation." Raab became curious about Whitmore and, after checking records on the case, also became suspicious about the validity of Whitmore's conviction. He began what was to become an eight-year investigation, in which he eventually proved, after going to WNET-TV, that Whitmore was somewhere else on the day of the killings and had been coerced into confessing. Raab also found in Puerto Rico a witness whose testimony exonerated Whitmore of rape charges in another case. Raab broke the story on a WNET-TV documentary and wrote a book about Whitmore's experience that later was bought by CBS and used loosely as the basis for the television detective series *Kojak*.

Raab was soon deluged with requests to free from prison others who may have been wrongly accused. He won parole for Carl De Flumer, who was legitimately convicted of murder in 1946 but sentenced to life imprisonment despite the fact he was then only fourteen years old. And he helped expose the perjury of the two key prosecution witnesses at the murder trial of former boxer Rubin "Hurricane" Carter, convicted along with grocery clerk John Artis of shooting to death three patrons of a Paterson, New Jersey, bar in 1966. By this time Raab had left WNET-TV after a not unusual public TV budget cut on *The 51st State* news show Raab produced. *New York Times* metropolitan editor Arthur Gelb, anxious to improve the *Times*'s local investigative reporting, hired Raab away from the station, not knowing at the time that Raab was bringing with him the Rubin Carter bombshell, which became a front-page story for the *Times* a few months later. As of this writing the Carter-Artis case is being newly appealed on the basis of the recanted testimony. Raab has since done for the *Times* a number of sophisticated investigative stories on the quality of justice and inner workings of law enforcement agencies in New York.

The one factor that could possibly bring more muckraking to the television screen in the future is the new technology that is making available smaller, more portable, and much less expensive cameras and videotape units. They promise to be easier to use and cheaper to buy for smaller stations, public television, cable television, and even independent groups. For example, videotape workshop groups from San Francisco and New York got together in 1972 to make revealing, behind-the-scenes documentaries of the national party conventions that were shown on cable television systems in several cities. A *San*

Francisco Examiner reporter wrote that the group's Republican convention documentary, "Four More Years," cost only $9000 to make, "less money than one network (NBC) spent on coffee in Miami Beach." Yet "Four More Years" captured better than any network coverage the essence of the convention as an American political experience, through the eyes, voices, and activities of individual delegates and observers, young Nixon supporters, street demonstrators outside, and reporters from the media. As cable television spreads slowly across the country and required public access channels became available in each community, almost anyone able to use the increasingly inexpensive videotape equipment will be able to put almost anything onto the air.

But will this new era of muckraking last that much longer for any of the media? Or will it end within a decade of its beginning—by the end of the 1970s—as the first golden age of muckraking did after the turn of the century? The outbreak of World War I marked the end of that era, although the muckrakers had long before begun to lose the interest of their readers. Their end was hastened by the attacks of Theodore Roosevelt, who was able to turn against the muckrakers without being himself publicly discredited, as Richard Nixon was nearly seventy years later. The original muckrakers also were far fewer in number than today's investigative reporters, and their output of nearly 2000 articles in less than ten years was confined largely to magazines. These national journals quickly became so filled with exposés that their editors, fearing that readers would become sated with scandal, began looking for more "good news" articles, while the muckrakers were still at their peak of popularity.

Several of the best-known early muckrakers became disillusioned with how little they had seemed to change the "system" of government and big business they had railed against. As *Forbes* magazine reassured its readers in 1972, while a new generation of muckrakers threateningly began to gather steam, "the U.S. capitalist system proved it could absorb and adapt" once before, making minimal reforms that temporarily inhibited the special interests the original muckrakers had exposed. "The lesson was that the curbing of special interests is sometimes necessary," *Forbes* pointed out, "not only for the survival of the nation as a whole but even for the survival of the special interests."

Today's muckrakers already have had a greater measurable impact on the nation, toppling a President, bringing about major reforms in political campaign financing, and opening up for public inspection the most secret and powerful organs of the government. They are more numerous than their turn-of-the-century predecessors and reach a much larger audience through newspapers and, to an extent, radio and television, in addition to magazines and books. They also seem, in this mass-media age, to have created more of a market for muckraking as muckraking, no matter what scandal is being revealed.

But if the act of muckraking were to become more significant than its substance, its purpose would be lost. After New York newspapers had been especially full of investigative reports on local nursing home scandals at one point in 1975, the *New Yorker* magazine, using the editorial "we" in its "Talk of the Town" column, observed that

there was something in all this that bothered us.

It was not, as Senator John Stennis said in the debate on the makeup of the special Senate committee to investigate the CIA, that the inquiries now going forward were likely to destroy worthy institutions. Nor was it, as one columnist maintained, that a new wave of "McCarthyism" had been unleashed. The investigators had, on the whole, been scrupulous. We had not seen a single fact that we would not have wanted uncovered. What bothered us was not the stories themselves but the way they were being handled. In part, the problem was the idea—implicit in the big headlines, and explicit in Assemblyman Stein's remark that the nursing home scandal might be "bigger" than Watergate—that the new headlines would fill a gap left by the tapering off of Watergate headlines. We wanted the investigations of scandals that have come to light more recently to go on, but perhaps with a little less fanfare . . . It is as though the country, having developed an appetite for sordid secrets, now had to be fed a steady diet of them. At the moment the mode of journalism, rather than the content of the story, often seems to determine the place of the story on the front page or its prominence on the television news: if it's "investigative," it gets heavy play.

The *New Yorker* went on to point out the need for close, sophisticated coverage of complicated but less hidden or seamy problems of our world: "the economic predicament, the energy predicament, the food predicament, the troubles in the Middle East, new difficulties in our relations with the Soviet Union . . . They call for a new kind of news reporting, as yet undiscovered, which will answer the special needs of our era as brilliantly and as daringly as investigative reporting met the special needs of the era of Watergate."

Although the era of Watergate may be ended, the need for investigative reporting remains, in part to deal meaningfully with some of the problems listed by the *New Yorker*. How much of our economic and energy and food problems result from morally neutral

Although the era of Watergate may be ended, the need for investigative reporting remains . . .

causes, and how many from dishonest or manipulative actions of special interests? Donald Barlett and James Steele, among others, have begun to reveal the manipulation of the world's oil resources by giant oil cartels and Middle East potentates. Dan Morgan of the *Washington Post* has begun to show how the American contribution to the world food supply could be greater, if government-sanctioned agricultural monopolies were not allowed to greedily maintain the high prices of certain commodities. A few muckraking authors have started to examine more closely the role of multinational corporations and the world's bankers in fluctuations in the international economy that somehow increase their profits at our peril. Diplomatic reporters need to focus more closely on the dangerous chicanery involved in superpower political maneuvers and arms deals in the Middle East. In each case, exposure of what is hidden beneath the surface could improve our now slim chances of coping with these problems successfully.

But to accomplish such ambitious tasks, investigative reporting must mature beyond titillating exposés of individual wrongdoing and embrace expert analysis of complicated subjects and institutions. The new breed of new muckraker exemplified by Barlett and Steele must prosper and multiply. Such reporters must learn how to use the sophisticated tools for fact-finding now available to others in our society: computers and other advanced forms of data processing, scientific surveys and public attitude polls, and research methods developed by social scientists. *Newsday* took a pioneering step in this direction in 1974 when it sent a team of reporters trained in survey, interviewing, and observation techniques into surrounding suburbia to find out how people really lived there, what their joys and problems were. The team was not after scandal, although it did turn up disturbing evidence of such problems as widespread drug use, ostracism of newly arrived middle-class black families, and the desire of most suburban families to shut themselves off from the outside world. These findings were not great surprises, but they are now documented facts for Long Island rather than mere journalistic supposition or cliché.

Editors of *Time* magazine concluded in a 1974 essay on muckraking, "the American press has a twofold task. It will have to carry out investigative reporting in areas far less obvious than the Watergate abuses . . . (and) even more important than investigation will be explanation. A shortcoming of the American press probably graver than any faults displayed during Watergate is the lack of expertise in many fields, a failure to develop the techniques necessary to inform the public on highly complicated subjects, to lay out the alternative choices and possible solutions in an increasingly baffling world." Morton Mintz has argued the need for "comparative journalism"—which would combine investigative reporting of local and national problems with exhaustive examinations of what has been tried in other societies. One could study the welfare systems of Scandinavian countries, national health care in Britain, the deemphasis of individual competition in Maoist Chinese society, or the technological revolution in Japan, not so much to find solutions, but rather because the trials, successes, and errors of people elsewhere may well give us productive ideas. "This is our real power," declared editor Harold Evans of the *Sunday Times* of London, after his newspaper forced Britain to do something about the misformed Thalidomide babies, "we can create an agenda for society."

In doing so the press must be accurate, responsible, and constructive whenever possible. There would be no point in its working to destroy society. Rather it must help improve society, perhaps by helping to bring about significant changes. There is no reason, however, for the press to make any post-Watergate reconciliation with government by abandoning its present adversary posture, as some panicky press critics like Irving Kristol, co-editor of *The Public Interest*, have urged. The press should not, of course, distort what those who run the government, or private industry, are doing and saying, but it should remain eternally skeptical of how they use their power. "The first principles of journalism," in light of Watergate were summed up nicely and succinctly by Mary McGrory, Pulitzer Prize-winning columnist for the *Washington Star*, when she concluded an essay on Woodward and Bernstein's *All the President's Men* with this advice to other would-be investigative reporters: "Ask, go back; be nice to people, but not to power."

A Short Bibliography

BOOKS:

Abell, Tyler, ed. *Drew Pearson Diaries 1949-59*. New York: Holt, Rinehart and Winston, 1974.

Alsop, Stewart. *The Center*. New York: Harper and Row, 1968.

Anderson, Jack. *The Anderson Papers*. New York: Random House, 1973.

Anderson, Jack, and Drew Pearson. *The Case Against Congress*. New York: Simon and Schuster, 1968.

Aronson, James. *Deadline for the Media*. New York: Bobbs-Merrill, 1972.

Barrett, Marvin, ed. *Survey of Broadcast Journalism, 1968-1969*. New York: Grosset and Dunlap, 1970.

Bernstein, Carl, and Robert Woodward. *All the President's Men.* New York: Simon and Schuster, 1974.

Caro, Robert A. *The Power Broker*. New York: Alfred A. Knopf, 1974.

Crouse, Timothy. *The Boys on the Bus*. New York: Random House, 1972.

Dennis, Everette E., and William L. Rivers. *Other Voices: The New Journalism in America*. San Francisco: Canfield Press, 1974.

Emery, Edwin. *The Press and America*, 2nd ed. Englewood Cliffs, N.J.: Prentice-Hall, 1962.

Harrison, John M., and Harry H. Stein, eds. *Muckraking: Past, Present and Future*. University Park, Pa.: The Pennsylvania State University Press, 1973.

Hersh, Seymour. *Cover-up*. New York: Random House, 1972.

Hersh, Seymour. *My Lai 4: A Report on the Massacre and Its Aftermath*. New York: Random House, 1970.

Hume, Brit. *Inside Story*. New York: Doubleday, 1974.

Johnson, Michael L. *The New Journalism*. Lawrence, Kan.: The University of Kansas Press, 1971.

Kaplan, Justin. *Lincoln Steffens*. New York: Simon and Schuster, 1974.

Krock, Arthur. *Memoirs*. New York: Funk and Wagnalls, 1968.

Leamer, Lawrence. *The Paper Revolutionaries*. New York: Simon and Schuster, 1973.

Newsday, its staff and editors. *The Heroin Trail*. New York: New American Library (Signet), 1974.

Stevens, John D., and William E. Porter, eds. *The Rest of the Elephant: Perspectives on Mass Media*. Englewood Cliffs, N.J.: Prentice-Hall, 1973.

Sussman, Barry. *The Great Cover-Up: Nixon and the Scandal of*

Watergate. New York: New American Library (Signet), 1974.

Stone, I. F. *In Time of Torment*. New York: Random House, 1967.

Stone, I. F. *Polemics and Prophecies, 1967-70*. New York: Random House, 1970.

PERIODICALS:

Bulletin of the American Society of Newspaper Editors.

The Columbia Journalism Review, published by the Graduate School of Journalism of Columbia University, New York.

[MORE], published by Rosebud Associates, New York.

FILM:

I. F. Stone's Weekly, a film by Jerry Bruck Jr., distributed by The I. F. Stone Project, Franklin Lakes, N. J.

Index

261

Composed in Times Roman by The New Republic Book Company, Inc.

Printed on 60-pound Warren's Old Style Laid and bound in Holliston Kingston Natural by Halliday Lithograph, Hanover, Massachusetts.

Designed by Gerard Valerio.